BAPTISM

A DIVIDER OF CHURCHES AND A CAUSE OF MARTYRDOM—IS IT A BASIS OF DIVISION OR A SOLUTION FOR UNITY

J. CLARENCE FORD, LittD

WESTBOW®
PRESS
A DIVISION OF THOMAS NELSON
& ZONDERVAN

WestBow Press books may be ordered through booksellers or by contacting:

WestBow Press
A Division of Thomas Nelson & Zondervan
1663 Liberty Drive
Bloomington, IN 47403
www.westbowpress.com
1 (866) 928-1240

ISBN: 978-1-4908-2393-5 (sc)
ISBN: 978-1-4908-2394-2 (e)

Library of Congress Control Number: 2014901594

Printed in the United States of America.

WestBow Press rev. date: 2/27/2014

THIS BOOK IS DEDICATED to my family who have given their support, my wife has been very patient, which has proven to be of immeasurable help. I wish to thank them and, also, those under whose ministry and service I have sat, but particularly I give my thanks to The Living Book, which I have read through at least 70 times with awe. It is the God-breathed Book!

CONTENTS

FOREWORD

" **B**uried with Christ in death and raised to walk in newness of life, I baptize you in The Name of The Father, The Son, and The Holy Spirit." You may recall these word or similar words as you fondly remember your own baptism experience. Whatever your own experience, this text serves to illuminate and clarify The Ordinance of Baptism and its role in the Christian Life.

In this scholarly text, J.C. Ford presents the Biblical origins and purpose of baptism and examines long-held religious beliefs. It is rich with references from both The Old and New Testament as well as other historical and academic works. He vividly tracks the History of baptism through the ages and explains its practicality and relevance to the believer in this postmodern era. In a logical and passionate manner, Pastor Ford takes on such topics as the prerequisites of baptism, the meaning of baptism, infant baptism and much more.

This volume provides meaningful insight and instruction for all who seek to know more about the beautiful Ordinance of Baptism. From the seminary student to the minister, to the new believer, all will benefit from the wealth of information contained within these pages. For those contemplating their own baptism, the evidence presented in this text will hopefully serve as the catalyst for you to proceed we trust this text will bless your life and deepen your understanding of baptism as it has ours. As we have had the opportunity to know and worship with Pastor Ford for several years, we hope that this documentary work offers the reader even a small glimpse into the life of the author as it reflects the integrity and fervor with which he preaches, teaches, and lives.

Dr. David Edwards, M.D.   **Dr. Robin Edwards, Ph.D.**

(The self-evident scholarship of these two highly valued scientific analysts is so deeply appreciated in their voluntary support of this investigation and work of structuring this volume in a clear, properly documented manner that we trust may be used of God to answer questions far too many people live and die without finding comforting answers.)

INTRODUCTION

I am deeply aware of the total chaos of the professing Church around us, with Bible ministers tip-toeing softly about. Baptism, and all that it represents, is not explained as it needs to be and its importance is tragically overlooked. Let Truth be thundered with the Power of The Holy Spirit of God and with the infinite Authority of Almighty God!! I fail to relate to a Church that ignores The Great Commission; and will not obey God! I believe the living Christ does, also. Further, I am stunned at the doctrines, activities, and indulgences that have been broadly and freely used by the 'church'.

Even Augustine, in his anti-Donatistic writings defends 'heretical' baptism (*baptizo*) by the following course of argument: "Baptism (*baptizo*) is an institution of Christ, shortly before his ascension, to be performed in the name of the Father, the Son and the Holy Spirit. It took the place of circumcision and was a sign and seal of church membership. It is the outward mark of Christian discipleship, the rite of initiation into the covenant of grace. It is the sacrament of repentance (conversion), of remission of sins and of regeneration by the power of the Holy Spirit. In the nature of the case it is to be received but once. It incorporates the penitent sinner in the visible church, and entitles him to all the privileges, and binds him to all the duties of this communion." HISTORY OF THE CHRISTIAN CHURCH, Philip Schaff, Vol. 1, p.466-467.

We must understand that there are a number of things in Augustine's statement that we would want to discuss with him; but, to try to make him an endorser of sprinkling for baptism, would hardly pass muster; and, to assume that he was an advocate of such procedure must be totally incorrect. I see nothing in Augustine that endorses sprinkling and immersion was not called into question until long after Augustine's time. You will please note there is no Scripture that states 'It (baptism) took the place of circumcision', or 'It is the sacrament of repentance (conversion).' A sacrament means that these things help to save the sinner, which is not true.

"And Jesus came and Spake unto them, saying, All power is given unto me in heaven and in earth. Go ye therefore, and teach all nations, baptizing (*Baptizontes)* them in the Name of the Father, and of the Son, and of the Holy Ghost: Teaching them to observe all things whatsoever I have commanded you: and lo, I am with you alway, even unto the end of the age." Matthew 28:18-20.

"AND WHEN THE DAY OF PENTECOST WAS FULLY COME, they were all with one accord in one place. And suddenly there came a sound from heaven like a rushing wind, and it filled all the house where they were sitting. And there appeared unto them cloven tongues as of fire, and it sat upon each of them.

"And they were filled with the Holy Spirit, and began to speak with other tongues, as the Spirit gave them utterance. And there were dwelling Jews, devout men, out of every nation under heaven. Now when this was noised abroad, the multitude came together, and were confounded, because every man heard them speak in his own language."

AND THEY WERE ALL AMAZED and marveled, saying one to another, Behold, are not these who speak Galileans? And how hear we every man in our own tongue, wherein we were born? Paarthians, and Medes, and Elamites, and the dwellers in Mesopotamia, and in Judea, and Cappadocia in Pontus, and Asia, Phrygia, and Palphylia, in Egypt, and in the parts of Libya about Cyrene and sojourners of Rome, both Jews and proselytes, Cretans and Araabians, we do hear them speak in our tongues the wonderful works of God. Acts 2:1-11.

HAD THERE BEEN a firm holding to The Scriptures, there would be no tongues movement! The modern Church is as pathetic as the Church of Corinth! Obviously, the real experience is here; and, the amazing thing is that "every man heard them speak in his own language." There is not a proper work when "every man does NOT hear in the "tongue wherein they were born!" The Church in Corinth is NOT the Church to imitate the folly of Corinth. HERESY BEGAN EARLY and it began with the tares (matthew 13:25) and the leaven (Matthew 13:33), but it spread like wild fire; legalism, changing of the fruit of the vine to the actual Blood of Christ, sprinkling for baptism, without warrant, etc.! The heresy of Covenant Theology did not begin in earnest until the 16th Century. Sprinkling came as a substitute for *baptize (immersion)* with the introducing of infants to baptism. Infants are shielded by the Blood of Christ until accountability, just as all creation belongs to Christ by right of redemption! (Matthew 19:14). The election process and progression is not to be cheated out of the repentance and active Faith process, when Faith has become a reality and a deliberate act.

(Covenant theologians COMPLETELY ignore *the meaning of the word: baptizontes.*) Exodus 40:12-16 "Washed with water" was the COMPLETE WASHING of Aaron and his sons for the work of the ministry. ALL BELIEVERS are 'believer priests'! Proselyte baptism was practiced before John the Baptist. ("Washed with water" "There is no instance in which it signifies to make a partial application of water by affusion or sprinkling, or to cleanse, to purify, apart from the literal act of immersion as the means of cleansing or purifying." See Broadus on Immersion) Systematic Theology, A.H. Strong, p.933.) II Corinthians 5:17.

Let the Character of God's standard of quality be administered to the Redeemed. "We ought to obey God, rather than men." Acts 5:2

WHY SHOULD CHRISTIAN BAPTISM cause division among earnest Church people who truly love God, since it is "The answer of a good conscience toward God?" I Peter 3:21

At a 1971 Winter Youth Retreat at a Baptist Camp, intelligent and earnest young people were asking the following questions out of their deep personal desire to know answers and truly please God:

(1) "why do so many different pastors give different views on certain points of the bible? A kid just doest know what is right or wrong."

(2) "Why do Baptists believe in being immersed instead of being sprinkled like Lutherans?"

(3) "Is it wrong to be sprinkled, as a way of baptizing? or is it better to be immersed?"

These were earnest, courteous questions which are deserving of the Bible's correct answer that is founded on what the Inspired Word of God teaches, and, on how the Church, in history, came to its present state of division.

DARE GOD'S LOCAL CHURCHES, entrusted with the Truth of Almighty God, continue to be like the two senators, a Democrat and a Republican, who met on a subway train which runs to the Capitol? They began discussing a bill they were about to vote on and found they were in perfect agreement on it.

"You know, this scares me," said one to the other, "This is the first time we have ever agreed on a matter of public policy." "I know!" Replied the other, "And it really makes me suspicious that I'm absolutely wrong in how I'm planning to vote."

The Church stands responsible before the Eternal and Infinitely Holy God to be OBEDIENT, to be accurate and diligently faithful, sounding the alert in teaching the Truths of His Holy Scriptures, even though some have been wrongly taught and must be very gently taught the truths, as they were Given by the Holy Spirit. This is not optional!! I Peter 2:2.

The King James Version has been used in all references. Where we have used literal translations this has been indicated. I would like to express deep appreciation to all authors for the texts that have been quoted; and have sought to give credit in each case.

THE PURPOSE OF THIS BOOK

WHEREAS "JESUS CAME and spoke unto them, saying, All Authority is given unto me in heaven and in earth. Go ye therefore, and teach all nations, baptizing them in the Name of the Father, and of the Son, and of the Holy Spirit, teaching them to observe all things whatsoever I have commanded you; and, lo, I am with you always, even unto the end of the world." Amen, and,

WHEREAS The Book of Revelation, Chapters two and three, provide The beautiful Biblical Outline of The Church Age, providing Infinite warning of Church apostasy; and, that this apostasy was persistent to near the point of infinity, as verified in the New Testament in many places, with the strong heralding of it in II Thessalonians 2:3-12, II Timothy 3, etc. sounding that alert like the blaring of a fog-horn; and,

WHEREAS I was stunned to read a book of 657 pages entitled "The Fundamentals" without a single reference to baptism, and, I mean NO reference, and,

WHEREAS The Great Commission is THE MISSION OF HIS CHURCH, through this age, as ordered of God, (Matthew 28:18-20), with the Church drifting madly from its moorings of ordered faith, from its very inception; and ordination, and,

WHEREAS in the current Church *is tragic evidence* that Satan, the destroyer, is daily using every weapon at his command to stop, hinder, distort and defy the Infinite eternal Work of God, I seek in this effort to counter as much of such destructive work as possible; and,

WHEREAS, knowing that I stand accountable to The Eternal God to make those facts known with the vehemence of infinity,

THEREFORE, be it resolved with full heart and voice, to give diligent attention to The Great Commission in all of its parts, particularly baptism, that the pages which follow shall provide in very concise and efficient way, The Holy Scriptures relative to Baptism and the reasons for martyrdom. We, therefore, very prayerfully send forth these pages!!

"The Unity of The Spirit" (Ephesians 4:1-3) is always to be sought in every part of The Church Age; making the vivid, living, vital message of the Gospel of The Death, Burial, and Resurrection of The Lord Jesus Christ the illuminating glow of Glory that it is! The Majesty, and Light that should surround His Holy Name which is above every name, and, at which every knee shall bow, this, Friend, most certainly must be seen!!

ON THAT PREMISE; AND, ON THAT ALONE, IT IS MOST CERTAINLY IN ORDER *THAT HIS OWN CHURCH BE OBEDIENT TO IT'S HIGH, Phil.3:14 HOLY II Tim. 1:9 AND HEAVENLY CALLING Heb. 3:1,* TO LOGICALLY PROCEED IN MAKING TRUTH KNOWN TO OUR LOST WORLD! FOR EVERY KNEE SHALL BOW TO HIM AND EVERY TONGUE SHALL CONFESS TO GOD! Isaiah 45:23,24; Romans 14:11,12; Philippians 2:9-11.

How can a disobedient Church call the world to The Obedience of Christ??

Dr. J. Clarence Ford, Litt.D.

CHAPTER 1
THE PRINCIPLES OF BAPTISM

" A ND JESUS CAME and spake unto them, saying, "All power is give unto me in Heaven and in earth. Go ye therefore, and teach all nations, baptizing them in the Name of the Father and of the Son, and of the Holy Ghost: Teaching them to observe all things whatsoever I have commanded you: and, Lo, I am with you always, even unto the end of the world. Amen." Matthew 28:18-20

"And he said unto them, Go ye into all the world, and preach the gospel to every creature. He that believeth and is baptized shall be saved; but he that believeth not shall be damned. And these signs shall follow them that believe; In my Name shall they cast out devils; they shall speak with new tongues; they shall take up serpents; and if they drink any deadly thing, it shall not hurt them; they shall lay hands on the sick, and they shall recover." Mark 16:15-18

"THEREFORE, LET ALL THE HOUSE of Israel know assuredly, that God hath made that same Jesus, whom ye have crucified, both LORD and CHRIST.

"Now when they heard this, they were pricked in their hearts, and said unto Peter and unto the rest of the Apostles, Men and brethren, ;what shall we do?

"Then said Peter unto them, Repent, and be baptized every one of you, in the name of Jesus Christ for the remission of sins, and receive the gift of the Holy Spirit.

"For the promise is unto you and to your children, and to all that are afar off, even as manay as the as the Lord your God shall call.

"And with many other words did he testify and exhort, saying Save yourselves from this untoward generation.'

"Then they that gladly received his word were baptized (*eBaptisthasan*): And the same day there were added unto them about three thousand souls." *Acts* **236-41**

"Father, Mother and John were having family worship. Dad was reading the Bible and came across this verse, "Thy Word is a lamp unto my feet and a light unto my path" (Psalm 119:105) John asked, "What does that verse mean, Dad?"

His father answered, "Thy Word means the Bible. The Bible guides us and lights our pathway. It shows us where we must go and how we must live."

mother said, "When I hear that verse I always think of something that happened when I was a little girl. One day my cousin from the city was visiting me. In the afternoon we took a walk up the mountain to look for wild flowers. We had a good time. We did not notice that the sun was setting. When it began to get dark, we decided that we must hurry home. Soon we found out that we were lost! We could not find the way home. It grew darker and darker.. How scared we were!

"Suddenly I saw something! Far below there was a light. I said 'look! There was a light coming toward us!' Soon we heard a voice calling us.

"We both shouted. The light kept coming toward us. Then Father appeared, carrying a lantern. How happy we were to see him! We followed him down the mountain. The lantern lighted our pathway until we reached home. Mother was anxiously waiting for us. She had a good supper ready."The Bible is like the lantern my father carried. It guides along the pathway to our Heavenly Home!

John said, "Oh, Mother I am so glad that God has given us a light for our pathway. I will always love Gods Word! Mrs Alice Marie Knight's stories for Children and youth, p. 8, 9.

"YE MEN OF ISRAEL, hear these words; Jesus of Nazareth, a man approved of God among you by miracles and wonders and signs, which God did by him in the midst of you, as ye yourselves also know:Him, being delivered by the determinate counsel and foreknowledge of God, ye have taken, and by wicked hands have crucified and slain: Whom God hath raised up, having loosed the pains of death: because it was not possible that he should be holden of it." Acts 2:22-24

"I BEHELD till the thrones were cast down, and the Ancient of Days did sit, whose garment was white as snow, and the hair of His Head like the pure wool: his throne was like the fiery flame, and His Wheels as burning fire.

"I saw in the night visions, and behold One like the Son of man came to the Ancient of Days, and they brought him near before Him.

And there was given Him dominion, and glory, and a Kingdom, that all people, nations, and languages, should serve Him: His Dominion is an everlasting dominion, which shall not pass away, and His Kingdom that which shall not be destroyed." Daniel 7:9,13-14.

"AND I SAW in the right hand of Him that sat on the throne a book written within and on the backside, sealed with seven seals .... And I wept much, because no man was found worthy to open and to read the Book, neither to look there on ... AND ONE OF THE ELDERS saith unto me, weep not: behold, the Lion of the tribe of Juda, the Root of David, hath prevailed to open the Book, and to loose the seven seals thereof.

"And, I beheld, and, lo, in the midst of the throne and of the four living creatures, stood a Lamb as it had been slain, having seven horns and seven eyes, which are the seven Sp;irits of God sent forth into all the earth. And He came and took the Book out of the right hand of Him that sat upon the throne." Revelation 5:1,4-7.

"The authorities quoted in Smith and Cheetham. 161. and more fully in Augusti, ie. *Ter mergitamur* "Immersion was very natural in Southern climates. We are not concerned with the 'natural' We are dealing with a principle! Our Lord came in "Southern climates." The baptistries of the Nicene Age were for immersion. It is the symbol of Death, Burial and Resurrection. DEATH to the 'old' and RESURRECTION to New Life! We are to walk in "Newness of Life."

Baptizo (Complete Immersion) not *Rantizo* (Sprinkling) is used for Baptism, even though it is used of blood, even water; but *Rantizo* never is it used of the Baptismal figure!**KNOW YE NOT that, as many of us as were baptized into Jesus Christ were baptized into His Death? ('into' is highly significant, having the total, absolute, transforming, 'new creation' significance.)**

"Therefore, we are buried with Him by baptism into death, that as Christ was raised up from the dead by the glory of the Father, even so we also should walk in newness of life." Romans 6:30-4

BAPTISM IS A STRIKING figure of death, burial, and resurrection; a symbol of release from earthly things; and, a transport into the eternal. The Old Testament speaks of Hades and of an eternal separation between the blessed and the cursed. A meddling in this realm (The realm of the dead.) is witnessed in I Samuel 28:7-20; but a cloud surrounds the realm and is not to be entered; whereas, those who choose to involve themselves with this treacherous realm find themselves clearly beyond the patience of G\The Holy Scriptures speak, in the Fifth Century B.C., in Daniel 12:2-3 of human experience arriving at the Bar of God: "And many of those who sleep in the dust of the earth shall awake, some to everlasting life, and some to shame and everlasting contempt."AND THEY THAT BE WISE shall shine like the brightness of the firmament; and they that turn many to righteousness, as the stars forever and ever." Daniel 12:3 The Spirit of God was stirring. John the Baptist with his fervent preaching had moved all Judea to repentance, with the exception of the religious leaders of the day. These were filled with fear of the Roman Empire.

Caesar, with his armies had stopped the wars between Egypt and Syria and something of a settled peace had brought the world into a rather tense submission, yet it was the only peace the world at large was to know!

"Now there was about this time Jesus, a wise man, if it be lawful to call him a man, for he was a doer of wonderful works, a teacher of such men as receive the truth with pleasure. He drew to him both many of the Jews, and the Gentiles. He was the Christ, and when Pilate, at the suggestion of the principal men among us, had condemned him to the cross, those that loved him at the first did not forsake him; for he appeared to them alive again the third day; as the divine prophets had foretold these and ten thousand other wonderful; things concerning him, and the tribe of Christians so named from him are not extinct at this day." JOSEPHUS *Antiquities,* xvii

"AND Jesus came and spake unto them, saying, All power is given unto me in Heaven and in earth. Go ye therefore and teach all nations, BAPTIZING THEM INTO (eis) THE NAME OF THE FATHER, AND OF THE SON, AND OF THE HOLY GHOST: TEACHING THEM TO OBSERVE ALL THINGS whatsoever I have commanded you: and Lo, I am with you alway, even unto the end of the world. Amen." Matthew 28:18-20.

May we begin by praying with David, "Search me, O God, and know my heart: try me, and know my thoughts: and see if there be any wicked way in me, and lead me in the way everlasting. Psalm 139:23,24.

John the Baptist, or John the baptizer, was moved greatly from birth, ultimately spending much time alone in the wilderness, in prayer and preaching with a passion that could not be resisted, having been filled with the Holy Spirit from the womb.

"Then went out to him all Jerusalem, and all Judea, and all the region round about Jordan, and were baptized of him in Jordan, confessing their sins." Matthew 3:5,6

"After these things came Jesus and his disciples into the land of Judea; and there he tarried with them, and baptized. And John also was baptizing in Aenon, near to Salim, because there was much water there; and, they came and were baptized." John 3:23-24.

"But when he (John the Baptist) saw many of the Pharisees and Sadducees come to his baptism, he said unto them, O generation of vipers, who hath warned you to flee from the wrath to come?

"Bring forth therefore fruits meet for repentance: and think not to say within yourselves, we have Abraham to our father: for I say unto you, that God is able of these stones to raise up children unto Abraham." Matt. 3:7-9.

Throngs by the thousands followed the Lord Jesus Christ in His Mission and ministry. He fed the multitudes, healed the sick, cleansed the lepers, restored sight to the blind and raised their dead. "But He was despised and rejected of men, a Man of Sorrows and acquainted with grief; and we hid as it were our faces from Him; He was despised, and we esteemed him not." Isaiah 53:3. THEN CAME THE HOUR of the crucifixion, Joseph of Arimathea, a wealthy man, used his own tomb, hewn in stone, for the burial of The Son of God! It appears that he believed God as Abraham did of the death of Isaac. (Hebrews 11:17-19). THE RESURRECTION and the forty days after the Resurrection, that were filled with stunning revelations! And, His Ascension was witnessed by more than 500 brethren at once! I Corinthians 15:6. Then, there was the message they proclaimed:

"There was a man of the Pharisees, named Nicodemus, a ruler of the Jews; "The same came to Jesus by night, and said unto Him, Rabbi, we know that thou art a teacher come from God; for no man can do these miracles that thou doest, except God be with him.

"Jesus answered, and said unto him, verily, verily, I say unto thee, Except a man be born again, he cannot see the Kingdom of God. John 3:1-3.

"As it is written, There is none righteous, no not one." Romans 3:10

"He came unto His Own, and His Own received Him not!"

"But as many as received Him, to them gave He the authority (*exousian tekna Theou genesthai*) "Authority the children of God to be" even to them that believe on His Name: (This is in the durative tense, meaning it is forever!!) Who were born, not of blood, nor of the will of the flesh, nor of the will of man, but of God." John 1:ll-13

There was literal terror when The Son of God arose from the dead! when Lazarus was raised panic had seized the leaders of Israel (Matthew 12:1-4) and the Pharisees were terror stricken (John 11:47,48)! Persecution is the fruit of fear! It appears that Caiaphas, being the high priest that same year, assumed from the revelation that the nation was, by this means, to escape the wrath of the Romans! John 11:49-52. (I think that is fascinating!)

Persecution began immediately, with the locked doors of the upper room! The raging of the Pharisees and of the Saducees (who say there is no resurrection of the dead), the Essenes and others who feared for their lives, lest they become victims of Caesar's wrath took refuge in the caves of Engedi!

IN CHAPTER FOUR of the Acts of the Apostles, persecutions began in earnest and the believers increased to about 5,000, the Apostles were put in the hold for overnight, the panic began and never ceased!

The wrath and raging of the Pharisees and Saducees continued to make havoc of the church, Stephen saw the Lord Jesus standing at the right hand of God; 'he was seen of Cephas, then of the twelve: and after that, he was seen of above five hundred brethren at once:' I Cor.15:5-7 he was seen of James; then of all the apostles, he was seen of Paul. My Mother saw little children, Mr. Knewtson, Sunday school superintendent saw an angel, Dwight L. Moody saw the Glory of God, many people who have been revived saw amazing things, need I say more???

"And the angel of the Lord spake unto Philip, saying, Arise and go toward the south unto the way that goeth down from Jerusalem unto Gaza, which is desert. And he arose and went: and, behold, a man of Ethiopia, an eunuch of great authority under Candace queen of the Ethiopians, who had the charge of all her treasure, and had come to Jerusalem to worship, was returning, and sitting in his chariot read Isaiah the prophet.

"Then the Spirit said unto Philip, Go near, and join thyself to this chariot. And Philip ran thither to him, and heard him read the Prophet Isaiah, and

7

said, Understandest thou what thou readest? And He desired Philip that he would come up and sit with him. The place of the Scripture which he read was this, He was led as a sheep to the slaughter; and like a lamb dumb before His shearer, so opened He not his mouth: In His humiliation His judgment was taken away: and who shall decare His generation, for His life is taken from the earth.

"AND THE EUNUCH answered Philip, and said, I pray thee, of whom speaketh the prophet this? Of Himself, or of some other man? Then Philip opened his mouth and began at the same Scripture and preached unto him Jesus. And as they went on their way, they came unto a certain water, and the eunuch said, see here is water: What doth hinder me to be baptized? And Philip said, If Thou believest with all thine heart, thou mayest. And he answered and said, I believe that Jesus Christ is the Son of God.

"AND HE COMMANDED the chariot to stand still: and they went down both into the water, both Philip and the eunuch; and he baptized him. And when they were coming up out of the water, the Spirit of the Lord caught away Philip, and the eunuch saw him no more: and he went on his way rejoicing." Acts 8:26-39.

IT IS NEEDFUL that I quote to you from Matthew Henry at this point, and I do so with aching heart because his description of the act of baptism is so absurd, simply because he ignores the cardinal meaning of baptism. We must proceed to show how he completely ignores this meaning:

"The confession of faith which the eunuch made in order to his being baptized. It is very short, but is is comprehensive and much to the purpose, and was sufficient: *I believe that Jesus Christ is the son of God.* He was a worshipper of the true God, so that all he had to do now was to *receive Christ Jesus the Lord.* (1) He believes that Jesus is *the Christ,* the true messiah promised, *the anointed One.* (2) That Christ is *Jesus – a Saviour,* the only Saviour of his people from their sins. And, (3) That this Jesus Christ is *the Son of God,* that he has a divine nature, as the Son of God, he is the *Heir of all things.* This is the principal peculiar doctrine of Christianity, and whosoever believes this with all his heart, and confess it, they and their seed are to be baptized.) (The N.T. promise that is made to his seed is conditional, based on the continued teaching of his offspring!)

(EVERY LEADER of any consequence agrees that immersion was baptism and that baptism was immersion, when the church started! The authority to 'change' it is without foundation!)

PERHAPS THE PLAIN, SIMPLE DESCRIPTION of the eunuch's baptism is one of the clearer scriptures on baptism and to read the full message, one should read Acts 8:26-40, but the matter of baptism is found in v.35-40: We proceed:

"Then Philip opened his mouth and began at the same Scripture (Isaiah 53), and preached unto him Jesus. And as they went on their way, they came unto a certain water: and the eunuch said, See, here is water; what doth hinder me to be baptized?

"And Philip said, If Thou believest with all thine heart, thou mayest. And he answered and said, I believe that Jesus Christ is the Son of God. And he commanded the chariot to stand still: and they went down both into the water, both Philip and the eunuch; and he baptized him. And when they were come up out of the water, the Spirit of the Lord caught away Philip, that the eunuch saw him no more: and he went on his way rejoicing. But Philip was found at Azotus: and passing through he preached in all the cities, till he came to Caesarea."

The eunuch's request is to be immersed; and that is precisely what Philip did. Now we proceed with Matthew Henry's 'interpretation of Acts 8:26-40):

"The baptizing of him hereupon. The eunuch ordered his coachman to stop, *commanded the chariot to stand still.* It was the best baiting (I believe this should be 'bathing') place he ever met with in any of his journeys. *They went down both into the water,* for they had no convenient vessels with them, being upon a journey, wherewith to take up water, and must therefore go down into it; not that they stripped off their clothes, and went naked into the water, but, going barefoot according to the custom, they went perhaps to the ankles or mid-leg into the water, and Philip sprinkled water upon him, according to the prophecy, which the eunuch had but just now read, for it was but a few verses before those which Philip found him upon, and was apposite to his case (Isaiah 52:15): *So shall he sprinkle many nations, kings and great men shall shut their mouths at him, shall submit to him, and acquiesce in him, for that which they had not heard shall they consider."* (This 'interpretation' of Holy Scripture is false and forbidden! It is handling the Word of God deceitfully!)

Neither Isaiah 52 or 53 has for its subject "baptism"! It is ALL about the Redeeming Blood Atonement. This Scripture states: "Behold, my Servant shall deal prudently, He shall be exalted and extolled, and be very high. As many were astonied (astonished) at thee; His visage was so marred more than any man, and His form more than the sons of men: So shall He sprinkle many nations; the kings shall shut their mouths at him: for that which had not been told them shall they see: and that which they had not heard shall they consider." Furthermore, the description of just how the baptism all happened is not stated in the Word of God, beyond the fact that it occurred. I consider it very dangerous to add to the Word of God. Revelation 22:18,19.

THE WORD TO THE WORLD was spread under terrible persecution. Acts 4 began the open rage and passion! Enraged rulers seeking the worship of the masses for themselves, refused to give glory to Him, while centuries rolled! Three hundred years of merciless blood baths swept the church under ten Emperors of Rome, seeking worship for themselves! Yet the Church grew like a living fire! Violent emperors drove the masses under ground and into the Catacombs; vicious imposters sowed the seeds of discord, yet it grew! Records of the Truth of God, baptisms, and lists of members were guarded with near infinite skill. During the first seven hundred years, the Word was spread throughout the Orient, Europe and North Africa, and some of the Islands. Separate houses were constructed with steps into pools for immersion.

"THE SICKENING CRACKLE of flames attracted the attention of residents near the Circus Maximus in Rome July 18, 64. Trumpets sounded the alarm, but winds whipped the fire into an inferno that spread across the Eternal City, roaring unchecked for a week. Thousands died, and hundreds of thousands became homeless. Rumors circulated that the fire had been started by the emperor himself—26-year-old Nero.

"Nero had become emperor ten years before, and almost from the beginning, the beginning the teenage emperor had gorged himself with eroticism. He arranged the murders of his mother, wives, rivals, and enemies. At the same time, he won praise for his artistic, and athletic pursuits. He began thinking himself a god, though he was actually 'a degenerate with swollen paunch, weak and slender limbs, fat face, blotched skin, curly yellow hair, and dull gray eyes.

"The arson rumors began because Nero had been wanting to raze and rebuild large portions of Rome, planning to rename the city for himself. A fire, people assumed, was just what the emperor had ordered. To divert blame, Nero pointed a finger at Christians. Tacitus wrote that the followers of Christ 'were put to death with exquisite cruelty, and to their sufferings Nero added mockery and derision. Some were covered with skins of wild beasts, left to be devoured by dogs; others were nailed to crosses; numbers of them were buried alive; many, covered with inflammable matter, were set on fire to serve as torches during the night."

Peter and Paul, according to tradition, were among the martyrs. Some were fed to lions, others were forced into gladiatorial conflicts. Let it be clear that baptism was not even an issue in the first 300 years of the Church. First the Jewish persecutions came because of the violent rejection of the Lord Jesus Christ and their total hatred of Him! Then the ten Empire persecutions came because Christ stood in total defiance of the Roman gods, Emperors and the unseen idols of Greek mythology. Crumbling chaos of agnosticism produced the panic that defied The Living God! This is why the insane, blind rage was used of Satan to retain his power!

"But what of the young emperor himself? Four years later he died, too, trembling and terrified in a cold cellar four miles from Rome while hiding from his own army. Trying repeatedly to commit suicide, he faltered and failed until a friend helped him plunge a dagger into his throat.

11

BAPTISM WAS TREATED as a deeply sacred obedience to God. Repentance, faith, and devout obedience to God preceded the confirmation of Faith by baptism, even though it was performed "the same day", at Pentecost!

"But within a short time, the church in Rome was stronger than ever; and, St. Peter's Cathedral stands today on the very spot where Christians were tortured in Nero's Circus." ON THIS DAY – By Robert J. Morgan

BUT, TEN CONSECUTIVE Emperors, leading the bloody Roman beast of Daniel's 4th empire, moved with blood dripping from its fangs and claws, in horrible persecution after horrible persecution, slaughtering thousands of loving, beautiful people who would die rather than follow the way of Rome or drop incense on the candle of the tyrant. They guarded their relationship with Christ much like the beautiful white ermine. When hunters find the ermine's lair, they grease the entry with coarse grease and the ermine will turn to the dogs and die rather than soil its beautiful coat!

THE EMPEROR CONSTANTINE legalized Christianity in the Roman Empire in A.D. 320 and the drama changed radically. "However, Licinius, who controlled the Eastern half of the empire, broke allegiance with the West and continued to suppress Christianity.

"When Licinius demanded that every soldier under his command sacrifice to the Roman gods, the forty Christian men of the 'Thundering Legion' refused. Their general, Lysias, had them whipped, torn with hooks, and then imprisoned in chains. When they refused to bow down and give up their worship of God, he ordered them stripped of their clothing and left in the middle of a frozen Alpine lake until they relented.

"A warm bath was poured for any who would give up their convictions. The men prayed together that their number would not be broken and began to sing, "Forty wrestlers, we, have been to Calvary." However, as it grew dark, one could not bear the cold any longer and ran to the warm bath. One of the guards who had watched the forty brave soldiers sing to Christ became angry that one would give in to Lysias's orders. His anger turned to conviction, and then his conviction turned to faith. He tore off his clothes and ran out to join the mighty forty on the icy lake, fulfilling their promise to be 'forty brave soldiers for Christ!' The forty died together that day (their voices rang out in song in the unbearably frigid, crisp night air, "Forty wrestlers we" until the last lone voice slowly, faintly faded away!) The one who gave up his faith for a warm bath also died that lonely night." EXTREME DEVOTION, the Voice of the Martyrs,

Warfare in the Empire gradually gave way before Constantine. "A purer form of missionary work, however, than that which went from Rome, spread from Ireland, through Scotland to Northern and Central Europe. Ireland first received the Gospel in the third or fourth century, through merchants and soldiers, and by the sixth century it was a Christianized country that had developed such missionary activity, its missions were working from the shores of the north sea and the Baltic to those of the Lake of Constance."

Augustine belonged to the Manichean sect, and was converted by the grace of God, entering the Catholic Church and at first held true evangelical views until the year 400. After this he was chose to advocate the persecution of 'heretics' by his doctrine of the so-called Christian State. At the same time, he urged upon the magistrates clemency and humanity! His noble maxim was "Nothing conquers but the truth, the victory of truth is love." And Neander quite properly observed "contains the germ of the whole system of spiritual despotism, intolerance, and persecution, even to the court of the Inquisition." Tertullian had condemnet heathen persecutors, reminding everyone that Christ and His apostles never persecuted anyone, declaring that god did not employ priest as hangmen! Many, such as Ambrose, Augustine, Gregory Nazianzen and Crysostom trembled at the responsibility of the office and had to be forced, to a great extent, to accept the responsibility of the Office;, but once there, a measure of hesitancy tempered their submission to the office. Gregory Nazianzen declared, "The priest must, above all, be a model of a Christian, offer himself a holy sacrifice to God, and be a living temple of the living God."

The brutal insistence of the State Church on 'having it's way', the horrible treatment of true believers, (roasting, the sword, starvation, etc, by 'whatever means' and the worldliness of the apostate church, the releasing of 'the natural man' who is given to doubt and drifting,' enforced by The State, even the most idolatrous actions, worship of Mary, etc. and blatant idolatry) for hundreds of years destroyed the Spiritual vitality of "The Church!" If this was not enough, then came Gibbon, Renan, Voltaire, and all the Greek Philosophers, Aristotle, Darwin and the 'Age of Reason' brought their blight.

By an illustration that could be multiplied ten thousand fold: Robert J. Morgan's "On This Day", in his devotional urges us to pause and consider; James Mitchel was a a covenanter in the Scotish Presbyterian assembly resisted the imposition of the Anglo Catholic forms of their churches.

"Their resistance drew fire from the monarchy and from the church itself, the chief tormentor being the Prelate, Archbishop James Sharp, who caught and killed Presbyterians like dogs.

"SOMETHING HAD TO BE DONE, Mitchell reasoned. On July 11, 1668, as the archbishop sat in his horse-drawn coach, Mitchell pointed a pistol at him and fired through the open door. He missed hitting another bishop in the hand. Eventually Mitchell was captured, imprisoned, and tortured with the boot, a tight box fitted around the leg into which staves were slowly driven, shattering the leg an inch at a time. Mitchell and his crushed limb were then thrown into a series of squalid prisons where he subsisted on snow water sprinkled with oatmeal.

On January 18, 1678, the preacher and would-be assassin were taken to the center of Edinburgh for execution. Loud drumming drowned out his last words, but he had hidden away two copies of his message, and with the scaffold he flung them to the crowd. The next day these words were plastered across Scotland:

"I acknowledge my private and particular sins have been such as deserved a worse death; but I hope in the merits of Jesus Christ to be free from the eternal punishments due me for sins, I am brought here that i might be a witness for His despised truths and interest in this land, where I am called to seal the same with my blood: and I wish heartily that my poor life may put an end to the persecution of the true members of Christ in this place, so much actuated by the perfidious prelates...

LECKY (*Hist. of* Europe, *Morals*) goes deeper than Gibbon, and accounts for the success of early Christianity by its intrinsic excellency and remarkable adaptation to the wants of the times in the old Roman Empire. "in the midst of this movement," He says, "Christianity gained its ascendency, and we can be at no loss to discover the cause of its triumph. No other religion under such circumstances, had ever combined so many distinct elements of power and attrition." HISTORY OF THE CHRISTIAN CHURCH, Vol. II, p. 16.

For a brief sketch and scan of the ages, to give us a brief by which to keep our perspectives, it is well to keep a broad picture before us to understand the drama of warfare of good and evil.

The baptisteries of the Nicene age, of which many remain in Asia, Africa, and Southern Europe, were built for immersion, and all Oriental churches still adhere to this mode." HISTORY OF THE CHRISTIAN CHURCH, Philip Schaff, Vol. II, p. 248, footnote.

The Russian, Greek-speaking, Orthodox Church has spoken: "The Russian Orthodox Catechism defines baptism as "a sacrament, in which a man who believes, having his body *thrice plunged in water* in the name of God the Father, the Son, and the Holy Ghost, dies to the carnal life of sin, and is born again of the Holy Ghost to a life spiritual and holy," HISTORY OF THE CHRISTIAN CHURCH, Philip Schaff, p.249 footnote.

IT IS AMAZING, but, very quickly the state controlled church was in command; and, although Constantine very likely meant well, the state masterminded church did not function under the Leadership of the Holy Spirit, as God intended. Two Heads for the Church was not acceptable to God. "For there is one God and one Mediator between God and men, The Man, Christ Jesus." Immediately, The State Church would have continued at the expense of the many groups that ran counter to their beliefs.

MARTIN LUTHER was caught in the octopus that had controlled the organization from the outset! Luther sought to restore immersion, but without effect. Calvin proceeded, viewing clearly "the handwriting on the wall," that would simply have dumped both Luther and Calvin, and have proceeded to resist the current of the times!

"Calvin, in his view of the impossibility of change, devised a system of theology that would be acceptable and the thirty years war was consoliidated and focused on the Anabaptist movement with intent to destroy all that did not agree with the Covenant Theology approach. Therefore, Calvin chose to make application of Sprinkling, pouring and immersion to be a matter of indifference, relative to baptism *inst.* Iv.CH. 1

"Whether the person who is baptized be wholly immersed *(mergartur totus)*, and whether thrice or once, or whether water be only poured *(infusa)* or sprinkled upon him *(aspergatur)*, is of no importance *(minimum refert):* but it should be left free to the churches according to the difference of countries and while ancient baptistries continue to be found, they were ignored."

A consolidated reference applying to part of this statement may be found in THE HISTORY OF THE CHRISTIAN CHURCH, Philip Schaff, Vol. 1, p. 251 (I believe this to be sinister; and, a clear break with the forthright teachings of Almighty God.)

DR. A. S. CRAPSEY, formerly an Episcopal rector in Rochester, made the following statement in the introduction to a sermon in defense of Infant baptism: "now in support of this custom of the church, we can bring no express command of the word of God, no certain warrant of Holy Scripture, nor can we be at all sure that this usage prevailed during the apostolic age. From a few obscure hints we may conjecture that it did, but it is only conjecture after all. It is true St. Paul baptized the household of Stephanas, of Lydia, and of the Jailor at Philippi, and in these household there may have been little children: but we do not know that there were, and these inferences form but a poor foundation upon which to base any doctrine. Better say at once and boldly, that infant baptism is not expressly taught in Holy Scripture. Not only is the word of God silent on this subject but those who have studied the subject tell us that Christian writers of the very first age say nothing about it. It is by no means sure that this custom obtained in the church earlier than in the middle of the second or the beginning of the third century." SYSTEMATIC THEOLOGY, A.H. Strong, p. 952

STANDING ON THE WORD OF GOD, ALONE, we are deeply troubled at the horrible treatment of "roasting" and "drowning" of immersion advocates by sprinklers who were backed by civil authority is under the curse of God! Just remember that the 'mother of harlots' of Revelation 17, had no other off-spring that we can trace, other than the multiplied diversity of the churches of Protestantism. (Whose practices coincide with sprinkling)!

DR. MARCUS DODS, "a" rite wherein by immersion in water the participants symbolizes and signalizes transition from an impure to a pure life, his death to a past he abandons, and his birth to a future he desires." HASTINGS DICTIONARY OF CHRIST AND THE APOSTLES.

AS REGARDS THE MODE OF BAPTISM, DR. DODS remarks: "That the normal mode was by immersion of the whole body may be inferred:

> "(a) From the meaning of *baptizo*, which is the intensive or frequentative form of *bapto* "I dip" and denotes to *immrse* or *submerg*, the point is that 'dip' or "immerse" is the primary, 'to wash' the secondary meaning *bapto* or *baptizo*.
>
> "(b) The same inference may be drawn from the law laid down regarding the baptism of proselytes." SYSTEMATIC THEOLOGY, A.H. Strong, P. 938

The Church began with a series of persecutions and beatings. The calm answer of Peter and the rest of the Apostles was "We ought to obey God rather than men." Persecutions first came from Christ-rejecting Israel who said "We will not have this Man to rule over us." The Apostles refused to scatter as they pled for repentance of Israel; and James pled with them well! The Apostles were almost as reluctant to go "into all the world" as Jonah. But, ultimately, they were scattered by blindly subjugated Israel; and, The Roman Empire, yet not before God had raised up Paul to care for the near infinite task of world evangelism. Every Apostle, with the exception of John (and James, who was martyred by Herod) was martyred in a foreign land, even John died in the foreign land of Asia Minor, some time after an effort was made to boil him in oil. (He died at Ephesus, and that after being carried into church for all services continually and so often crying, "Brethren, love one another!" Authorities were terror stricken when the fire would not burn under his martyrdom kettle)! So they exiled him to the Isle of Patmos where he composed the final book of the Bible, Revelation!

DOLLINGER, KIRCHE AND KIRCHEN, 337- "The Baptists are, however from the Protestant point of view, unassailable, since for their demand of baptism by submersion they have the clear Bible text; and the authority of the church and of her testimony is not regarded by either party"- *i.e.* by either Baptists or Protestants, generally. Prof. Harnack, of Giessen, writes in The Independent, Feb. 19, 1885. "*I. baptizein* undoubtedly signifies immersion *(eintauchen)*. 2, No proof can be found that it signifies anything else in the N.T. and in the most ancient Christian literature. The suggestion regarding a 'sacred sense' is out of the question. 3. There is no passage in the N.T. which suggests the supposition that any New Testament writers attached to the word *baptizein* any other sense than *eintauchen=untertauchen* (immerse, submerge) See Com. Of Meyer, and Cunningham, Croall Lectures. SYSTEMATIC THEOLOGY, A.H. Strong, P. 935.

Dr. Broadus makes John's 'baptism unto repentance' mean baptism in order to repentance, repentance including both the purpose of the heart and the outward expression of it, or baptism in order to complete and thorough repentance. But the work of St. Peter and of his fellow Apostles was no mere continuation of that Baptism.

Their baptism was to be into (eis) the Name of the Father and of the Son and of the Holy Spirit. St. Peter's address (Acts 2:36-40) had been directed to the proof that Jesus was the Christ, and it was only natural that the acknowledgment of the cogency of that proof should form the ground of admission to the Christian Church: the ground of the admission to baptism was the recognition of Jesus as the Christ.

Apostelgeschichte is said to bring this out more clearly than (en). It certainly should not be thought strange, that the passage in the *Didache, vii.,3, is cited to prove the early existence of the Invocation of the Holy Trinity in baptism,* and is closely followed by another which we read (ix.5).

A TERRIBLE PERSECUTION, already begun in 64 A.D., spawning hatred of those who refused to bow to civil authority, as the apostles did, drove them into the catacombs! Many leaders of the Church perished in the vicious carnage of nine previous emperors' rage; and, this was continued under Diocletian in 303. Successive decrees ordered all churches destroyed under Diocletian and Christian Scriptures were confiscated, bishops and lesser clergy were put to the torture until they sacrificed to Caesar's image, and ordinary Christians were forced to sacrifice likewise.

But before the persecutions had gone very far, Diocletian retired from the burdens of office and left four coordinate "CAESARS" IN CONTROL. There after, the persecutions became more sporadic. Clashes among the Caesars soon upset the balance among them, and the son of one of them, a man favorable to Christianity, named Constantine, finally overcame all opposition and became, in 323, the sole ruler of the empire." MAN'S RELIGIONS, John B. Noss, P, 460.

"The Oriental and the Orthodox Russian churches require even a *threefold* immersion, in the name of the Trinity, and deny the validity of any other. They look down upon the Pope of Rome as an unbaptized heretic, and would not recognize the *single* immersion of the Baptists.

The Longer Russian Catechism thus defines baptism. "A sacrament in which a man who believes, having his body *thrice dipped* in water in the name of God, the Father, the Son, and the Holy Ghost, dies to the carnal life of sin, and is born again of the Holy Ghost to a life spiritual and holy" Marriott (in Smith and Cheetham, I., 161:) *tripple immersion,* that is thrice dipping the head while standing in the water, was all but universal rule of the church in early times," and quotes in proof Tertullian, Cyril of Jerusalem, Chrysostom, Jerome, Leo, I, etc. But he admits, on page 168 sq, that *affusuion* and *aspersion* were exceptionally also used, especially in clinical baptism, the validity of which Cyprian defended (*Ep.*76 or 69 *ad Magnum*). This mode is already mentioned in the *Didache* (ch. 7) as valid; see my book on the *Did.*, third ed., 1889, pp29 sqq sgg." HISTORY OF THE CHRISTIAN CHURCH, Philip Schaff, Vol. 1, p. 469, 470. (*footnote!*)

I very strongly object to: (1) placing this as a footnote, rather than in the text. This tip toeing on the issue is objectionable. (2) nobody is sick or dead, but the reformation church could take a stronger stand without creating large issues. (3) the teachings of Tertullian, Cyril of Jerusalem, Chrysostom, Jerome, Leo, I, has been expunged, Why? (4) Trine immersion is really unnecessary. I Tim. 2:5; John 10:30. "For there is one God".....

THE MOST EMINANENT GREEK FATHERS of the Nicene age,... adhered to the position of Cyprian and Firmilian, Athanasius, Gregory Nazianzen, Basil, and Cyril of Jerusalem, regarded, besides the proper form, the true Trinitarian faith on the part of the baptizing community, as an essential condition of the validity of baptism. The 45th of the so-called Apostolic Canons threaten those with excommunication who received converted heretics without rebaptism. But a middle view gradually obtained even in the East, which settled at last upon a compromise.

Constantine, leading the forces of Gaul, Spain, and Britain, crossed the Alps under the banner of the cross, to face Maximilian at Milvian Bridge, defeating him, under the sign of The Cross! Maxentius and his army of veterans perished in the waters of the Tiber on Oct. 27 312." It was 323 before this monarch was in absolute control, and, he could declare the Roman Crown obedient to the Cross of Christ, bowing the knee to The Savior.

But he was still Chief Priest of the heathen and a large portion of the century was consumed in the effort to make Christianity the religion of the Empire.. The first proclamation of 312 (which is now lost) was "that every man had a right to choose his religion according to the dictates of his own conscience and honest conviction without compulsion and interference from the government."

This passed into a second edict in 313, Maxentius was forced to comply shortly before he committed suicide. But the successors of Constantine were not so generous and they executed all who did not comply. Consolidation was complete and all seized property of believers was restored at the expense of the Imperial Treasure. Those who refused to comply were ultimately labeled "heretics" and continued to preach and work and grow as "the hunted!" The transition took a number of years. Constantine was seated as head of the organized church clothed in his royal garments and red boots at the Council of Nicea. Constantine's movement underwent the usual struggle in the formation of the empire. Great segments of the Church were left 'outside the camp.' Heb. 13:13. This began a very long period of turmoil and chaos.

Montanists, Novatians, and Donatists, possibly others, were a few of the immersionists who refused to bow in the shattered, persecuted church! These were treated as "heretics" in the centuries that would follow!

"It was doubless hoped by many that when organized Christianity had gained power to enforce its decisions there would be an end of controversy. Yet never had controversy raged so fiercely as in the fourth and following centuries. A MANUAL OF CHURCH HISTORY, Albert Henry Newman, p. 20.

CATHERS OR PURITANS, from the time of Constantine, continued to die for what they believed, being hunted by the Catholic (The Universal) church. Donatists and Novatianists, Arians, Manichaeians, Pelagians, had their issues, but the Donatists were strongly Biblical and very zealous, keeping records for which the authorized 'church' searched. The tares of Matthew13:25; and the leaven of v.33 were strongly at work, (even radically in the Catholic System) and even in the earliest years of the Church.

"Julian, nephew of Constantine, was born in Constantinople in 331 and was made governor and defender of Gaul in 356. There, Julian distinguished himself and his troops proclaimed him Emperor in 361. Constantine died that same year. "The Donatists appealed to him, and he issued an edict annulling whatever had been undertaken against them and restoring to them their churches." See, A MANUAL OF CHURCH HISTORY, Albert Henry Newman, p.322; WORLD BOOK, Julian p.151.

"The Donatist schism was still unabated at the beginning of the fifth century. Augustine, bishop of hippo, was impelled, not only by the high idea of church unity, but also by the annoyance that the schism caused him personally to write against them and to seek to compass their overthrow. The leading points on which Augustine bases his attacks are:

(1) Their persistent *separatism* from the church, which led them to refuse to enter even into social relations with the Catholics.

"(2) Their insistence on the *rebaptism* of the Catholics as a condition of communion with them. This offered the greatest obstacle to the union, necessitating a complete surrender on the part of the Catholics in order thereunto.

"3) He rebuts their charges of persecution on the part of the Catholics by setting forth the *intolerance* of Donatists themselves, citing as the instances, the refusal of Donatists, in a town in which they were predominant to sell bread to Catholics, and the forcible manner in which, in a schism in a Donatist church, led by Maximianus, the stronger party, had seized the church property. The fact that the schism was afterward healed, without requirement of rebaptism on either side, he uses against the Donatists to show their inconsistency in requiring rebaptism of Catholics. The deeds of the fanatical 'circumcelliones' are also used to show the intolerant, persecuting spirit of the Donatists.

The Donatists appealed to Constantine, and he issued an edict annulling whatever had been undertaken against them to seek their overthrow. Constantine made Julian Governor and defender of Gaul. Julian distinguished himself and his troops proclaimed him emperor in 361. Civil war almost resulted, but Constantine died the same year. It will likely the truth of the matter will never be known. (everything was classed as 'heretic' which was not Catholic).

For three centuries, the adamant persecution by the Emperors threatened the Church! Belief flourished that Constantine had brought rest to the Church, but this was not to be! "Constantine having expressly excepted the Donatists' from the privileges conferred on Christians at the beginning of His reign, they appealed to him (then in Gaul) to name judges in that country to inquire into the nature of the divisions at Carthage (313).

Constantine referred the matter to Melchiades, bishop of Rome, and five Gallic bishops before whom he accused Caecilian and ten African bishops, before whom the accused Caecilian and ten African bishops from each side were summoned. A hasty decision in favor of Caecilian resulted.' A MANUAL OF CHURCH HISTORY P. 320.

"In the early fourth century baptism was not performed on children. For a normal catechumen—one who wished to become a member of the Christian Church—the Sacrament of baptism was the culmination of a course of instruction lasting up to three years. Origen, we may recall, was an instructor of catechumens, and he and others employed the prescriptions of the church orders to determine who might and who might not receive baptism. (Constantine became ill while on this excursion for war with Persia, and died within six days, made preparations very quickly for baptism).

"Intensive preparation during lent of those who would be received into the Church, and the initiation ceremony took place at the end of the Easter vigil on Holy Saturday. In 337 Holy Saturday fell on 2 April, and it had passed before Constantine left Constantinople. But the emperor was no ordinary catechumen, and his progression was expedited. The awesome mysteries that attended those admitted into the Christian Faith were performed by Eusebius of Nicomedia: exorcism, the tripple immersion in water, the laying-on of hands. Reborn, the emperor cast aside his purple and crimson garments, the color of power but also of blood, and henceforth wore only pure white robes. He was reborn so that he might die and live forever.

"When the tribunes and senior officers of the armies filed in and lamented, bewailing their own immanent bereavement and wishing him long life, he answered them too by saying he enjoyed true life now and only he knew the good things he had received.' It is at this point that Eusebius' narrative, the only contemporary account of Constantine's final journey, that we realize that the emperor is on campaign, bound for Persia. He was desperately ill. "Eusibius and those who followed him obscured this fact, to dwell on the culmination of Constantine's spiritual journey. Constantine died on 22 may 337." CONSTANTINE, Roman Emperor, Christian Victor, Paul Stephenson. Donatism was by far the more important schism in the church of the period before us (2nd & 3rd Centuries, proceeding on into the 4th and 5th), taking issue with Constantine sweeping into the Church of every foul spirit,

ONE OF THE FIRST problems regarding baptism, was stumbling over the obvious: Belief that Baptism was essential to Salvation! We are NOT redeemed with corruptible things! But, because "visible baptism" could be seen, the Unseen Baptism (I Cor. 12:13) had already occurred! The visible WITNESS was confused with the efficacious fact. I know my conversion (at age 3) was complete and instantaneous for I began to grow even then! I was not baptized until I was 16.

'Justin Martyr gives the following account of baptism: "Those who are convinced of the truth of our doctrine, and have promised to live according to it, are exhorted to prayer, fasting and repentance for past sins; we praying and fasting with them. Then they are led by us to a place where is water, and in this way they are regenerated, as we also have been regenerated; that is, they receive the water-bath in the name of God, the Father and Ruler of all, and of our redeemer Jesus Christ, and of the Holy Ghost. For Christ says: except ye be born again, ye cannot enter the kingdom of heaven. (John 3:5) thus, from children of necessity and ignorance, we become children of choice and of wisdom, and partakers of the forgiveness of former sins.... The baptismal bath is called also, illumination *(psywtismos)* because those who receive it are enlightened in the understanding.'" HISTORY OF THE CHRISTIAN CHURCH, Vol. II, Philip Schaff, p. 247, 248.

AUGUSTINE (354-430) WAS BORN IN Tagaste, a city in northern Africa near what is now Constantine, Algeria. His name in Latin was Aurelius Augustinus. His mother, Saint Monica, was a devout Christian. His father was a pagan. As a young man, Augustine pursued worldly success and was attracted to several non-Christian movements. He described his early life and spiritual struggles in *Confessions*, one of the great autobiographies.

IN THE EARLY 380's, Augustine taught rhetoric in Carthage and Rome and then in Milan, Italy. Some friends in Milan encouraged him to read the works of the Greek philosophers called neo *neoplatonists.* (see Neoplatonism). These writings and the sermons of Saint Ambrose, the bishop of Milan, convinced Augustine to accept Christianity. In 386, he decided to devote himself to the faith, and Ambrose baptized him the next year.

BECAUSE of the overwhelming heed paid to Augustine, I have chosen to give him space. Apparently he was immersed and continued in the good graces of the system in which, by a balancing act, he could continue. His beliefs are obviously moderated and given expression in almost innumerable ways. Soon afterward, Augustine returned to Tagaste, where he organized a community of monks. In 391, he traveled to nearby Hippo. The Christian congregation there persuaded him to stay. He was ordained as a priest in Hippo in 391. From 396 until his death, he served as bishop of Hippo.

HIS BELIEFS can be divided into three main groups: I1) God and the soul (2) sin and grace, and (3) the church and the Sacraments.

GOD AND THE SOUL. Augustine's study of neoplatonism convinced him that God existed in the soul of every human being. He believed that people should direct their attention to God and not be distracted by the cares and pleasures of the world.

SIN AND GRACE. Augustine preached that people could not change their sinful ways unless helped by the grace of God. He believed that God chooses only certain individuals to receive His grace. This belief forms part of a doctrine called *predestination* or *election.*

AS TO THE CHURCH AND THE SACRAMENTS Augustine believed that people could not receive God's grace unless they belonged to the church and received the sacraments. A group of clergymen in northern Africa said that grace could not be given unless the clergy itself was perfect. But Augustine declared that God could bypass human weakness through the sacraments. Augustine's longest book *City of God,* presents the history of mankind as a struggle between those who depend on God and those who rely on themselves. WORLD BOOK A, P.864

"For all have sinned and come short of the Glory of God. Being justified freely by His Grace through the Redemption that is in Christ Jesus:

"whom God hath set forth to be a Propitiation (a mercy seat *hilastnrion*) through faith in His Blood, to declare his righteousness for the remission of sins that are past, through the forbearance of God:

"to declare, I say, at this time His righteousness: that He might be just, and the Justifier of him which believeth in Jesus." Romans 3:23-26.

"One day, as my friend and I were walking down the street, we found ourselves behind a disheveled mother with a grubby little boy in hand. She was angry at the child and was walking much too fast, towing him at a pace his little legs couldn't maintain.

"We reached a busy intersection where the child abruptly stopped and his hand slipped out of his mother's grasp. She turned around, spat out a curse, and trudged on. The little boy sat down on the curb and burst into dears. Without a moment's hesitation, my friend sat down next to him and gathered the little guy in his arms.

"The woman turned and looking at the child, began to curse again. My friend sighed and looked up. "Lady," he said softly, "If you don't want him, I'll take him." Our Daily Bread. March 24th.

Many an aching heart, bitter, angry, helpless and exasperated as this child which had sat down and burst into tears know exactly how he feels! Can't you just hear God's gentle Voice, "Lady, If you don't want him, I'll take him!!" "If you don't want her, I'll take her!" Bring to the Savior your heart cry! HE LOVES YOU! Please! PLEASE DONT make the one fatal mistake!

When I was a teenager, taking one's own life was *very* rare; and, was no solution! ***It isn't now!!*** Hell is forever! CALL SOMEONE, 785 749 5294! Thousands have made the mistake of ignoring God! Please, please don't.

Gellet was the best hunting dog Llewllyn had ever had. One day, when Llewellyn decided to go hunting, the dog was missing. With anger in his heart Llewellyn rushed into the house. In the room where the baby was sleeping in her cradle, he saw Gellet lying on the floor, covered with blood.

Llewellyn glanced toward the cradle. When he didn't see the baby, who was covered with a blanket, he shot the dog, thinking that he had hurt or perhaps killed the baby.

When the sound of the gun awakened the baby, and she began to cry, Llewellen realized how wrong he had been. But it was too late—Gellet was dead.

Then Llewellyn noticed the trail of blood that led to the back door. He followed it and just outside the door he found a dead bear which Gellet had killed to save the baby. How sorry Llewellyn was that in anger he had killed the faithful dog that had saved his baby! ~ ALICE MARIE KNIGHT

ONE MUST BE SHOCKED TO SILENCE that so much wrong is done through misunderstanding, yet it obviously was not misunderstanding alone and it must be faced for what it is: men are fallible, self-seeking, and capricious. (Read the list: Romans 1:28-32) There is a way that seemeth right unto a man, but the end thereof are the ways of death! The wages of sin is death; but, the gift of God is eternal life, through Jesus Christ our Lord!

"Wherefore, as by one man sin entered into the world, and death by sin; and so death passed upon all men, for that all have sinned." Romans 5:12.

"For the wages of sin is death; but the gift of God is eternal life through Jesus Christ our Lord." Romans 6:23.

"BUT GOD commendeth His Love toward us, in that, while we were yet sinners, Christ died for us.

"MUCH MORE, then, BEING NOW JUSTIFIED BY HIS BLOOD, we shall be saved from wrath through Him.

"For if, when we were enemies, we were reconciled to God, by the death of His Son, much more, being reconciled, we shall be saved by His Life.

"And not only so, but we also joy in God through our Lord Jesus Christ, by Whom we have now received the Atonement."(*i. e.* Reconciliation). Romans 5:8-11

"We give thanks to God always for you all, making mention of you in our prayers.

"Remembering without ceasing your work of faith, and labor of love and patience of hope in our Lord Jesus Christ, in the sight of God and our Father;

"Knowing, brethren beloved, your election of God.

"For our gospel came not unto you in word only, but also in power, and in the Holy Ghost, and in much assurance; as ye know what manner of men we were among you for your sake.

"And ye became followers of us and of the Lord, having received the Word in much affliction, with joy of the Holy Ghost.

"So that ye were ensamples to all that believe in Macedonia and Achaia." I Thess.1:2-7.

"But as many as received Him, to them gave He the power to become the sons of God, even to them that believe on His Name. Who were born, not of blood, nor of the will of the flesh, nor of man, but of God. John 1:12-13.

"And this is the record, that God hath given us eternal life; and this life is in His Son." He that hath the Son hath life; and he that hath not the Son of God hath not life. These things have I written unto you that believe on the Name of the Son of God; that ye may know that ye have eternal life, and that ye may believe on the Name of the Son of God." I John 5:11-13

In acts 19:1-5 "And it came to pass, that, while Apollos was at Corinth, Paul having passed through the upper coasts came to Ephesus; and finding certain disciples, He said unto them, have ye received the Holy Ghost since ye believed? And they said unto him, we have not so much as heard whether there be any Holy Ghost.

"And he said unto them, unto what then were ye baptized? (e'Baptisthae)? And they said, Unto Johns baptism (Baptisma), then said Paul, John verily baptized (e'Baptisma) with the baptism of repentance saying unto the people that they should believe on him which should come after him, that is on Christ Jesus. When they heard this, they were baptized (e'Baptisthasan) in the name of the Lord Jesus." Acts 19:1-5

These dear people did not realize The Lord Jesus had come. They were overjoyed and were baptized in the Name of The Lord Jesus.

"Conant, Appendix to Bible Union of Matthew, 64 has samples drawn from writers in almost every department of literature and science; from poets, rhetoricians, philosophers, critics, historians, geographers; from writers on husbandry, on medicine, on natural history, on grammar, on theology; from almost every form and style of composition, romances, epistles, orations, fables, odes, epigrams, sermons, narratives: from writers of various nations and religions, Pagan, Jew, and Christian, belonging to many countries and through a long succession of ages. In all, the word has retained its ground-meaning without change.

From the earliest ages of Greek literature down to its close, a period of nearly two thousand years, not an example has been found in which the word has any other meaning. There is no instance in which it signifies to make a partial application of water by affusion or sprinkling, or to cleanse, to purify, apart from the literal act of immersion as the means of cleansing or purifying." See Stuart, in Biblical Repos., 1833: 313; BROADUS ON IMMERSION, 57, Note MEYER, Com. *In loco "ean ma' Baptizwntai"* is not to be understood of washing the hands (Lightfoot, Wetstein), but of immersion, which the word in classic Greek and in the N.T. everywhere means; here, according to the context, to take a bath." The Revised Version omits the words "and couches," although Maimonides speaks of a Jewish immersion of couches; see quotation from Maimonides in Ingham, Handbook of Baptism373- "whenever in the law washing of the flesh or of the clothes is mentioned, it means nothing else than the dipping of the whole body in a laver; for if any man dip himself allover except the tip of his little finger, he is still in his uncleanness.... A bed that is wholly defiled, if a man dip it part by part, it is pure." Watson, in Annotated Par. Bible, 1126.

It was on a Sunday morning and as the invitation was given to take The Lord Jesus, as Savior and Lord. A precious boy of eight or nine years stepped out and came forward like an adult, and said, "I would like to receive the Lord Jesus as my Savior."

I carefully led him to Faith in Christ, when he bowed to pray calmly to receive the Lord Jesus as his Savior. Then, with shining eyes, he asked, "May I tell these people what I have done?" "Of course you may," I replied. Then he stood and matter-of-factly said, with happy heart and smiling face, "I have taken the Lord Jesus to be my savior."

(I suspect that his witness was given freely to his mother and her 'live in', for he beheaded the child and threw him in the river! This child, that day, was added to God's martyrs for The Faith as he moved into the glorified ranks of God's beautiful people in eternal glory!! May God have mercy on the wretch's eternal miserable soul who could behead such a beautiful child! I will never forget this darling boy!!)

Baptism is mentioned 12 times in the Epistles of Paul (not even once is it called 'sprinkling'): Four of those speak of Spirit Baptism, One of Moses, Five of Paul's baptism, Two mentions of baptisms for the dead. **MUCH BLOOD** has been spilled over "Infant Baptism"! Yet *Calvin and Luther forthrightlty declared their belief that ALL baptism 'from the beginning' was by immersion!*

"Paul's letters are our primary source for our knowledge of the beginnings of Christianity, for they are the earliest debatable Christian documents the most important of them having been written between eighteen and thirty years of the Death of Jesus." "Apostle of the heart set free" F.B. Bruce. P. 16.

THERE ARE TWENTY (20) word forms (all of them meaning uniformly immersion) in the New Testament. They are in agreement with the eight tenses of grammar: *Baptizei; Baptizein;Baptizeis; Baptizomai; Baptizonmai, Baptizomeoni; Baptizontai;Baptizomenoi;Baptizontai;*

Baptizontes; Baptizw; Baptiswn; Baptai; Baptisantes; Baptisei; Baptise\theis; Baptiwstheis; Baptisthentes; Baptisthentos; Baptisthenai; Baptisthanesthe; Baptisthatw!!

Baptizw *(baptize)* dip, immerse, baptize (966); *Baptw (bapto)* dip *(970) Baptismos (baptismos), dipping, washing (968) Baptisma (baptisma)* baptism (967) *Baptistns (baptistes)* baptizer, Baptist (969)

CHAPTER II

THE PROPER BASIS
FOR BAPTISM

England's Reformation, inaugurated by Henry Viii, Elizabeth I, and James I, was largely political. The genuine reformers, the puritans and separatists, were opposed. But then, so were the Roman Catholics.

"Good Queen Bess" used fines, gallows, gibbets,; racks, and whips against those who said Mass, honored the pope, or harbored a priest, Reputed Catholics had no peace. Often in the middle of the night, thugs would burst in and drag them away to be scourged, fined, or seared with glowing irons.

Nicholas Owen, probably a builder by trade, designated countless hiding places for endangered Catholics. He hid them in secret rooms and between the walls and under the floors, he hid them in stone fences and in underground passages. He designed nooks and crannies that looked like anything but hiding places.

He was a slight man, nicknamed "Little John", so the royalists long discounted him of hiding so many. He seemed too small to move stones, break walls, and excavate the earth. But he viewed his work as divine. He always began construction of a hideaway by receiving the Eucharist. He prayed continually during the building, and he committed the spot to God.

He also proved a master at devising getaways for helping Catholics escape prison. He was an escapist himself, having several aliases and disguises. Perhaps no one saved the lives of more Catholics in England during those days than Nicolas Owen.

But Nicholas was at last betrayed. Taken to the Tower of London, his arms were fixed to iron rings and he was hung for hours,; his body dangling. Weights added to his feet increased the suffering, yet not a word of information passed his lips. The tortures continued till March 2, 1606, when "his bowels broke in a horrible way" and he passed to his reward. He was canonized by the church and is honored each year on March 22, in Catholic tradition the feast day of St. Nicholas Owen. ON THIS DAY, Robert J. Morgan.

"I HAVE BEEN CRUCIFIED with Christ, nevertheless I live; yet not I, but Christ liveth in me; and the life which I now live in the flesh I live by The Faith of the Son of God, who loved me and gave Himself for me." Galatians 2:20 (Paul's witness to his experience)

"THE PENTECOSTAL BAPTISM. The Risen Lord had charged His disciples 'Not to depart from Jerusalem, but to wait for the promise of the Father, which, said he, ye heard from me: for John indeed baptized with water; but ye shall be baptized with the Holy Ghost not many days hence' Acts 1"5)."

"And when the day of Pentecost was fully come, they were all with one accord in one place.

"And suddenly there came a sound from Heaven like a rushing Mighty Wind, and it FILLED ALL THE HOUSE where they were sitting. (They were immersed in the Holy Spirit)

"And there appeared unto them cloven tongues as of fire, and it sat upon each of them."

The house where they were sitting became a huge baptistry, conforming to the meaning of *BAPTIZO.* There is most certainly significance in each part of Holy Scripture and the wise will take note. (Speaking with tongues (and they all understood in the language into which they were born) The questions were all answered regarding those present at Pentecost, In the division with the Samaritans, in the house of Cornelius, and with the dozen men in Acts 19. This completed all the doubtful). There is One

Calvary and One Pentecost, for all who are learning faithfully! For others, I Cor. 14:38, I believe this relates to stubborn, blind ignorance of those who believe 'tongues' are added to believing; also, that gibberish is 'tongues', although I doubt there is a people on earth who could understand the folly of those who believe it to be needful! *(Believers NEVER sought baptism with the Holy Spirtf!!)* **We are never told that even the Corinthians sought it. But Paul, rather than create issues, gave them I Corinthians 13.)**

"Ye have not chosen Me, but I have chosen you, and ordained you, that ye should go and bring forth fruit, that your fruit should remain; that whatsoever ye shall ask of the Father in My Name, He may give it you." John 15:16.

TRANSFORMED LIVES (as nearly as possible) was to be the thrill of their experience as they began a walk with God, rejoicing in Him as they began that walk as transformed men, moving into all the world preaching and teaching the Eternal Word of God; and, preaching the Gospel to every creature.

But until we have IMMERSED every person earth, in the Name of The Father, and of The Son, And, of The Holy Spirit, we have not completed the command of our Lord Jesus Christ.

The issue is clear: *Baptizo* does not have seven meanings! It means to "plunge into" to "totally submerge"! It cannot possibly have another meaning. Why should anyone even dare to call "sprinkling" and "Pouring" *Baptizo...* *but..* they DO dare call it baptism.....though every leading advocate of sprinkling and pouring acknowledges that the original Church immersed its converts!! Let it not become a matter of blame. Let's fix it.

"TACITUS in his *Annals* illustrates vividly the dynamic of The Great Commission and also the diabolical opposition to the spread of the Christian Gospel, (Nero's being musically inclined did not exempt him from being merciless) as Tacitus says of him, in his account of the great fire in Rome in 64 A.D.:

"but all the endeavors of men, all the Emperor's largesse and the propitiation of the gods, did not suffice to allay the scandal or banish the belief that the fire had been ordered. And so, to get rid of this rumor, Nero "set up as the culprits and punished with the utmost refinement of cruelty a class hated for their abominations, who are commonly called Christians. Christus, from whom their name is derived, was executed at the hands of procurator Pontius Pilate in the reign of Tiberius.

"Checked for the moment, this pernicious superstition again broke out, not only in Judea, the source of the evil; but, even in Rome, that receptacle of everything that is sordid and degrading from every quarter of the globe, which there finds a following. Accordingly, arrest was first made of those who confessed (sc., to being Christians)' then, on their evidence, an immense multitude was convicted, not so much on the charge of arson as because of hatred of the human race. Besides being put to death they were made to serve as objects of amusement; they were clad in the hides of beasts and torn to death by dogs; others were crucified, others set on fire to serve to illuminate the night when daylight failed.

"Nero had thrown open his grounds for the display, and was putting on a show in the circus, where he mingled with the people in the dress of charioteer or drove about in his chariot. This gave rise to a feeling of pity, even towards men whose guilt merited the most exemplary punishment; for lit was felt that they were being destroyed not for the public good but to gratify the cruelty of an individual." (xv.44)" THE LIGHT IN DARK AGES, Dr. V. Raymond Edmond. (Foreword).

Dr. Edmond says, "They were to go into all the world, to teach and preach, to baptize and to make disciples, to be witnesses unto Him and to care for His sheep. The Word of God was to be the basis of their message of light and their unfailing weapon against their adversaries; the Spirit of God was to be their power; the whole world was to be their parish. The program was to be The Word to the World in the dynamic of the Spirit. Centuries later the Moravaians paraphrased thus the spirit of the Great Commission: *"To win for the Lamb that was slain a reward for His sufferings.* It was to proclaim "Thus Saith the Lord," to those who knew not His truth: it was to bring Light to those who sat in darkness and in the shadow of death." LIGHT IN DARK AGES, Dr. V. Raymond Edmond, p. 13.

"If the closest relationships of life clash with the claims of Jesus Christ He says it must be instant obedience to Himself. Discipleship means personal passionate devotion to a Person, Our Lord Jesus Christ. There is a difference between devotion to a Person and devotion to principles or to a cause. Our Lord never proclaimed a cause: He proclaimed personal devotion to Himself. To be a disciple is to be a devoted love-slave of the Lord Jesus. Many of us who call ourselves Christians are not devoted to Jesus Christ. No man on earth has this passionate love of the Lord Jesus unless the Holy Ghost has imparted it to him." MY UTMOST FOR HIS HIGHEST Oswald Chambers July 2nd p..184

"It is sometimes supposed that Scripture is not sufficient for the guidance of the churches without the addition of at least, early traditions, on the ground that it was by the early church councils that the canon of Scripture was fixed. This of course could only refer to the New Testament." THE PILGRIM CHURCH, E. H. Broadbent, p 22

THERE is a very solid basis for Immersion in the Bible. It is not at all optional whether one BE Baptized! Nor is it optional WHY one should be Baptized! Nor is it optional HOW one is Baptized! What IS optional, is the highest privilege of being committed to Christ in the absolute!! What is amazing is all of the chaos that surrounds the subject until the minds and hearts of humanity at large are completely confused, paralyzed and dead!

FOR CENTURIES political dominance made all publicly received records open to the revision of the 'legal' body. Ambiguity of the facts and deletion of records confuse the issue!

The idea of Baptism: "It was solemnly instituted by Christ shortly before his ascension, to be performed in the name of the Father, the Son, and the Holy Spirit.... It is the outward mark of Christian discipleship, the rite of initiation into the covenant of grace...It is the sign of absolute commitment. Regeneration by the power of the Holy Spirit has already occurred, and the cry goes out: "What will you do with Jesus Who is called Christ?"

The absolute commitment of the Redeemed, inducting the believer into the beautiful glory of righteousness. Baptism is the forthright declaration that this is fact and is spoken of as "obedience to the faith. It incorporates the penitent sinner in the visible church and entitles him to all the privileges and frees him to walk in righteousness. In the nature of the case, it is to be received but once, by faith. Infant baptism is never addressed in Scripture but there is much Scripture which follows the pattern of Deuteronomy 6:1-12. In due course, it should be anticipated that the child shall seek baptism, voluntarily, and should be encouraged to do so.

"The church has always held the principle that the mere want of the sacrament does not condemn, but only the contempt. Otherwise all un-baptized infants that die in infancy would be lost. This horrible doctrine was indeed inferred by St. Augustine and the Roman church, from the supposed absolute necessity of baptism, but is in direct conflict with the spirit of the gospel and Christ's treatment of children, to whom belongs the kingdom of heaven." HISTORY OF THE CHRISTIAN CHURCH, by Philip Schaff.

"The oriental and the orthodox Russian churches require a threefold immersion, in the name of the Trinity, and deny the validity of any other. They look down upon the Pope of Rome as an un-baptized heretic, and would not recognize the single immersion of the Baptists. The Longer Russian Catechism thus defines baptism: "A sacrament in which a man who believes, having his body thrice plunged in water in the name of God, the Father, the Son, and the Holy Ghost, dies to the carnal life of sin, and is born again of the Holy Ghost to a life spiritual and holy." Footnote, P.468, HISTORY OF THE CHRISTIAN CHURCH by Philip Schaff. Vol.1

"As to the subject of baptism: the apostolic origin of infant baptism is denied not only by the Baptists, but also by many Paedobaptist divines. The Baptists assert that infant baptism is contrary to the idea of the sacrament itself, and, accordingly, an unscriptural corruption. For baptism, say they, necessarily presupposes the preaching of the gospel on the part of the church, and repentance and faith on the part of the candidate for the ordinance; and as infants cannot either understand preaching, nor repent and believe, they are not proper subjects for baptism, which is intended only for adult converts." HISTORY OF THE CHRISTIAN CHURCH, by Philip Schaff, VOL. 1, P.469, 470.

It is frankly admitted by Calvin, Zwingly and Luther that baptism 'at the first" was by immersion. It is pathetic that by the 15th Century there had been enough bloodshed over the issue for literally hundreds of thousands had given their lives in the cause that must be whitewashed. The legal force was almost always on the side of Sprinkling, confirming that "the god of this world" is Satan.

"After the council of Carthage, A.D., 256, we find it a regular part of the ceremony of baptism, preceding the baptism proper, and in some cases it would seem, several times repeated during the course of catechetical instruction." Footnote, p. 250 "POURING AND SPRINKLING WERE EXCEPTIONAL IN THE NINTH CENTURY ACCORDING TO Walafrid Strabo. (*De Rel. Eccl, c* 26) but they made gradual progress with spread of infant baptism, as the most convenient mode, especially in northern climates and came into common use in the West at the end of the thirteenth century," HISTORY OF THE CHRISTIAN CHURCH, Philip Schaff Vol. II, P.251

"Their energies into were spent in incessant traveling, and they were successful in spreading the Gospel and founding churches as far as the most remote parts of Asia. In the fourth century, when the churches in the Roman world had respite from persecution they had suffered, those in Persia and the east entered into a time of fiery testing such as they had not hitherto experienced. They endured and, their faith and patience prevailed.!

"Already the *vandals* had moved from their homeland in western Germany (406), first into Gaul (France), and over the Pyrenees into Spain; and later across the straits of Gibraltar into North Africa (429), to found an empire whose capital city was Carthage. In the year 455 they crossed the Mediterranean to capture Rome and to plunder it as had the Visigoths a generation earlier. The destruction wrought by these barbarians has been immortalized in the term "vandalism." Among the treasures alleged to have been removed to Africa were the sacred vessels from the Temple in Jerusalem, brought to Rome by Titus, and undisturbed since the year 70. the *Burgundians* moved into the upper reaches of the Rhine, while the *Franks* crossed the lower Rhine into northern France." THE LIGHT IN DARK AGES, DR.V. RAYMOND EDMOND., P.11.

Having already permeated Europe, great restlessness and very chaotic conditions moved Saxons, Angles, Ostrogoths and Huns called the "scourge of God" while Mongols plundered central Europe until driven back by Visigoths and Romans at Chalons (451). It is another turbulent, chaotic force with which the Christian Church was forced to deal, a Satanic onslaught creating crisis after crisis!

"This ordinance (baptism) was regarded in the ancient church as the sacrament of the new birth or regeneration, and as the solemn rite of Initiation into the Christian church, admitting to all her benefits and committing to all her obligations. It was supposed to be preceded in the case of adults, by instruction on the part of the church, and by repentance and faith (*i.e.* conversion) on the part of the candidate, and to complete and seal the spiritual process of regeneration, the old man being buried, and the new man arising from the watery grave. Its effect consists in the forgiveness of sins and the communication of the Holy Spirit. Justin calls baptism "the bath of conversion and the knowledge of God." It is often called also illumination, spiritual circumcision, anointing, sealing, gift of grace, symbol of redemption, death of sins, &c." HISTORY OF THE CHRISTIAN CHURCH, Philip Schaff, Vol.II, P. 253

THE SEARCH of the modern mind and heart of The Word of God, The Will of God, The Witness of God and for The True Church that lives in The 21st Century, will be best helped by giving a very simple reading of Holy Scripture, since the Bible is the Infinite, Eternal, Word of God.

THE BASIC TEXT *used in this work is The 1611 King James Version of Holy Scripture, with current language in those parts where English Text is clarified, with current words where Original Text meanings might be helpful. Many current translations use of some questionable and doubtful manuscripts that have not been carefully examined, in their use of documents found by archeologists since 1611; and, often with wording that cannot be sustained by The Original Text. None of those later, possibly accurate, possibly inacurate, manuscripts justify any doctrinal change in our current Text of The Word of God.*

IN EPHESIANS 4:1-3, THE APOSTLE PAUL pleads that believers endeavor to keep the Unity of The Spirit in the bond of peace. The Church in our modern world is in tragic straits in its shattered, complex, infiltrated form. It is adding tragically to the confused state of an already blinded and confused world! Its multiplicity of conflicting voices, Satan's most destructive work, is being done from inside the "false front" of a highly complex Christendom. Read Nehemiah 6 to see the near infinite efforts of Satan to confuse!

Believing God has called me to this effort; and, that many hearts hunger for broader church harmony, existing facts are here used in this effort to draw believing hearts into a more unified spirit of obedience to our Lord and the joys harmony always brings!

Hopefully, this will prove to be a useful means for shedding abroad the Love of Christ, to unite hearts around our wonderful Lord. Laxity of pure doctrinal teaching has permitted Satan to enter, carve, and destroy, thus blurring the Truth even more in the eyes of man, making man even less receptive to God's Spirit's Strong Efforts to keep the Unity of the Spirit in the Bond of Peace! (i.e. II John 7-11; III John 9-11; I Corinthians 3:1-3, Hebrews 2:1-4, etc.).

"The distinguishing principle of the Waldenses bore on daily conduct and was summed up in the words of the apostles, "We ought to obey God rather than men." This the Catholics interpreted to mean a refusal to submit to the authority of the pope and prelates." (The Waldenses kept rigid and implicit written records of the Centuries carefully hid and persistently kept.") HISTORY OF THE CHRISTIAN CHURCH, Vol. V. p. 502.

"As for the administration of baptism, there were also differences of view between the Waldenses of Italy and those of France. There was a disposition (firmness) in some quarters to deny infant baptism and to some extent the opinion seems to have prevailed that infants were saved without baptism." HISTORY OF THE CHRISTIAN CHURCH Vol. V, p.504 (c.1179)

(The principles of Transformation defy "water" as the element of Transformation)

COVENANT THEOLOGY, which was formulated by John Calvin bred a strong and strange ideology. Water baptism is made to have saving efficacy and yet sprinkling is the mode. Awe surrounds the experience of baptism; yet, there is not the forthright facing of the real meaning of Baptizo; and, trembling fear is clearly present. Therefore, it strongly fosters doubt and insecurity. Let us hear his thought and apprehension:

"The matter still remains uncertain, unless we understand who are the weak and who the Pharisees; for if this distinction is destroyed I see not how in regard to offenses, any liberty at all would remain without being constantly in the greatest danger. But Paul seems to me to have marked out most clearly, as well by example as by doctrine, how far our liberty, in the cases of offense, is to be modified or maintained. When he adopts Timothy as his companion, he circumcises him: nothing can induce him to circumcise Titus (Aacts 16:3; Gal. 2:3). INSTITUTES of the CHRISTIAN RELIGION, John Calvin, Vol. III., p 138,

"During the administration of Bernard Guy, as inquisitor of Toulouse (1306- 1329), forty-two persons were burnt to death, sixty-nine bodies were exhumed and burnt, three hundred and seven were imprisoned, and one hundred and forty-three were condemned to wear crosses." HISTORY OF THE CHRISTIAN CHURCH Vol. V. p. 528

Possibly there were diversified reasons for the persecution, but quite obviously much of it was because of the baptism of believers. Faithful, obedient followers of Christ have labored diligently to build His Church in harmony with the clear teachings of Holy Scripture! The materials used in this book have been used of Him to build harmony where I have served under His Calling! It is striking that the Catholic Church near Waterloo, Iowa (c. 2000) was constructed with a baptistry for immersion!!

"The union of Church and State was in all times looked upon by many of the Lord's disciples as contrary to His teaching; but whenever the Church had the power of the State at it command, it used it for the forcible suppression of any who dissented from its system or in any way refused compliance with its demands; and, great numbers through indifference, antagonism or fear, have been untaught. Thank God, hungry hearts have been kept warm to the desire to follow Christ and keep the teachings of His Word, crying out for the Truth of God; and, for the doctrine of the Apostles. These were continually objects of persecution, in history." THE PILGRIM CHURCH, Ch. III, Paulicans and Bogomils (50-1473) p. 57

"Baptism, the original form of which was immersion, cleanses from original sin and incorporates into the body of Christ. Children of Jews and infidels are not to be baptized without the consent of their parents." HISTORY OF THE CHRISTIAN CHURCH, Vol. V. p.671

TERTULLIAN does not make mention of John's martyrdom, but Origen mentions the Roman Oil-martyrdom of John, when the fire refused to burn and seems to point to the persecution under Nero. Epiphanius puts the banishment under the reign of Claudius, which seems to be much too early, but Eusibius says definitely that John returned from Patmos to Ephesus after the death of "the tyrant," John is buried at Ephesus, (under the name of 'John the Presbyter'), after a very long life, when he was carried to services, and his last words seem to have been "Little Children, love one another!" Jerome assigns the exile and the composition of the Apocalypse to the reign of Domitian. I find "love" mentioned 33 times in the Book of I John. (A.D. 51-96) SO we love the saints "Immersed" and "Sprinkled"; but we must stand by the truth, faithfully; and, Immerse.

The Ten Great Persecutions which occurred under ten consecutive Roman emperors, makes the conserving of records extremely difficult, they began with Nero and terminated with The Conversion of Constantine; from The Catacombs through the ages of time to the Mayflower Charter. The Constitution of the United States gave great respite to the followers of The Lord Jesus Christ and they have refused to give up the Truths which they knew to be His Teachings! The world at large has continued the slaughter of God's own precious people! There are well over one million souls that have been slaughtered within the past century.

HISTORY HAS PRESERVED FOR US, with volumes of records of the evil leaven at work within the professing church. Aristotle's philosophy from the 11th to the 17th century held an enormous influence over the church, with devastating effect! Unsaved have been welcomed into the professing church; and infant baptism has been a disaster! This has had the highly corrupting effect illustrated by The Lord Jesus, in Matthew 13:33, likening the receiving of unconverted humanity into the church, with the corrupting effect which He likened to leaven in baking dough!

POLYCARP who lived c.69 to 155 A.D., disciple of St. John, absorbed much of the beauty of the gracious, tender caring of his teacher and was martyred triumphantly after servint the church for 86 years, declaring "eighty and six years have I served my wonderful Lord. He has done me no wrong!" Therefore he went joyously to his death!

TERTULLIAN c.160 to 230, OBSERVED the conflict of the ages, as Satan had violently attacked the church and great confusion had already begun! He noted how some who were already dead without being baptized, were being immersed in water in the waters of baptism, also that infants were beginning to be baptized, when there was no warrant in Scripture for it. He very strenuously objected to both problems and this can be read in his works.

The North African church had the immersion baptistries in the period before us. (311-600) For a whole century it divided the North African churches, for there were many unanswered questions, particularly in those areas where the Greek language was not well understood.

"The beginnings of the Donatist schism appear in the Diocletian persecution which revived that controversy concerning church discipline and martyrdom. The rigoristic party favored by Secundus of Tigisis at that time primate of Numidia and led by the bishop Donatus of Case Nigrae rushed to the martyrs crown with fanatical contempt of death and saw in flight from danger or in the delivering up of the sacred books only cowardice and treachery which should forever exclude from the fellowship of the church." HISTORY OF THE CHRISTIAN CHURCH Philip Schaff Vol. III P. 260-261.

"THE DELIVERING up of the sacred books" it appears to me was caused by a passionate determination on the part of 'the controlled body of the church' to 'edit' the books to make them conform to please themselves. The Holy Scriptures were forbidden to 'the church' under the excuse "they had to be interpreted" in large blocks of Europe and wherever Catholicism was spread. Translators took their lives in their hands in daring to translate the Holy Scriptures into 'the language of the people!

Terror reigned for centuries; the bones of Wm. Tyndale, e.g., were exhumed, burned and strewn upon the Thames! May God have mercy on the professing church!

The professing church's mass acceptance of members, without conversion, or baptism, in 'state church' blocks, recognizing heathen idolatrous meeting places as churches! This occurred in 313 B.C., following the conversion of Constantine and set the stage for the strong heresy problems; from that time, even further complications of the interpretation of The Inspired Holy Scripture; and, the rampant apostasy which made a fertile setting for 'fabricated' doctrines! E.g., The farce of "The Mother of God!"

The dissenting movement started with the people and not with the schools or princes. As much provocation as the princes had for showing their resentment at the avarice and worldliness of the clergy: and, (their proneness to use the realm of civil authority), (conflicts were frequent.) The vast majority of those who suffered punishment, as heretics, were of the common people. The heresy of a later period, the fifteenth century, differs in this regard, having scholars among its advocates."...... "Underneath all this discontent was the spiritual hunger of the masses. The Bible was not an altogether forgotten book. The people remembered it. Popular preachers like Bernard of Thiron, Robert of Abrissel, and Vitalis of Savigny, quoted its precepts and relied upon its authority. There was a hankering after the Gospel which the Church did not set forth. (ref.) THE HISTORY Of

THE CHRISTIAN CHURCH, Philip Schaff, Vol. V, (The Middle Ages. A.D. 1049-1294) p. 462, 63.

"The church historian, Eusebius of caesarea (c260-c.340), to whom we are indebted for almost all of our information about Origien's life, presented him as an ideal Christian scholar and saint in the sixth book of his Ecclesiastical History. Unfortunately, Eusebius wrote fifty years after Origen's death, and had relatively little reliable information at his disposal about Origenl's life, especially his early years. Furthermore, he suppressed some evidence that did not place Origen in the best possible light, accepted hearsay evidence that a modern historian would reject, and made questionable inferences from the information he did have. This has made it very difficult to write convincingly about Origen's life." ORIGEN, Joseph Wilson Trigg, p. 9.

In the time of The German Reformation, A.D. 1517 to 1530, Philip Schaff's History of The Christian Church states: "Luther thanks God. He agrees essentially with the Roman doctrine, and considers baptism as a means of regeneration;.. "As to the *mode* of baptism, he gives here, as elsewhere, his preference to immersion, which then still prevailed in England and in some parts of the Continent, and which was not a point of dispute either between Romanists and Protestants, or between Protestants and Anabaptists; while on the question of *infant* baptism the Anabaptists differed from both." THE HISTORY OF THE CHRISTIAN CHURCH, Philip Schaff, Vol. VII, p.218

Roman Catholic churches were built with large baptisteries for immersion as late as the 12th Century; and, in some areas as late as the 16th Century. Eastern Greek Orthodox churches never ceased to immerse; and, accept no other action as valid baptism, as those who understand their own language well until today, because that is what the word *baptize (baptidzo)* signifies.

The Greek *baptizo* was 'transliterated' into the English word 'baptize', as The King James Version to get approval by King James and The Church of England, blurring the meaning of *baptizo*, so that the significance and proper practice of the Greek *baptizo* was ignored, and the enemy came in like a flood!

"in the report of the Council of the archbishop of Cologne about the 'Anabaptist movement,' to the Emperor Charles V, it is said that the Anabaptists call themselves 'true Christians', that they desire community of goods, 'which has been the way of Anabaptists for more than a thousand years, as the old histories and imperial laws testify.' At the dissolution of the Parliment at Speyer it was stated that the 'new sect of the Anabaptists' had already been condemned many hundreds of years ago and "by common law forbidden.' It is a fact that for more than twelve centuries baptism in the way taught and described in the New Testament had been made an offense against the law, punishable by death." THE PILGRIM CHURCH, E.H. BROADBENT, p 154 Par. 2.

From the 4th Century onward, some sprinkling and pouring were done at the request of the infirm, not as The Church's practice; and, was termed by The Church, at that time, as "clinical baptism" in justifying its usage.

However, the stature of those within The Church, as Constantine was falsely stated to have been sprinkled. Not so! (Constantine experienced 'trine-immersion') and Augustine (I find nothing in Augustine, but EVEN WERE HE TO BE VAGUE ENOUGH IN HIS VOLUMINOUS WRITING, *IT IS NOT FOUNDED ON THE WORD OF GOD!!*

In approaching death without their having been baptized, IS SAID TO use of 'clinical' baptism, or sprinkling! That is not true! Read the record. It is in this book! This had a broad influence on the entire Church. Later, those who refused to accept the standard of 'clinical' baptism were burned as heretics by The State Church body. Their teaching caused the bold embrace of infant baptism. We must not base our stand on the numbers of adherents of a practice; but, rather, we stand firmly on our Lord's Command; and, base our faith on The Revelation of God, our Holy Bible, with His Explicit Command clearly outlined in The New Testament Text, the Word of our Eternal God!

"We are of God: he that knoweth God heareth us; and he that is not of God heareth not us. Hereby know we the spirit of truth, and the spirit of error." I John 4:6

So with a very uniform, clear understanding by all that *baptizo* and *baptizion* for centuries meant the complete immersion of the individual in water, it was understood that the whole person of the baptized, in the Western Church as well as in that of The Eastern Church was meant. We must also uphold and maintain this uniform teaching of Holy Scripture, without wavering. All proper use of the word baptized, from the beginning was universally understood to be the immersion of the whole person in water; therefore, may we continue to rest our faith and practice on The Biblical Text; and help His Church to continue that practice of true Obedience to our Lord's Command!

PLEASE REMEMBER that the 'harlot' of Revelation 17 had children!

"Little children, it is the last time: and as ye have heard that antichrist shall come, even now are there many antichrists; whereby we know that it is the last time.

They went out from us, but they were not of us; for if they had been of us, they would no doubt have continued with us: but they went out, that they might be made manifest that they were not all of us." I John 2:18,19.

On what basis and with what authority could any individual, church body, or, ecclesiastical order declare either sprinkling or pouring to be 'baptism'? And upon what basis should the matter have even become an issue in the last five hundred years; much less, for sprinkling and pouring to be defended, based alone on the ground that more people have been sprinkled than immersed? If the number of adherents "who were sprinkled or pored" were 'more,' then I suppose all those tadpoles are well on their way to becoming squirrels!

The fourth century dawned with Diocletian's determined effort to bring order out of chaos by the leadership of the strong man. The Emperor (A.D. 284-305) INSTITUTED SWEEPING ADMINISTRATIVE AND MILITARY REFORMS, WHICH UNDOUBTEDLY STRENGTHENED THE DISEASED BODY POLITIC, and postponed its demise. The vast empire was placed under four Emperors, (each assisted by a "Caesar"). All vestige of republican government was abandoned, and the Empire became an undisguised absolutism, oriental in its outward splendor and in its utter disregard for human rights. The sword of the tyrant was the only remaining security of the state, and that sword was turned against any foe, actual or potential. The persecutions of the Christians by edict of Diocletian followed the pattern of the previous century, only with redoubled fury against he alleged "atheists" whose unwillingness to worship the emperor was regarded as dangerous to the safety and stability of the state. The sun of empire had begun to decline markedly, and the long shadows, uncertain and insidious, began to deepen, despite the dynamic leadership and reforms of Diocletian." THE LIGHT IN DARK AGES, V. Raymond Edmond, p. 9.

IN VIEW OF THE INCORRECTLY INTERPRETED TEXTS of Holy Scripture, I readily understand the frustration of modern reformed theologians; and, fully realize no change shall come until there is first a clear, Infinitely Achieved change of heart, which only God, in answer to prayer, can Effect in a dramatic way: e.g., (Try prayer. It works!) Doctor William G.T. Shedd:

"The *mode* of baptism which is by far the most common in the history of the Christian church is sprinkling or pouring. From the time of Christ to the present, a vastly greater number have been sprinkled than have been immersed. At the present day, sprinkling is the rule throughout Christendom, and immersion the exception. The former mode is catholic; the latter is denominational." DOGMATIC THEOLOGY, *Wm. G.T. Shedd, Vol. II, p. 578.* (Only because they had the authorities on their side and murdered, slaughtered, and roasted without question, those who immersed their converts.) Again, the minority speaks. Satan is called 'the god of this world'.... until our Blessed Redeemer Comes!! Better wake up, friend!

More than human courage is required in this modern age to fully obey God. It takes God at work in Regeneration through the Transforming Word of Scripture to return His Church to the kind of Holy Spirit Generated Unity that God has ordered! His Clear Instruction has been pushed aside by the professed church even from before the beginning of the dark ages of disobedience; and, The Truth of God, Administered by The Holy Spirit, must be embraced afresh in modern times, to produce Regenerated Thinking and Belief in hearts that have been Born of God, producing regenerated, obedient Lives, transformed by God's Own Power:

'The story appeared in a Communist Russian newspaper around 1960. It read in part, "young boys and girls sing spiritual hymns. They receive the ritual baptism and keep the evil, treacherous teaching of love toward the enemy." The story went on to disclose the shocking reality that many young people in the Communist Youth Organization were secretly Christians.

"We must believe our Savior as the first Christians did," Pastor Serebrennikov told his youth group. "for us, the principal law is the Bible. We recognize nothing else. We must hurry to save men from sin, especially the youth."

The pastor was thrown in prison when the Communists discovered a letter written by one of his converts. The teenage girl had written, "I send you blessings from our beloved Lord. How much he loves me!" EXTREME DEVOTION – Voice of The Martyrs, p.1

CHAPTER III
THE PRECISE WITNESS
OF BAPTISM

"**A**S YE HAVE, THEREFORE, RECEIVED Christ Jesus the Lord, so walk ye in him, Rooted and built up in him, as ye have been taught, abounding therein with thanksgiving." Colossians 2:6,7.

"THERE WAS A MAN sent from God, whose name was John." John 1:6. Herodias requested his beheading and Herod twice took credit for it. Matt 14:10; Mark 6:16, 27. This was the pattern of persecution for hundreds of years.

BAPTISM: "Christian Baptism is the immersion of a believer in water, in token of his previous entrance into the communion of Christ's Death and Resurrection—or, in other words, in token of his regeneration through union with Christ." SYSTEMATIC THEOLOGY, Augustus Hopkins Strong, D.D., LL.D.

THE SIGNIFICENCE of the Word *Baptizo* means "to dip, perf. Pass. *BeBaptismai* aor.1 pr. *to dip, immerse; to cleanse or purify by washing; to administer the rite of baptism to baptize;* met. With various references to the ideas associated with Christian baptism as an act of dedication, e.g. marked designation, devotion, trial, etc; mid. *to procure baptism for one's self, to undergo baptism,* Acts 22:16.

Baptisma, atos, to (4. tab. D.c) pr. *immersion; baptism, ordinance of baptism,* Mat. 3:7; Rom 6:4, et al.; met. *Baptism,* in the trial of suffering, Matt. 20:22,23; Mar. 10:39.39. Heb. 6:2; *an ablution Mar. 7:4,8; Heb. 9:10. N.T. Baptistas, ou, o (2. TAB. B.C), Matt. 3:1;11:11,12, et al N.T.,*

WEBSTER: 'A dipping in< Gr. *Bapisma* Immersion *Baptizein,* immersion; baptzein, to plunge, immerse. 1. A baptizing or being baptized. **specifically,** the ceremony, or sacrament of admitting a person into Christianity or a specific Christian Church by dipping him in water (and. following the open practice, he is forced to add "by sprinkling water on him" with which he departs totally from the meaning of the word. "Sprinkling' has absolutely NO connection with *Baptzein.* He first gave the meaning of the word.

BAPTZEIN has to do with death and resurrection. Sprinkling has to do with neither. The full import of death and resurrection best places the total experience in a capsule.

THE EMPEROR TRAJAN, (53-117) born, Marcus Ulpius Trajanus, widely traveled, and, a scholar of the philosophers, received a military education, devoted large amounts of time assisting the hungry, building bridges for the betterment of his people, reducing poverty, after his conversion, gave as his testimony of Christ: "When I was paying earnest heed to what was profitable, some barbarian writings came into my hands which were too old for Greek ideas and too divine for Greek errors. These I was led to trust, owing to their simplicity of expression, and the unstudied character of their authors, owing to their intelligible descriptions of creation, their foreknowledge of the future, the excellence of their precepts, and the fact of their embracing the universe under the sole rule of God. Thus my soul was instructed of God, and I understand how other teachings lead to condemnation, whilst these writings abolish the bondage that prevails throughout the world and free us from a plurality of rulers and tyrants innumerable" LIGHT IN DARKAGES, IV. Raymond Edmond, p. 36.

"Baptism symbolizes the previous entrance of the believer into the communion of Christs's Death and Resurrection; Baptism, more particularly, is a symbol: (a) of the Death and Resurrection of Christ. (b) Of the purpose of that death and resurrection,- namely, to atone for sin, and to deliver sinners from it's penalty and power." A. H. Strong, theology, p. 940

The graphics of baptism are beyond words when properly and wisely done. It is a vivid witness: Romans 6:3,4: "Know ye not, that so many of us as were baptized into Jesus Christ were baptized into his death? Therefore we are buried with Him by baptism into death: that like as Christ was raised up from the dead by the glory of the Father, even so we also should walk in Newness of Life.(I Cor. 12:13).

I Cor. 15:3-4 "For I delivered unto you first of all that which I also received, how that Christ died for our sins according to the Scriptures: and that He was buried, and he rose again the third day according to the Scriptures:"

Col. 2:12 "Buried with him in baptism wherein also ye are risen with Him through the faith of the operation of God, who hath raised Him from the dead."

I Cor. 10:1-2 "Moreover brethren, I would not that ye should be ignorant, how that all our fathers were under the cloud, and all passed through the sea:

2. And were all baptized unto Moses in the cloud and in the sea."

QUENCH NOT the Spirit; despise not prophesyings; prove all things; hold fast that which is good." I Thessalonians 5:19-21.

In the Cathedral Church of Copenhagen, amid Thorwaldsen's famous group of the Twelve Apostles, stands the figure of a grave and meditative man, with earnestly questioning face, rule and measure in hand, as though prepared to bring all things under strict verification, whose name no one needs to ask, so plainly does the statue stand for the doubting Thomas. Thomas was, according to traditions of the Early Church, a born skeptic, a constitutional questioner, whose faith followed his understanding, who could not rest on external authority, who brought even Christ's words to the bar of reason, and failing to elicit an intelligible answer, withheld his assent—in short, a genuine Rationalist. Yet this Thomas was one of the twelve disciples a full member of the Apostolic College who carried the message of Salvation to the people of India.

IT IS INTERESTING that Satan works with such passion! The amazing thing is that there is a light burning! And, that we have the Bible, in spite of it all! The Record of the Book of Acts reveals the diverse methods of Satan and the record of history continues to show two things: A. The carnage of the diversity of God's Infinite works which shine forth in the Absolute; and, B. God's beautiful perfectionism in our Holy Redeemer and viewing us in Him, anticipating the day and hour when we shall be conformed to the image of His Son! You and I do not know when that hour shall come; we trust it will be soon, even as we pray, "even so, come, Lord Jesus!" God disciplines His Children with this in Mind; and, we shiver to think of the chilling, undeviating way that God mocks the wicked.

The Light covers a land, flourishes, flickers, it is rejected! Awful, horrible darkness follows! Out of the night comes the screams and wretchedness of the souls that are forever lost in that eternal night where there is weeping and wailing and gnashing of teeth! Should we not snatch the fagots from the burning?? How many have we, personally, led to Christ?

Time after time it occurs. Most of the world was enlightened at one time or other! The end times rumble, earthquakes, signs in the heavens, the darkness deepens! God pity our land!

"And when the day of Pentecost was fully come, they were all gathered together into one place." Acts.2:1

"Then they that gladly received His Word were baptized: and the same day there were added unto them about three thousand souls". Acs 2:41!

"And they, continuing daily with one accord in the temple, and breaking bread from house to house, did eat their meat with gladness and singleness of heart,

"Praising God, and having favour with all the people. And the Lord added To the church daily such as should be saved." Acts 2:46-47

The word *invariably* used for Baptism is some form of the Word *"Baptizontes"* (So used in Matthew 28), which means to "totally submerge".

Some form of the Word Sprinkle *"rantismon"* is used in the New Testament a total of seven times (Heb.9:13, 19,21; 10:22; 11:28; 12:24; I Pet. 1:2), **NEVER,** in the sense of *Baptism.*

After the 6th century, the baptisms of Adults was rare in the State church, but let it be clear that the baptisms in the underground church flourished and while the records of the underground church were not readily available, we are left to judge the persecuted element and the thousands of baptisms there were totally undaunted by the violent persecution from the state church that sought to extinguish the light! It is intensely interesting that the arrest of 'heretics' required the 'surrender of records!' The 'expunging' of records is amazing! Thank God the inspired record cannot be 'expunged!'

THE WORD OF GOD is a fire that cannot be put out, even though strong efforts were made to keep the Holy Scriptures out of the hands of the people and fervent, even vicious efforts were exercised with the stern statements that "the common people could not understand the Scriptures. Some paid for their efforts to get the Word of God to the people with their lives.

Attempts were made to 'confiscate records' of the underground church but they were guarded very carefully for the protection of those who were baptized.

"Besides the images of Christ, representations were also made of prominent characters in the sacred history, especially of the blessed Virgin with the Child, of the wise men of the east, as three kings worshipping before the manger of the four Evangelists, the twelve Apostles, particularly Peter and Paul, of many martyrs and saints of the times of persecution, and honored bishops and monks of a later day." HISTORY OF THE CHRISTIAN CHURCH, Vol. III, p. 571.

"The definition of baptism excludes all un-baptized children, dying in infancy, from heaven. That mystic and lovable divine, Hugo of St Victor, whether the children of Christian parents may be saved who happen to be put to death in a city besieged by pagans and die un-baptized. He leaves it unanswered, remarking that there is no authority for saying what will become of them." Duns Cotus makes it plain that children yet unborn are under the law of sin, not because of their own bodies. He mercifully excepts from the law of perdition unborn infants whose mothers suffer martyrdom or blood baptism. The Reformers, Zwingli excepted, shared the view of the mediaeval theology that un-baptized children dying in infancy are lost. The Reformers, Zwingli excepted, shared the views of the mid-evil theology that un-baptized children dying in infancy are lost." At later date, about 1740, Isaac Watts and other Protestant theologians, as a relief from the agonizing thought that the children of non-Christians, elaborated the view that they are annihilated. It remained for still later Protestant period to pronounce in favor of the salvation of all such children in view of the super-abounding fullness of the Atonement and our Lord's Words, "for of such is the kingdom of heaven." HISTORY OF THE CHRISTIAN CHURCH, Vol. V, p. 711.

We have just noted in the 20th Century, even when evil does its utmost, The Eternal Truth of God goes on, Taught By The Holy Spirit, even in the most vicious and wicked climates! The True Church in China, along with that noted occurring in Russia, in the 20th and 21st Centuries are classic illustration that 'The earth is the Lord's and the fullness thereof!' Psalm 24:1.)

Doctor Wm G.T. Shedd writer and Reformed Theologians at large seems more concerned with the numbers of adherents in their practices, than in having a heart concern for faithful obedience to The Holy Scriptures of God. These are tragic attitudes that have continued to move the professed church of God into its current full-blown apostasy of radical unbelief apostasy and confused view of Holy Scripture! The Church is under Orders to **OBEY!** *Sprinkling* is hardly to be equated with **OBEDIENCE** of our Lord's **COMMAND to be baptized** (baptizo)! I am deeply impressed with the knowledge many of the 'heretics' had relative to the deep things of God and to the nature of Holy Scripture! They obviously excelled in this matter.

"Behold, to obey is better than sacrifice, and to hearken than the fat of rams." rebellion is as the sin of witchcraft, and stubbornness is as iniquity and idolatry. Because thou hast rejected the word of the Lord, He hath also rejected thee....." I Samuel 15:22, 23

The Protestant Reformation was a break with The Roman Catholic Church, which had, from 315 A.D., embraced all heathen religions of the day, including emperor worship:

"If Replacement Theology is true, then certainly God has an opinion about it—one He states clearly and teaches visibly in Scripture. Conversely, if it is not plainly taught, then Replacement Theology must be the fictitious creation of men." Israel, My Glory, P.28, 2012.

Emperor Constantine declared Christianity to be the State Religion! As a 'State Religion', carrying the label 'Christian', all religions were swept into it, thus beginning with a profuse mixture of experiences and practices! The unconverted within the professed church had become a dominant factor in its teaching departures from The Truth of The Holy Scriptures, even then; and, many types of unbiblical practices had mushroomed by the middle ages to press Martin Luther into his deep heart concerns, sufficient to generate his 95 Theses; and cause him to confront the Catholic System with them!

THE CLIMATE OF CHURCH HISTORY IS FRAUGHT with examples of tragic and monstrous persecutions. The following is a mere example of the blood and slaughter of over 1500 years of the rage of Satan!

"In Languedoc and Province in the South of France,...Pope Innocent III required of the Count of Toulouse, Raymond VI, who ruled in Province, and of the other rulers and prelates in the South of France, that the hermits should be banished. This would have meant the ruin of the country. Raymond temporized, but was soon involved in a hopeless quarrel with the Pope, who in 1209 proclaimed a crusade against him and his people. "Indulgences, such as had been given to the crusaders who went at great risk to themselves to rescue the Holy places in Palestine from the Mohammedan Saracens, were now offered to all who would take part in the easier work of destroying the most fruitful provinces of France. This, and the prospect of booty, and license of every kind attracted hundreds of thousands of men. Under the presidency of the high clerical dignitaries and led by Simon de Montfort, a military leader of great ability and a man of boundless ambition and ruthless cruelty, the most beautiful and cultivated part of Europe at that time was ravaged, became for twenty years a scene of unspeakable wickedness and cruelty and was reduced to desolation.

E. H. Broadbent, in "THE PILGRIM CHURCH" has done a very masterful work, calling attention to very large Christian settlements and their horrible sufferings because they refused to conform to Roman Catholicism and faced death joyfully as martyrs. I strongly commend the work. Many of these devout believers were faithful; and, their adherence to Scripture in a very disciplined manner produced believers with a character that was outstanding in their obedience to Holy Scripture.

THE REFORMERS, Martin Luther, Ulrich Zwingli, John Calvin and others who declared their faith on the basis of their understanding of The Teachings and principles of Holy Scriptures, first pleaded with Rome concerning radical practices and indulgences. It was only when Rome called for their death that The Reformation began; and, it was with broken hearts that these rejected the edicts and sentences from Rome!

The following excerpt from THE PILGRIM CHURCH records, gathered and recorded by E. H. Broadbent, open a very telling and illustrative window on church trends, crises, conflicts and courage in the history of The Church, in one segment of time; and, trend out of which current development is quite astonishing! I commend his excellent handling of facts, problems, emotions and exercises of activities in the progress of Christian Church History:

The Swiss Reformation is said to be divided into two separate efforts. It was begun in 1517 under Zwingli who had lived from 1484, and began his work from 1517 to 1531 and after his death, Calvin, who had lived from 1509; taking up the work in 1531 and carried it forward to 1564. this had become a very strong area for the Anabaptists who carried the Biblical Immersionist doctrine forward; they called themselves "brethren" or Christians", they were self-denying and heroic, but restless and impatient. They accepted the New Testament as their only rule of faith and practice, and so far agreed with the Reformers, but utterly broke with the Catholic tradition, and rejected Luther's theory of forensic, solifidian justification, and the 'Real Presence'. They emphasized the necessity of good works and deemd it impossible to keep the Law. While both Zwingli and Calvin, had readily acknowledged that The Church, at it's outset practiced immersion, they, believing that God was through with Israel, had in essence fabricated 'another gospel'. Zwingli, who had been quite pleased to fellowship with the Anabaptists until there came to be the choice made, very likely after the development of Calvin's Institutes of Religion. Whatever caused the collusion, The Reformation Church carried forward what had been The Roman Catholic doctrine and philosophy of baptism, with these, The Anabaptists took violent exception.

The first and chief aim of the Radicals was not the opposition to infant baptism as such, still less, it is said, to the sprinkling or pouring in baptism, but the establishment of a pure church of converts in opposition of a church mixed with the world. The problem was that of obedience; and there could not be obedience to the Word without submission to THE TRUTH! In observing the history of The Church, the very first deviation from the truth is like the hole in the dyke...it gets bigger!

The opposition to the mixed state-church or popular church, which embraced all the baptized as our Lord commanded led to the rejection of infant baptism. A true church must be an obedient church. The blood of saints of all the church age is stunning and runs into the millions of believers. No wonder we read in Isaiah 63:1 "Who is this that cometh from Edom, with dyed garments from Bozrah? This that is glorious in his apparel, traveling in the greatness of His strength? I that speak in righteousness, mighty to save!" Surely God is tired of blood!

"Wolfgang Brandhuber, who, together with seventy members of the assembly, was put to death (1528). So, in place after place, the Lord's witnesses were raised up by the preaching of Jesus Christ and Him crucified, and in the most literal way followed in His footsteps. Troops of soldiers were sent through those countries to search out and to kill those called "heretics", without trial. Though they were called *Anabaptists*, (* German footnote) it was not the form of baptism that gave them courage to suffer as they did. They were aware of immediate communion with their Redeemer; no man and no religious form came between their souls and Him." THE PILGRIM CHURCH, E.H. Broadbent, pps. 167-171.

What has been placed before us in this text is a mere sampling of the people of God, throughout the history of The Church, who are classic examples of the greater part of His people who earlier experienced like rejection by the world and were honored in The Divine History of His Old Testament saints preserved for is in Hebrews 11:32-40. His people through these last 2,000 years have continued the characteristic experience of rejection by a lost world, deluged in sin, quietly laying down their lives and firmly refusing to deny Him!

The professed church reflected in Matthew 13:24-30,33, had drifted into multiple errors, eventually expanding radically even to the selling of indulgences. This is still reflected in our time in the modern Mardi gra event, demonstrating the practices with which the Pope, in The Middle Ages had built massive wealth, even as he declared blandly to Thomas Acquinas, as he opened Rome's massive room filled with silver and gold, "Look! We no longer have to say as Peter did, "Silver and gold have I none!" God's servant said quietly to him, "Neither can the church now say as Peter did: 'In the Name of Jesus Christ of Nazareth, rise up and walk!'"

The indulgences drove Martin Luther to The Reformation and to his nailing of his Ninety-Five Theses' to the Castle Church door on October 31, 1517! Luther had found 95 ways in which The Catholic System had departed from Holy Scripture. HOWEVER, he was in that proverbial position of being 'between a rock and a hard place.' Most of his own people he wished to take with him in his break were those who had also been sprinkled, as Luther, himself, had been!

He made the decision to break and take his people with him, rather than become a martyr in that break! Martin Luther was a person of strong inflexible character; and, final break with Rome was initiated by the Catholic Church hatred that sought his death! The martyrs of the time are clear proof of what Martin Luther's fate would have been, had he rejected his own baptism and that of his people. Besides, Anabaptists had already become 'outcasts' of the society of the day; and, were not to be eagerly embraced! Never underestimate the strong hold that tradition, heredity and environment have over the spiritually subjugated human!

An elderly gentleman, with whom I visited on his front porch as a college student was obviously near death, with his greatly enlarged body and limbs, but he refused to allow me to read The Bible to him, pointing to his church steeple; and, saying, "That church will take care of all my need as I leave this world."

Many of the broadly read church scholars of history have valued their existing position as recipients of infant baptism; and, the false stand on false premises of a fabricated Covenant Theology matters which vie with any complete obedience to God; because, (1) Promises God made to Israel will be fulfilled to Israel, not to The Church; (2) A Covenant Theology, embraced without warrant by the professing church, has no Bible Authorization, but is, in all honesty, a fabricated, dangerous false teaching introduced by The State Church, that has caused both deep sorrow and serious error relative to the experience of Salvation.

Many rest this vital experience upon the waters of infant baptism and Israel's Covenant, wrongly appropriated by The State Church in taking its position under its Covenant Theology. No Scripture, without monstrous false assumptions, justifies this action. Nor does any command whatsoever exist to justify this action by The Church. Certainly the Nation of Israel will be restored and exalted at His Second Coming! The Church is commissioned to diligently embrace, practice, teach; and, herald to the world, The Whole Counsel of God, properly teaching the complete Bible. Our own children are to be lovingly, gently and firmly guided to bring them to a like embrace, practice and proclamation of Holy Scripture, in a developing maturity and in evangelistic outreach!

Is this not that real human nature with which each of us grapple?! Ties with parents and church heritage by means of infant baptism, for most people, immunize far too many of those adherents to having any openness to their choosing the Biblical positions that require Faith alone resting on

The Word of God alone! This problem did not develop yesterday; and, only God's Spirit gives strength to embrace Total Obedience to The Holy Spirit. Yet each will not only answer to God; but, will only inhibit their own growth experience in all that God has individually designed for each of His Regenerated children. A Right Foundation must be personally embraced by each of His children for a true life structure, built on The Foundation of God: I Corinthians 3:11.

Salvation in Christ is a unique personal transaction, by Faith alone, based upon The Eternal Covenant made between God and His Son, Transacted by His Holy Spirit in each heart that individually makes its own distinct personal choice by Faith, to trust Our Redeemer's Finished Work on our behalf. Christ died for our sin; and, we love Him and His Finished work us, by personal faith in Him. Israel has a Family Covenant, as descendents of Abraham, Isaac and Jacob! The New Covenant is between the individual heart and our Eternal God; and, this Heart Transformation is God's Own Designed Process by which He grants individual New Birth; and, thus grows His Family in a New Order, which He has designated as "My Church!" Matthew 16:18, His *Ecclecia,* (His Called Out Assembly) His Body, under direction from The Head, designed to do His Work under His direct Lordship, with His Holy Spirit placed in Absolute Charge of The Church Age in the present world! Romans 8:9,14.

We submit that we have no authorization for substituting another act for the one commanded! I feel very deeply for those who are caught and taught in the ridiculous, troubling, folly of Sprinkling and pouring. It is an extremely difficult thing to step outside of! There is a word for 'sprinkle' and there is a word for 'pour' and there is a word for baptizing in the Greek New Testament! ***Baptizontes; Matthew 28:18-20;***

IN EPHESIANS 4:4-6 "There is one body, and one Spirit, even as ye are called in one hope of your calling: "One Lord, One faith, one baptism, One God and Father of all, who is above all, and through all, and in you all."

"In Ephesians 4:5 it is noticeable that, not the Lord's Supper, but baptism, is referred to as the symbol of Christian unity. A.H. Strong, Cleveland

J. Clarence Ford, LittD

Sermon, 1904- "Our fathers lived in a day when simple faith was subject to serious disabilities. The establishments frowned upon dissent and visited it with pains and penalties. It is no wonder that believers in the New Testament doctrine and polity felt that they must come out from what they regarded as an apostate church. They could have no sympathy with those who held back the truth in unrighteousness and persecuted the saints of God. But our doctrine has leavened all Christendom. Scholarship is on the side of immersion. Infant Baptism is on the decline. The churches that once opposed us now compliment us on our stedfastness in the faith and missionary zeal. There is a growing spirituality in these churches, which prompts them to extend to us hands of fellowship. And there is a growing sense among us that the kingdom of Christ is wider than our own membership, and that loyalty to our Lord requires us to recognize His Presence and blessing even in bodies which we do not regard as organized in complete accordance with the New Testament model. Faith in the larger Christ is bringing us out from our demonstrational isolation into an inspiring recognition of our oneness with the universal church of God throughout the world." SYSTEMATIC THEOLOGY, A. H. Strong, p. 944

CHAPTER IV
THE PRECISE CLARITY
OF BAPTISM

J ohn Clough was called to the harvest field while working in one. He had grown up without religious inclinations, and in college seemed resistant to evangelistic efforts by friends. His roommate tried to read the Bible and pray with him each evening, but John, growing exasperated drew a chalk line down the middle of the room, forbidding prayer or Scripture on his side of the line.

But the Holy Spirit worked on his heart, and one evening, unable to study and overwhelmed with his need, he crossed the line and knelt by his roommate. Shortly after, hearing a missionary sermon, he was atop a four-horse reaper breaking off grain when a farmhand approached him with a letter from Boston. Clough wiped away his sweat and tore open the news from the Baptist Foreign Mission Board. "What do you know!" he shouted "They want me to go to India as a missionary!"

Missions officials wanted to send him to "Folorn Hope" – Telegu, India- where 17 years of painful plodding effort had produced no apparent results. On November 30, 1864, Clough and his wife sailed from Boston on a tiny ship, hardly seaworthy, called the *James Guthrie*. It rolled and pitched its way across the ocean, finally limping into India the following April. John, leaping into service, was immediately confronted with a dilemma. The higher caste of Indians refused to attend church with the lower caste and outcasts. Praying for wisdom, clough randomly opened his bible and read in I Corinthians 1:26-29 of God choosing the lowly. Across the room at the same moment, his wife randomly opened her Bible to the same place. Clough, amazed, took is as divine guidance. He announced that all were welcome in his church, that he would not accept a segregated congregation.

He started preaching, and conversions multiplied. Fifteen months later two Indian preachers stood in a river and began baptizing the converts. When they grew weary, other preachers relieved them. By five o'clock 2,222 had been baptized, and the baptisms continued for two more days. ON THIS DAY, Robert J. Morgan

"FOR IF WE HAVE BEEN PLANTED together in the likeness of His Death, we shall be also in the likeness of his resurrection; knowing this, that our old man is crucified with him, that the body of sin might be destroyed, that henceforth we should not serve sin." Romans 6:5-6.

The command to baptize is a command to immerse. From the meaning of the original word *baptize, this is to immerse.* We have a slight problem with sprinkling inasmuch as we do not 'plant' something by sprinkling dirt on it, "we have been 'planted' "in the likeness of His Death'! They rolled a great stone across the entrance to 'bury' Him! The entire process of the Crucifixion; and, being buried in the likeness of His death is that a new creation is coming! II Corinthians 5:17. "the 'swoon' theory' and 'pop and hamburger communion' are on their way! No wonder the pop gun has replaced the Sword of the Spirit! WE NEED REVIVAL!!!!

From the usage of Greek writers —including the church Fathers, when they do not speak of the Christian rite, they, and the authors of the Greek version of the Old Testament, (the Septuagint), are somewhat prone to make vague mention of the occasion in passing.

In the International Critical Commentary, see Plummer on Luke, p.68-"It is only when baptism is administered by immersion that its full significance is seen. It has been attempted to fill up the gap by establishing the existence, prior to the Gospel era, of *a jewish proselyte baptism.* Many of the more learned inquirers into Biblical antiquities, including Buxtorf, Lightfoot, Selden. Schottgen, Wall. &c, have been of the opinion that the

Jews were in the habit of admitting proselytes to the Jewish faith by an ordinance of baptism accompanying the rite of circumcision."

Obviously the Jews knew the significance of the word, *baptizo,* they knew the meaning, and clearly a proselyte would not have been received, if one little toe had been unwashed; more than this, the word "sprinkle" is used a few times, less than ten in the New Testament, (but, none of them is used in regard to baptism).

A FALSE MODE of administering the ordinance has so obscured the meaning of baptism that it has, to multitudes, lost all reference to the death of Christ, and the Lord's Supper is assumed to be the only ordinance which is intended to remind us of the atoning sacrifices to which we owe our salvation. (which is tragic). For evidence of this, see the remarks of President Woolsey in the Sunday School Times: "Baptism it (the Christian religion) could share in the doctrine of John the Baptist, and if a similar rite had existed under the Jewish law, it would have been regarded as appropriate to a religion which inculcated renunciation of sin and purity of heart and life. But (in the Lord's Supper) we go beyond the province of baptism to the very *pinnacle* of the gospel, to the efficacy and meaning of Christ's death.

"Baptism should be a public act. We cannot afford to relegate it to a corner, or to celebrate it in private, as some professedly Baptist churches of England are said to do. Like marriage, the essence of it is the joining of ourselves to another before the world. In baptism we merge ourselves in Christ, before God and angels and men. The Mohammedan stands five times a day, and prays with his face toward Mecca, caring not who sees him. Luke 12:8 "Every one who shall confess me before men, him shall the Son of man also confess before the angels of God." SYSTEMATIC THEOLOGY, A. H. Strong, p. 54

So awesome is the reality of identification with The Lord Jesus Christ in His Death and Resurrection, Baptism symbolizes purification, but purification in a peculiar and Divine way, namely, through the death of Christ and the entrance of the soul into communion with Him in

that death. **It is to radically change the significance of Baptism to inject sprinkling and pouring, which does not point to Christ's Death as the procuring cause of our purification!**

THE WITNESS OF CHARLES SPURGEON: "SIX YEARS AGO TODAY, as near as possible at this very hour of the day, I was in the gall of bitterness and in the bonds of iniquity, but had yet by divine grace been led to feel the bitterness of that bondage and to cry out by reason of the soreness of its slavery.

Seeking rest and finding none, I stepped within the house of God and there afraid to look upward lest I should be utterly cut off and lest his fierce wrath should consume me. The minister rose in his pulpit, and, as I have done this morning, read this text, 'Look unto me, and be ye saved, all the ends of the earth: for I am God, and there is none else, Isa. 45:22. I looked that moment. The grace of faith was vouchsafed to me in the self-same instant, and now I think I can say with truth,

> "E'er since, by faith, I saw the stream
> Thy flowing wounds supply,
> Redeeming Love has been my theme,
> And shall be till I die"
> -William Cowper
> As told by C. H. Spurgeon, regarding himself!

BAPTISM (*baptizo*) is so transparently clear that it is impossible to define baptism by saying "He was immersed in sprinkles of water.!" If that sounds strange, I think so, too. Quietly, discerningly, Dr. Chafer said, "the force of this is to say "He that believeth and is drowned" shall be saved!" That is precisely the meaning! The Old man goes down; and, The New Man emerges. Or, The Old Man is plunged under the water, and the New Man comes out! He is to be forever changed! And, that is precisely the point!

THE PRECISION of the meaning of baptism, that the Infinite, Holy, Eternal Word of God is Absolute; any deviation from the fine line of its richness will appear to be totally ignored until it reaches the point where wickedness prevails; then, it's over! We have seen this so VERY evident in the Far East, the Gospel was there very early! in India, where the Apostle Thomas was clubbed to death with a halberd (an ax), The Gospel was there! In Russia, the Gospel was carried there VERY early! One of the richest places of theological advance was in Germany, in England, and, now, in America! May God help us!

You will notice that in these regions, India is the land of 6,000 gods, In Russia, atheism,; in Germany, Nazism, here is the very nest for Biblical Criticism, etc. "And he cried mightily with a strong voice, saying, Babylon, the great is fallen, is fallen, and is become the habitation of devils, and the hold of every foul spirit, and a cage of every unclean and hateful bird." Revelation 18:2.

The obedience of the believer portrays the complete transformation of the 'New Creation', by the complete burial of the 'old man', and, the rising from the waters as a transformed creation, made into the complete likeness of the Redeemer! (Something like the Phoenix.) This is why believers were fearful of being baptized, and put it off until their death bed. However, the plan of God is that we be 'kept by the power of God' through faith unto salvation, being walking evidences of being in the likeness of 'His' Resurrection! I John 1:9. It is an order from God that we live like Him!! The believers in Antioch did just that! And, those who observed, declared it by calling them 'Christians', that is, they were like Him!! Immediately following this, those who claimed sprinkling had to scramble and "fill up the holes in the old wine bottle" without a shred of Biblical evidence to sustain, as the Spirit of God descended from heaven on the transformed creation. Matthew 3:16,17. Think about it!

The Baptism of believers is universally administered in Christian Churches under the formula: "In Obedience to His Command!"

The Verbal, Plenary Inspired Holy Scriptures God gave to be "obeyed" are NOT obeyed, unless that obedience fulfills the requirement of The Holy Text of **The God-breathed Book**; and, the climate produced by deliberate 'adjusting' of what was Commanded has produced its own fruits of tragic, further departure from The Faith of God:

Covenant Theology is premised on the erroneous beliefs:

1. That God cancelled all of His Promises to The Nation Israel!
2. That humanity should hate Israel for rejecting God's Son!
3. That baptism is the replacement of The Covenant of Circumcision!
4. That The Church is Spiritual Israel and should adapt their covenants!
5. That, therefore the Christian family is responsible for securing the baptism of all infant family members as they arrive in the world, in maintaining the family covenant!
6. That Canaan was symbolic of our Heavenly Home, instead of being a place of warfare and triumph! (Symbolic, rather, of the victorious Christian life)!
7. That The Church will be successful in converting the world; and, that

Then, the Kingdom of Heaven will prevail and Christ will return, thus overcoming the world: John 16:33; I John 5:4.

1. Every Promise God ever made to anyone will be kept in The Absolute to the one to whom the promise was made! God is not finished with Israel. Every Promise He made to Israel will be kept with Israel, as it was given! Israel is the only nation on earth that has unconditional national promises!

(Tragically) belief that God cancelled His Covenant with Israel and gave it to His Church, has been cause for doubts of our Eternal Promises in Christ, and has raised such question in the minds of believers that far too many have not been able to hold fast "the faithful word as he hath been taught, that he may be able by sound doctrine both to exhort and to convince the gainsayers." Titus 1:9! At a future day, Israel will have a national Conversion Experience: Israel has unique promises. The Church has a "far more exceeding and eternal weight of glory" awaiting. II Corinthians 4:17.

2. Those who crucified Christ were Romans, not Jews! In fact, it was your sins and mine (and, that of all humanity) that nailed Him to The

Cross, that horrible instrument of death, that stood on the hill called Calvary, which, itself stood on the form of a human skull (form of a mountain)...such a striking place for all humanity to die in the Form of our Magnificent, Majestic, Infinite Divine-Human Substitute!

3. It was Romans who invented the unspeakable and totally fabricated false story that the trembling disciples who had run away in terror at His attack by the mob, had boldly returned to take His Body from armed guards! Those guards were paid handsomely to tell the story that the disciples came by night while the guards slept and took away his body, leaving the tomb empty! (Matthew 28:12-15). This lie was boldly spread by the embarrassed guards with the guarantee of assured Roman Government protection to them for their having spread the lie that 'His disciples came by night, while the guards slept, and took His Body away!' The interesting fact is that their story is an official confirmation that after three days, THE TOMB WAS EMPTY; AND, HAD BECOME EMPTY WITH THE ROMAN GUARD PRESENT!!

The human race loves and invariably, publicly chooses its vile, most unreasonable 'beliefs', before embracing The Truth of God.

Assurance of security with the added money was adequate to generate even the modern continuation of human denial, to form the premise for humanism in all of its forms and under its multiple philosophies!

4. The Church, as it was formed on The Day of Pentecost, consisted exclusively of Jews and Proselytes. These graciously shared the message with Gentiles; yet their sacrificial efforts were rewarded by theft of their promises, with adaptations of these (without Biblical warrant) to The Church and its individual families! And by the Ten Great Persecutions!

The Mosaic Family Covenant was to be inherited by Abraham's natural children, who walk in the steps of their father, Abraham! Abraham was given both 'The Dust Covenant' of Genesis 12:1-3; 13:14-18; 15:18-21; and, 'The Star Covenant', Genesis 15:5-6; with Israel owning The Dust

Covenant; and, leading in The Star Covenant'! Even though we, as those embracing Abraham's 'Star Covenant of Faith, are declared to be children of our father, Abraham, Romans 4:11-12, this does not cancel Abraham's Dust Covenant; and, all the land from the Nile to the Euphrates is still reserved for the nation of Israel, as owners, alone, of that Covenant and of that entire territory in The Middle East! Genesis 15:18-21.

THE FALSE CONCEPT that God had cancelled His Covenants with Israel; AND, that that Israel's Covenant had been cancelled by The Cross, has provided fertile soil for the false Armenian belief: 'If God cancelled His Covenant with Israel, do not believers stand in constant peril of losing their Salvation, as well??' Also, in believing Salvation is by water baptism, since it is a Church Ordinance, most Reformed teachings continue to rest security on infant baptism, thus confusing that experience with the Spirit Baptism declared in I Corinthians 12:13; and, which is experienced in New Birth when God's Spirit does His Regenerating Work at the very instant the human heart grasps by Faith The Infinite Work Accomplished by our Redeemer in His Finished Work on behalf of sinners, by His Death on The Cross; and, is justified eternally by His Triumphant Resurrection from the dead! Galatians 6:14.

The Entire Body of New Testament teaching is that Conversion comes by believing; that believers are New Creations, possessing Eternal Life; (II Corinthians 5:17) and, that believing must precede baptism.

The Salvation of the believing thief on the cross should clarify the fact that water baptism cannot be a requirement for salvation! Many throw doubt on Christ's Promise to the thief on the cross in arguing against our rest in Christ's Completed Work! So that many still pray, "And, finally in Heaven save us", refusing to rest in His Own Completed Work, fearing their potential misstep could doom them forever; (Hebrews 10:14) not understanding God no longer deals with us as servants, but as sons! Galatians 4:4-7; I John 3:1-3; 5:11-15.

Scripture is transparently clear that Salvation is by Faith plus nothing! Covenant Theology initially made baptism essential to Salvation, creating confusion in the ranks of Covenant Theologians; and creating life-long anguish in the hearts of parents unable to get their new born baptized before death came! Today, some still make baptism essential. Also, out of those ranks arose the Pentecostal movement with no assurance of Eternal Salvation, living daily in the fear of 'falling from Grace'; and the continued State Church premise is disaster, teaching that there is no need for a 'New Birth experience by personal choice.'

IT IS, HOWEVER, ESSENTIAL that ALL PEOPLE understand that every human is under God's Sovereign Redeeming Work of The Lord Jesus Christ Who 'tasted death for EVERY human', Hebrews 2:9. Our God is a Just God and when we depart from belief in a Verbal, Plenary Inspired Bible, we have moved away from His Foundation, I Corinthians 3:11! In fact, His Redeeming Work returned every facet of His Creative Work to His Own Authority. This is spelled out in The Great Commission, Itself! No infant will EVER burn in Hell!

Is it any wonder the 21st Century Church is in chaos, calling into question the Inspiration of Holy Scripture, The Virgin Birth, The Deity of our Redeemer, His Resurrection and every cardinal doctrine of The Bible, abandoning belief in The New Birth, which Our Lord stated is required for seeing The Kingdom of God? John 3:3, The modern church is deceived by false science, pressured by culture; and starved spiritually by abandoning The Strict Text of Holy Scripture! (Every text stands alone, so does its own corruptions.) The proper building of life requires it to be built and to stand complete on The Only Foundation. I Corinthians 3:11.

Church apostasy has gendered a climate of doubts that destroys man! When church bodies move from Scripture Authority, to human logic, man loses his Foundation for Faith; and, Christendom is resting on a totally imaginary foundation, leaving individuals, drifting in delusion, to manufacture their own level of logical behavior! This leaves man adrift in a sea of deceit, abortion and broken homes, with every man doing that which is right in his own eyes. Judges 17:6.

America, established to provide freedom to worship according to The Bible, has become like Babylon, 'the hold of every foul spirit, and the cage of every unclean and hateful bird.' Revelation 18:1-5. 85% of Americans drink alcohol that deadens the human senses. Half of the younger generation is said to have at least experimented with drugs. Prisons are filled with human lives that at birth, had just as much potential as productive humans anywhere; and, whose actions might have been far different, had their foundations for life from earliest days of childhood been nurtured in The Truth of The God of The Bible; and, fortified against the universally corrupting influences of the wicked forces of evil that destroys humans everywhere The Bible has not given protection! This must correctly be laid at the door of the modern, poorly, or totally wrongly informed, unfaithful professed churches of Christendom everywhere!

"Therefore we ought to give the more earnest heed to the things which we have heard, lest at any time we should drift from them! (*pararuomen*) – Hebrews 2:1; 6:16-20.

II Timothy 2:15 forbids the mishandling of The Eternal Word of God; and, false teachers must answer to the Almighty. Those who have been shown God's truth by the Holy Spirit have nothing to be arrogant about; and, are deeply responsible to God as well as to our fellow man, to lovingly help make clear the Spirit-revealed Truths of Holy Scripture. Hebrews 10:19-25.

THE ONLY WAY TO PLUG THE HOLE IN THE DIKE is to return to The Bible; and, obey our beautiful Revelation from The Hand of Almighty God. Far more progress would be made in helping others, if we used the Bible God has used in America for 400 years, with a dictionary for words we do not understand, which in reality are very few in number. Multiple versions have done more to confuse than to make The Bible meaning clear.

Our King James Version, in its 400 year history, did more to build lives, build families, comfort families, and individual hearts, over our departed loved ones; and, in death's sorrows in general, building character, ideals, countering the wicked spirit of Antichrist fostered by the tragic spiritual blindness that is fallen on human society; and, in the educational molding of our youth with a false science born of strong agnosticism.

Until recent time, The Bible was found to have provided strength to establish right standards for living, raising admirably strong families, to produce the greatest nation, and greatest society on earth today; surpassing all other factors combined in the development of America, because The Word of God was reverenced and obeyed much better than is the case today, with our 43 variations of renderings of The Original Holy Scriptures!

Our advances in life and knowledge, that has opened vast and awesome realms of the infinitely expanding fields of human knowledge, which God has opened, as He foretold in Daniel 12:4; and, have been only the scratching of the surface, had Americans been faithful to read and heed The Bible, as it has come with us into this 400th year of its Supernatural Influence; and, in Its enlargement of the fields of human knowledge with It's Influences of Integrity, efficiency and abundant warnings!

It is self-indicting to us that we have not strongly sustained Bible readership, and provided study guides as teaching tools. We had further responsibility to strongly encourage and warn to diligent obedience, carefully, gently, and lovingly helping our children to appreciate The Bible's mentally and spiritually enhancing features in assisting their personal development and excellence in all facets of life and opportunity.

Within the last 75 years 43 finished efforts have been made to antiquate our King James Version with more current language, more colloquial, lucid speech of 'common' people, believed to be more easily understood by today's American public!

But the result has not been one of betterment; but, has quite obviously reduced devout reading of it; and, greater boldness in the arrogant disdain of unbelievers! We now have fewer people who read it, more folk confused about what it says, and a society that holds the Word of God in the lowest esteem in the entire course of our American history! So, what is the extended result?

Our prisons are stuffed, Johnny can't read! Our criminal activity, drug use, disrespect for other humans, immorality; some one of the thirty sexual diseases being carried by one in five in our generation, as we are told; and the physical deterioration of our youth is declared by our armed forces to be at a level where only one in four stand at a level that might qualify for acceptance for military training and service.

Churches can no longer read the Word of God together because a dozen different renderings of the Original Scriptures are present in nearly any sizable congregations; and, respect for the Bible takes second place to the morning newspaper...! Shall I continue, or are we prepared to agree that the wicked one has scored again; and it is later than high time to deal with this matter properly by returning to a reverent, diligent, faithful teaching of the deep significance of Holy Scripture in daily life; and making efficient use of The Bible to build up believers in The Faith Once Delivered to the saints? II Timothy 3:16,17; II Peter 1:1-8.

"And this is Life Eternal, that they might know Thee, the only true God, and Jesus Christ, whom Thou hast sent.... And now I am no more in the world, but these are in the world, and I come to Thee. Holy Father, keep through Thine Own Name those whom thou hast given me, that they may be one, even as We are One." – *From our Lord's Prayer in John 17:1-26 (vvs.1 and 11)*

OUR HOLY REDEEMER has issued Command to every believer: "Come unto Me, all ye that labour and are heavy laden, and I will give you rest.

"Take my yoke upon you, and learn of Me; for I am meek and lowly in heart: and ye shall find rest unto your souls. For My yoke is easy, and My burden is light." Matthew 11:28-30

Doctor Lewis Sperry Chafer, Presbyterian from birth; and, having done music ministry in the interdenominational evangelistic campaigns of both D.L. Moody and Billy Sunday, has perhaps provided believers in these last days the most elaborate, easily read and refined analytic outlay of Christian Doctrine to be found in modern times. Educated in The Presbyterian climate of the Spiritual Life of his day, he has done enormous service to The Church. I respect him highly, as I do Martin Luther; and, recognize his work as exceptional in thoroughness. But inasmuch as there are no perfect humans, we all are to search The Scriptures, like The Bereans, 'who searched the Scriptures daily' whether the things they were being taught were true facts! Acts 17:10-11.

From that scholastic heritage, he has included a chapter on "The Cup Baptism." But many of his students, upon reading it, went from class to obtain baptism by immersion, in order to obey Scripture! No one is perfect; and, no writing except Holy Scripture is Inspired of God! In other fields, he is most obviously a master theologian with a very refined grasp of Biblical Truth and having the organized mind of a master scholar, produced his Systematic Theology, with The Truth of God in excellent, practical working order for teaching, training and diffusing into the service of the ministry, that local church work might have an orderly form, a smoothly working exercise in doing the broad, full activity of true Christian service both to the membership and through the membership into full outreach in local and extended witness of The Gospel, for the developing of the saints for the work of the ministry. His work in developing a masterpiece of organized Bible Concepts for structuring an efficient order for fulfilling The Great Commission, from the service oriented form to the deeper strong meat diet for personal development of individuals who through study, meditation and witness glorify God, in true fellowship with Him!

It is our responsibility as Bible believers to "take upon us The Yoke of our Holy Redeemer; and, Learn of Him." Using information from all Biblical Revelation and subject to The Holy Spirit's teaching in the Holy Scriptures, He has commanded us to walk in the light as He is in the Light. His Spirit bears witness with our spirit, not only that we are the children of God (Romans 8:16), but He confirms what is truth and what is not truth, if we pray. I very well remember when God opened an entire, life-changing truth to my heart. "But we all with open face beholding as in glass (mirror) the Glory of the Lord, are changed (transfigured) into the same image from glory to glory even as by the Spirit of the Lord. II Corinthians 3:18. It has always been like that in doctrine after doctrine and it is incumbent on me to be obedient to what He has taught. Our Appointed Teacher seals God's Truth to our hearts and minds. with our absorbing and rejoicing in the glory of sweet fellowship with Him; and, to the best of our ability to discern, receive and obey The Wisdom that He, alone, can confirm.

I recall being stunned and thrilled as a young believer, sitting at the feet of one capable Architect of Character, unfolding the simple Gospel message from the most obscure passages of Old Testament Scriptures, my soul was deeply joyful as The Holy Spirit burned into my heart vivid Truths that stood out in a glory that absolutely thrilled the soul! There was no mistaking the reality of the Heavenly Truths brought forth in simple terms that a child might appreciate. He gave me a set of his books that prolonged my wonder!

Recognizing that wrong concepts of the meanings of words of Holy Scripture lay an inadequate and faulty foundation for Biblically building up the Saints on the granite foundation of Absolute, Infinite, Eternal Truth of God, as It has been entrusted to us, under The Holy Spirit's Tutlage, for:

1.- The Calling Out of a Regenerated company of His New Creations in Christ!
2.- Teaching and training new converts to be prepared and equipped to serve God commendably!
3.- Structure a properly prepared congregation for worship!
4.- Put in order a plan of operation for local church ministry!
5.- Activate and keep in order His Program for reaching our lost world!

This man was of the Brethren mold; and, I was supernaturally blessed by his ministry.

PLYMOUTH COLONY was settled in 1620 by pilgrims, steeped in Church of England teaching and was hardly ready for Obadiah Holmes' ministry. "In 1651, Holmes was arrested for preaching Baptist doctrine in nearby Lynn, Friends tried to pay his fine, but Holmes refused. On September, 1651 he was taken to Boston Commons, stripped to the waist, and tied to a whipping post. He later wrote:

"As the man began to lay the strokes upon my back, I said to the people, though my flesh should fail, yet God would not fail. So it pleased the Lord to come in and fill my heart and tongue; and with an audible voice I broke forth praying unto the lord not to lay this sin to their charge. In truth, as the strokes fell upon me, I had such a manifestation of God's Presence as the like thereof I never had or felt, nor can with fleshy tongue express; and the outward pain was so removed from me, that indeed I am not aable to declare it to you. It was so easy to me that I could well bear it, yea and in a manner felt it not although it was grievous, the man striking with all his strength (spitting on his hands three times as many affirmed) with a three corded whip, giving me therewith thirty strokes. When he loosed me from the post, having joyfulness in my heart and cheerfulness in my countenance, I told the magistrates, "You have struck me with roses."

"If so, they were covered with thorns. The whipping was so severe that blood ran down Holmes's body until his shoes overflowed. A friend reported: 'Holmes was whipt thirty stripes in such an unmerciful manner that in many days, if not some weeks, he could take no rest, but lay on knees and elbows, not being able to suffer any part of his body to touch the bed'

"But the suffering wasn't wasted. The trial and whipping of Obadiah Holmes occasioned the conversion of Henry Dunster, President of Harvard, to the Baptists, and led to the organization of Boston's first Baptist Church." ON THIS DAY, by Robert J. Morgan, September 6.

To understand the significance of baptism, it is very important to begin where our Lord, Himself begins His Own instruction relative to the matter:

Matthew 13:17 "many kings and prophets have desired to see the things which you see, and have not seen them; and to hear the things which ye hear, and have not heard them. Blessed are your eyes, for they see; and your ears for they hear."

CHAPTER V
THE PRACTICAL CONCEPTS IN BAPTISM

A CHRISTIAN MAN asked his father, who was visiting him, to go to church with him. The sermon was on Christian missions. "I am sorry that I came here today," said the father. "I don't believe in missions. It is a stupid waste of time and money."

The young man made no reply at the time. When they reached home, however, he asked his father to listen to a story.

"A few years ago," he said, "a young man left his father's farm. He went to the Canadian northwest. There he got into bad company. One day his companions left him by the road, drunk and unconscious.

Nearby in a sod-covered shack lived a young missionary who found the young man and carried him to his shack. He placed him in a warm bed! He worked over him, until he brought him back to consciousness

The missionary cared for the young man several days and fed him. He talked earnestly to him and prayed with him. AT LAST THE YOUNG MAN CONFESSED HIS SINS AND SOUGHT GOD'S MERCY AND DELIVERANCE FROM DRINK. HEARD HIS PRAYER AND SAVED HIM.

"NOW THE YOUNG MAN IS AN HONORED CITIZEN. HE IS AN OFFICER IN HIS CHURCH. IN ORDER TO ADD TO THE COMFORT OF HIS AGED FATHER, HE SENDS HIM FIVE HUNDRED DOLLARS A YEAR. FATHER, YOU KNOW WHO THAT YOUNG MAN IS? I AM THAT MAN! I TREMBLE TO

THINK WHAT I WOULD HAVE BEEN NOW WITHOUT THAT FAITHFUL MISSIONARY. *I BELIEVE IN MISSIONS!* KNIGHT'S CHILDREN'S STORIES. Alice Marie Knight.

HAUK, referring to New Testament baptism remarks: "Baptism probably always took place through immersion in flowing water." 'As regards the subject of baptism he has the following: That in the New Testament is found no direct trace of infant baptism must be regarded as firmly established; attempts to prove its necessity from the manner of its institution, its practice from such passages as Acts 2:39; I Cor. 1:16 suffer from the defect that the thing to be proved is presupposed.' A MANUAL OF CHURCH HISTORY, Henry H. Newman, Vol. 1, p. 136.

"LOVE NOT THE WORLD, neither the things that are in the world. If any man love the world, the love of the Father is not in him. For all that is in the world, the lust of the flesh, and the lust of the eyes, and the pride of life, is not of the Father, but is of the world. And the world passeth away, and the lust of it; but he that doeth the will of God abideth forever." I John 2:15-17.

Origin, born in 185 A.D., of Christian parents, treated himself with extreme severity and would have joined his father in prison, but his mother hid his clothes; he wrote to his father, urging constancy! He was diligently listened to by bishops, censored by Demetrius of Alexandria and finally excommunicated in 231. but he stands as one of the more brilliant scholars of his time. After the bloody persecutions of Decius, he remained strong and held strong influence which lived on after his death in 254 from persecutions he received 5 years earlier at Tyre. One of the ten Emperors, wrote that 'the persecutions was small and easily counted', but soon after, under Decius, (whose persecutions were hideous) they threw Origin into prison, at Tyre, and very cruelly treated him.

"Baptism, at its deepest level, symbolizes the Logos' purification of the soul so that it may obtain the knowledge of God. The actual rite of immersing in water, on a far more superficial level, makes Christians members of the church and provides them a powerful motive not to sin. The Christian tradition, as it came to Origen, taught that baptism instantaneously forgave sins as it empowered and obligated the Christian to sin no more.

"Origen echoed this teaching when he preached on the miraculous healing of the syrian officer Naaman, who found himself cured of leprosy when he obeyed Elisha's command to bathe in the Jordan. Just as Naaman's formerly scabby skin became instantaneously as smooth as a baby's, so the newly baptized Christian is as innocent of sin as a newborn child. ("For to me to live is Christ; and to die is gain) The scapegoat in Leviticus 16 gave him an opportunity to preach to his congregation on the danger of sinning after baptism. Since the goat is a clean animal, fit for God's altar, it must symbolize a baptized Christian.

"Yet the people expel the goat into the desert, bearing away sins. (another symbol and view of the Lord Jesus) It must therefore represent the Christian who has sinned after baptism and, in consequence, suffers expulsion from the church. (we are corruption, period! But in Christ we are new creations, complete in Him, Colossians 2:10)

"Caesarean Christians had better not yield to licentious temptations, or they will suffer the scapegoat's fate. Origen recognized that some leaders in the church considered such sentiments too rigorous to be practical, but he warned them not to provide people pretexts for sinning under a cover of a seemingly reasonable recognition of human weakness. While the moral level of the church by no means satisfied him, he was confident that Christians did at least meet minimal standards. Since Christians do not steal, break oaths, or abuse deposits, Moses' laws on those topics must be interpreted allegorically." ORIGEN, Joseph Wilson Trigg, p. 191, 192.

NO, THE SCAPEGOAT DOES NOT REPRESENT A CHRISTIAN THAT HAS SINNED AFTER BAPTISM!!! The scapegoat is another portrayal of THE LORD JESUS CHRIST in His being 'despised and rejected of men, a Man of Sorrows and Acquainted with Grief' For by One Offering He has Perfected Forever them that are sanctified! Hebrewss 10:14 This is another fruitage of a fabricated 'Covenant Theoology!'

The absence of any use of the word in the passive voice with 'water' as its subject confirms the conclusion that its meaning is 'to immerse'. Water is never said to be baptized upon a man.

While every extreme under heaven appears to have existed quite early in the church age, "infant baptism" as such, was not at all discussed until 195 A.D., when strong disapproval of the practice was expressed. But, my personal experience of knowing good and evil causes me to agree with Origin that children, not infants, are suitable subjects for baptism. At the age of 3, I was clearly discerning and capable of being instructed in Salvation truth. When told the concept of being 'totally depraved', this was *very* clear to me, and I felt totally dirty, with deep feeling, when told how the Lord Jesus was wounded and died, because of my sin!

Origen believed that little children (not infants) understood and believed and were suitable recipients of baptism and spoke approvingly of the baptism of little children, addressing the well established custom of the churches. I further believe, as Israel did, that at the age of 12, children should be faced with the accountability of decision, although the matter of being 'lost' may be dependent on instruction to the age of 20; Imbalance in the teen years is tragic! Exodus 30:13;38:26;Lev.27:3,5, considering the grace of God!

Origin believed that children could understand and needed remission of sins. He, however, believed in the necessity of baptism for the remission of sins, which I do not believe is required for Salvation, (believing that water is included in the 'corruptible things' of I Peter 1:18, but Salvation is through the precious blood of Christ, alone, as meeting the One Incorruptible Quality of Redemption. He spoke disapprovingly of infant baptism.

PERHAPS the practical concepts of Baptism created in the heart and mind of James and John, and, especially in the heart of their mother, very suddenly some awesome glory of what it would mean to have her very own sons seated on either side of The Lord Jesus, on thrones of glory in His Infinite Kingdom was passionately desired!

As the mother of James and John came with them to become their intercessor to The Lord Jesus Christ, her request that her two sons be seated on His Right Hand and on His Left, in His Kingdom, received this response:

"But Jesus said unto them, Ye know not what ye ask: can ye drink of the cup that I drink of? And be baptized with the baptism that I am baptized with? And they said unto him, We can, And Jesus said unto them, ye shall indeed drink of the cup that I drink of; and with the baptism that I am baptized withal shall ye be baptized." *(e to baptisma ho ego baptizomai baptisthenai)* (Mark 10:38-39) (The cup was that which it was impossible for sinful man to drink of) His Father had given Him the full responsibility to pay in full, every single element of the complete reconciliation of His universe; and He trod the winepress alone! But, the baptism was that in which His Substitutionary Death, took us with Him in perfection through the entire event; and, the payment in full was complete!) "But I have a baptism to be baptized with; and, how am I straightened till it be accomplished" (Luke 12:50)! My friend, it is Glory Unspeakable for you and me!

Obviously The Savior linked baptism with the new Life in Him. He was to experience the dramatic change of moving from his limited Human Form to the Resurrection Transformation form, full and complete; and, in doing so, He specifically selects, not the cup He which he was to drink of; but, in his totally transformed self, therefore, he selects the word 'baptism,' in the infinite and absolute In Volume V, p.72, of Systematic Theology, Doctor Lewis Chafer I, as one who learned much from this scholarly theological work have a deep respect for this great scholar but his concept of the cup as a baptizing agent, I believe to be wrong. Two experiences of the believer are stressed in this awesome passage of Scripture: "can you drink of the cup that I drink of" *(dunasthe piein to potarion 'o egw pinw)* and "be baptized with the baptism that I am baptized with?" *(e to baptisma ho ego baptizomai baptisthenai)!*

To equate and merge into a single experience these two challenges cannot be Biblically accomplished by man!! Obviously, the cup He must drink of related to His bitter experience of separation from The Father in bearing the Judgment of God upon sin, as the sin of all humanity was laid upon Him. You and I have no concept of the agony entailed in His separation from The Father in His eternally putting away the horrid curse of sin on behalf of humanity! He must tread the wine press alone and He must also drain the cup, complete with the bitter dregs!

You and I can't even go there! He removed the sting of death for us. Baptism by The Holy Spirit into The Body of Christ is painless experience for us. (I Corinthians 12:13). The equally painless experience of water baptism is our assigned action to declare our identity with Him for all the world to witness, to give the world His call to them to follow Him!

We drink of His Cup by being faithful witnesses, living as crucified with Him (Galatians 2:20) and as Risen with Him (Colossians 3:1), in this Christ rejecting world, where passionate persecution has been the experience of His Own throughout The Church Age; and, some of His most faithful have drained the cup to its bitter dregs in martyrdom! Every believer should be prepared to die for Him and never deny Him! Those subject one to extremely distasteful experiences! But, Our Lord was first *baptistheis* by His forerunner, John the Baptist, or baptizer by being immersed by John, who was baptizing in Aenon, near to Salem, (or, near Jerusalem) because there was much water there! (John 3;23).

Dramatic efforts have been made to place 'Salem,' at various and sundry places. "A place mentioned with Aenon, to indicate that spot, where John was baptizing during the latter part of his ministry; Salim, being the well-known town or district; and, Aenon a place of many waters, fountains, or streams, near it, Many conjectures have been made as to the locality of Salim and Aenon the place of many waters, fountains or streams, near it. John 3:23. Many conjectures have been made as to the locality of Salem. Some have looked for it in the valley of Scythopolis, where Jerome supposed it to have been, mistaking Salimas for Salem." FAIRBAIRN'S IMPERIAL STANDARD BIBLE ENCYCLOPEDIA, Patrick Fairbairn.

In Genesis 14:18 we read "And Melchizedek king of Salem brought forth bread and wine: and he was priest of the Most High God, Possessor of heaven and earth. And He blessed him, and said, 'Blessed be Abram of the Most High God, Possessor of Heaven and Earth.' And blessed be the

Most High God, which hath delivered into thy hand. And he gave Him tithes of all!" Genesis 14:18, 19.

"In Judah is God known: his name is great in Israel. In Salem also is his tabernacle, and his dwelling place in Zion." Psalm 76:1-2

Hebrews 7:1,2 "For this Melchisedec, king of Salem, priest of the Most High God, who met Abraham returning from the slaughter of the kings, and blessed him;

"To whom also Abraham gave a tenth part of all; first being by interpretation King of righteousness, and after that also king of Salem which is, king of peace:" Hebrews 7:1-2. (Jerusalem, as strange as it may seem, is the city of peace)

The King of Jerusalem, Melchisedec, is a Fascinating Person. It is our reference to the City of Jerusalem. It was originally known as Salem.

It is one of the oldest cities on earth, having been destroyed and rebuilt some 20 times, as is confirmed by archeologists, "Because there was much water there."

PLEASE understand that I am deeply grateful for Philip Schaff, for Calvin, for Zwingli, and Luther, for the diversity of their ingenious thought patterns, even for the complex genius of Catholicism because it is out of this spectrum of the Church's radical complexity that we are able to discern truth. We may define truth and fit each beautiful truth into it's maize.

However, it is needful to understand that it is totally impossible for Covenant Theology to be correct, for infant baptism was never dreamed of for over 315 years; and, Covenant Theology was not 'born' until the time of the Reformation in the 15th Century! Israel is still a reality! And, has promises that have not yet been fulfilled! Each of them *MUST BE FULFILLED!! So stop and smell the coffee!*

No Scripture warrants belief in infant baptism, theft of the covenants, etc. I Would call your attention to the following discrepancies:

"The usual FORM of baptism was immersion. This is inferred from the original meaning of the Greek *baptizein* and *baptismos;* from the analogy of John's baptism, in the Jordan; and from the apostles' comparison of the sacred rite with the miraculous passage of the Red Sea, with the escape of the ark from the flood, with a cleansing and refreshing bath, and with burial and resurrection; finally, from the general custom of the ancient church, which prevails in the East to this day. But sprinkling, also, or copious pouring rather, was practiced at an early day with sick and dying persons, and in all such cases, where total or partial immersion was impracticable." HISTORY OF THE CHRISTIAN CHURCH, Philip Schaff, Vol. l, p.468.

"But sprinkling, also, or copious pouring rather, was used at an early day with sick and dying persons, and in all such cases where total or partial immersion was impracticable. Some writers suppose that this was the case even in the first baptism (I disagree) of the three thousand on the day of Pentecost; for Jerusalem was poorly supplied with water and private baths; the Kedron is a small Creek and dry in summer; but there are a number of pools and cisterns there." (This is just 3 1/2 years after John! And this conclusion is highly doubtful, because we have shown that Jerusalem had very ample access to water!) HISTORY OF THE CHRISTIAN CHURCH by Philip Schaff. Vol. 1, p. 46

First, it was Israel doing the persecuting! Then: The horrible persecutions under the first ten emperors from 64 A.D. onward, Israel having heeded the baptism of John were terribly confused by the blind Pharisees. "From its earliest days, Christianity spread throughout the empire, despite severe persecutions at the hands of imperial officials, who feared it as alien and subversive. Yet despite long sufferings and martyrdoms the new faith slowly won grudging toleration. Christians established influential churches and schools in the great cities and communication hubs, benefiting from the empires peace and stability, Christians spread along the protected trade routes, and to the familiar languages of the ruling elites. The ecclesiastical hierarchy closely mirrored the old imperial structure of cities and provinces, and when the empire faded away, the Christian church survived on its ruins." THE LOST HISTORY OF CHRISTIANITY, Philip Jenkins, p.49.

It is impossible to trace the massive Nestorian heresy in the east and it is all but impossible to decipher which are the true believers; and, if the Holy Spirit able to give light and truth, through real conversion!! It is extremely difficult to know how much of The Word of God was carried and to tell what was really believed. Just how much of the Truth traveled in the regions of India, Russia and China, and "the regions beyond!" Were believers immersed? What was the impact of the true Gospel?"

'Imagination' and 'Assumption' have been used to fabricate an entire ideology and structure an entire philosophy of behavior in attempting to "erase" the Biblical Command to Baptize! There is certainly no need for lack of water at Jerusalem, for John's ministry was conducted "in Aenon near to Salem, (Jerusalem) because there was much water there." Also, that the priests could go out and visit freely as we have shown; It merely shows to what lengths Pedo-Baptists are forced to go, to have sprinkling, pouring, etc., as fulfilling the required action. Their entire system collapses in reality, but "the beat goes on!" On what premise do they proceed when "baptism" and "Immersion" are synonyms?

Three and one half years later, He still faced the drinking of 'The Cup' from His Father: Matthew 26:39! In no way are we to confuse these two graphic teachings! We can in no way obey our Lord's Command to be baptized by *(baptistheis)*, using The Cup!

(It is the drinking of the cup of which Our Redeemer Said, "The cup which My Father giveth me, shall I not drink it?)" John 18:11. It has nothing to do whatsoever with "*baptism!*"

Please note, relative to Isaiah 52:15; Ex. 24:6,8; Lev. 6:27; Lev. 8:19,24; Heb. 12:24 (Symbol of the Holy Spirit) the sprinkling done was with blood, not water! No water is mentioned in that text. But the "so shall He sprinkle many nations" Text of Isaiah 52:15 signifies three things:

(1) It was in the Blood, that 'many nations' were affected by the sprinkling, as God calls out of every nation, tongue and language, a people for His Name! Most of the 'sprinkling' done in the Mosaic Law was with blood: Ex. 29:20,21; Lev. 1:5; 1:11; 3:2;

3:8; 3:13; 4:17; 5:9; 7:2, and in a very large number of other places. It was also used of oil, symbol of the Holy Spirit, Who is God's Messenger to the human heart over His entire earth! When Moses sprinkled the children of Israel (Exodus 24:8), it was not with water, but blood, sprinkled to make clear to that nation 'that they are not all Israel who are of Israel. A sprinkle of blood was all that was needed to cleanse the 2 ½ million Israelites in the company! Every adult Israelite, except Caleb and Joshua, including Moses and Aaron, died without enjoying their promise of their own land! (Romans 9:6,27; 11:5,7,27).

(2) The sprinkling of many nations provides the Gentile nations with the Gospel of Salvation, because man's Redeemer tasted death for every human; (Hebrews 2:9), but, all are not saved as a result! All are, however, savable! Romans 10:13.

(3) As you notice in the text, Acts 8:26, the eunuch was traveling through desert country; and, anyone should know he had more water with him than a small canteen, going through a desert, traveling in style in his chariot, with proper attendants for such official position, reading, which suggests he had a driver, at least, who would be kept very busy selecting his road and keeping the animals moving; and, with no limited resources as the queen's treasurer! (I do consider MY logic valid! But, I'm NOT going to tell you he was wearing a blue suit and had two servants fanning him in the blazing heat! When we boldly violate the meanings of Holy Scripture, we sin!)

PROFESSOR GOODWIN of Harvard University, February 13, 1895, says: "The classical meaning of *baptizo,* which seldom occurs, and of the more common *bapto,* is to dip, (literally or metaphorically), and I never heard of its having any other meaning anywhere. Certainly I never saw a lexicon which gives either sprinkle or pour, as meanings of either. I must be allowed to ask why I am so often asked this question, which seems to me to have but one perfectly plain answer."

This book on water baptism was developed to give questioners with troubled hearts answers from The Bible and from the history of The Church for real healing of wounds which have divided local churches, families, and, even broader communities of relationships, who were suffering from the need for mutual common ground. This work in embryo, in manuscript form, served its original intent very well, it seems; and, was so deemed by those it served; as well as by other friends, to be vital enough to the common good of The Church to be put into fuller book form.

I AM RICHLY BLESSED to have children who love the Lord and have provided means for us to travel; and, to observe some of the great museums and sites of early American history, also, foreign, even to the gruesome Tower of London, where saints have suffered; and, to see the surrounding region; the golden vessels from which royalty drank, the changing of the Guard, memoirs of Richard the lion hearted, Henry, The VIII, etc., the European setting of The Reformation, and the Pacific battle fields where the heroes of freedom with their renouned accomplishments, where memories live on, even a relative by the same name, in silent, sacred tribute! I stand in awe of their supreme sacrifice that we may continue our Faith, treasuring the fundamentals of our faith, to be baptized as God Instructs, giving Worship and service to our Heavenly Father and to His Christ! I bow in thanksgiving to Almighty God for the beautiful privilege of surveying, first hand, these landmarks of 'Our Heritage'; as well as the bloody trail of the serpent, Satan! While history was being carved with blood and battlefields, it was my privilege to look down on the Arizona with it is trove of treasure, to observe that records, thank God, are left, THAT WE MIGHT REMEMBER AND GIVE THANKS! 'Lest we forget! Lest we forget'

Hermenigildus was a Gothic prince and the eldest son of Leovigildus, a king of the Goths, in Spain. He was originally an Arian but became a convert to the orthodox faith, having been led to the Lord by his wife, Ingonda. When his father heard of his conversion, he stripped him of his command at Seville, where he was governor, threatening to put him to death unless he renounced his new Faith. His son took a posture of defense against his father to stop the menacing threats his raging parent had chosen to execute. Christians stood for this new convert to the Christian Faith! The king, being outraged by his son, chose to begin a bloody persecution against the saints of God, and marched against his son with his armies. The son was captured and loaded with chains, taken to Seville. During the Easter Festival, he refused to receive the Eucharist from an Arian bishop, which enraged the king even more and ordered his guards to cut the prince in pieces, which they performed on April 13, 586.

In A.D. 655, Martin the Bishop of Rome, born at Todi in Italy, a highly virtuous man, had been given by his family a masterful education! He very strongly opposed the heretics, the Monothelites, the patrons of Emperor Heraclius. He was taken to Constantinople, exposed in the most public of places to ridicule of the populace, divested of all Episcopal marks of distinction and treated with absolute scorn and persecution after having lain for months in prison. Martin was taken to an island some distance away and cut in pieces!

It is well that we remember those who have valiantly carried the torch of Christianity, through the ages that we might have the Truth, held in our own hands to read freely! John, the Bishop of Bergamo, in Lombardy, France, was a scholarly man and a devout Christian! He labored valiantly to remove every type of heresy from the Church from the errors of Arianism that was being practiced in the Church! He had joined John, the Bishop of Milan and became highly successful in resisting this false teaching of Arian, who had claimed that Jesus was not of the same substance as God, but simply the very highest of humans. He was treacherously assassinated on July 11, 683 a.d.

Ireland's evangelism has suffered from myths; and it is difficult to know just how St. Patrick, called a British Bishop, with the dates of birth and death being from 389 to 461, is said to have brought Christianity to Ireland. But the Faith once delivered to the saints was clearly there. Killien, born in Ireland, was given by his parents a great education, which he developed and brought to fruition in troublous times. He was given the Roman Pontiff's license to preach to the barbarians in Franconia, Germany. At Wurtzburg he converted Gozbert, the governor and the larger part of his people within two years. But when he condemned Gozbert for marrying his brother's widow, the enraged Gozbert had him beheaded in 689 A.D.

89

It has, likewise been developed for the even larger purpose of candidly teaching The Eternal Truth of God, to encourage living, dynamic Faith and deep *Agapao* Love in the heart of man both for our Eternal Loving God to give fuller depths of understanding which The Holy Spirit may use, as He does all facets of The Truth of God, to reveal God to us on behalf, also, of our Holy Redeemer and our Loving Heavenly Father, whose passion, as our Triune Eternal God, is that we share His Eternal Love freely and fully with every person around us, thus extending His Message to ALL. II Peter 3:9.

Therefore, this writing is produced with the singular prayerful purpose of serving God to the best of my ability in seeking the furtherance of the common good of His Church, answering to all His Call; and, my cry to our Wonderful Loving God is that He would be pleased to use it to strengthen the harmony of all believers in our common Biblical Faith in unified Love, for the larger, more efficient use of His Church in true, faithful, diligent, yes fervent, larger service and witness for God to build His Church, fulfilling His Great Commission.

Individuals and families have strongly voiced appreciation for the effort, for having profited much as relationships were healed to their benefit. Had uniformity of teaching maintained from the beginning of The Church relative to baptism, there would be far fewer divisions among His Own. Many hearts have been broken; and, untold numbers of lives, families and homes have suffered ruin as The Unity of The Holy Spirit has been given second place to personal opinions promoted improperly; and without careful seeking of The Mind of The Holy Spirit; or, without due respect for The Oneness of the people of God!

Many personal, emotional, even physical sufferings and even hatreds have stemmed immediately out of the singular service of baptism. It has been the purpose of this writer to simply give unaltered facts to assist in healing in some measure, The Church's many schisms, in concentrating the Scriptures; and, Recorded Church History to this end for the betterment of The Church's many services, so grossly and grotesquely hindered in these last days, when the harvest has all the appearance of an over-ripe wheat field wasting in neglect; with so many great opportunities gone, with an infinite number of eternal souls *Lost FOREVER!* May God help us to *WAKEUP!!*

SOPge in the Roman and Byzantine Periods, 140 B.C. to 1,000 A.D. – "*baptidzo, to dip, to immerse, to sink...* There is no evidence that Luke and Paul and the other writers of the N.T. put upon this verb meanings not recognized by the Greeks."

God loves every one of His own; and, permitted His Own Precious Son to die in our place to shield you, me, and every human from God's Wrath, by bearing for each of us, personally, God's Judgment, on the single condition that we receive it by faith; and, giving to all who will receive His Love and Salvation, Perfect, Absolute Family Status as God's sons and daughters, His Own Personal, gracious gift, at horrible cost to Him! Please don't miss His free gift of Family Standing and our Heavenly Home He has for you.

Water baptism is not Salvation, nor is it a sealing element. Ephesians 4:30. It is the believer's first act of obedience, designed for witness of personal faith; and, to provide a public visual, as an easily comprehended witness to our faith; also, to state our public declaration of commitment to begin the experience of a new walk of OBEDIENCE in following our Lord.

The Lord Jesus Christ's Baptism in Jordan by John The Baptist, was His declared eternal identification with sinful mankind, as pictured by offerings under the Mosaic Law, where sinners laid hands on heads of an innocent, clean animal, which became the victim sin offering, to declare a belief that there would come The Perfect One Who would pay sin's debt for man, by dying as The Perfect Substitute for sinners, the Innocent One, paying by His Death for the guilty, as The Just for the unjust, thus canceling judgment for the repentant guilty; and, in that same Transaction, purchasing eternally God's Perfect Righteousness for all who believe and receive it.

"ONE OF THE LAST of those who had personally known any of the Apostles was Polycarp, bishop of Smyrna, who was put to death in that city in the year 156, at the age of 86, saying "eighty and six years have I served

Him and He has done me no wrong." He had long been instructed by the Apostle John, and had been intimate with others who had seen the Lord. Irenaeus is another link in the chain of personal connection with the times of Christ. He was taught by Polycarp and was made bishop of Lyons in 177.

THE FATHERS, even those who unconsciously did the most service to Rome, and laid the foundation for its colossal pretensions, yet had no idea of ascribing absolute supremacy and infallibility to the pope.

CLEMENT OF ROME, the first Roman Bishop of whom we have any authentic account wrote a letter to the Church at Corinth not in his name, but in the name of the Roman Congregation; not with an air of superior authority, but as a brother to brethren—barely mentioning Peter, but eulogizing Paul, and with a clear consciousness of the great difference between an APOSTLE AND A BISHOP OR ELDER.

"THE VERY WORD *BAPTIZE SIGNIFIES TO IMMERSE (MERGERE); AND IT IS CERTAIN THAT IMMERSION WAS THE PRACTICE OF THE ANCIENT CHURCH."* HISTORY OF THE CHRISTIAN CHURCH, VOL 1, P. 251.

IGNATIUS OF ANTIOCH, UNDER TRAGAN, (PROBABLY BETWEEN 110 AND 116) WAS CONDEMNED TO DEATH, TRANSPORTED TO ROME, AND THROWN BEFORE WILD BEASTS IN THE COLOSSEUM AND IS CHARACTERISTIC OF THE LEGENDARY MARTYROLOGY OF THE ANCIENT CHURCH. HE HIGHLY EXTOLS THE EPISCOPACY AND CHURCH UNITY IN HIS SEVEN EPISTLES, ONE OF WHICH IS ADRESSED TO THE ROMAN CHRISTIANS, MAKES NO DISTINCTION OF RANK AMONG BISHOPS, BUT TREATS THEM AS EQUALS.

"The practice of baptizing believers on their confession of faith in the Lord Jesus Christ, as taught and exemplified in the New Testament, was continued in later times. The first clear reference to the baptism of infants is in a writing of Tertullian in 197, in which he condemns the practice beginning to be introduced of baptizing the dead and of baptizing infants."
– THE PILGRIM CHURCH, E. H. Broadbent, p. 8, 9.

THE SPIRITUAL WARFARE which has troubled all humanity through the ages, lingers treacherously, demanding our dependence absolutely on The Holy Spirit, to keep our vision clear and our hearts warm! Satan's evil rebellion and theft of one third of the angelic host in Ezekiel 28 and Isaiah 14 demand militance! Israel's deceptions by him brought awesome tragedy!

He was permitted of God to bring evil upon evil, corruption upon corruption to Israel! They must have the opportunity to love and serve God by choice; and, not as those who had no choice. Satan, the tempter, is allowed his continued activity that each human shall have opportunity for that same choice, with a mind and will of our own with which to decide and take action. Every person, in our free nation, is likewise free and responsible to make personal decisions that determine our eternal destiny.

Because of the deeply personal nature of baptism there is a person in the spirit world who through the ages has gendered strife. He is involved in all of human experience; and, as discussions most often have gendered anger and division, rather than the seeking of a proper solution to differences of belief, great sorrow has resulted, even hatred, war, and strife, with an undercurrent of animosity, not with the Spirit of Love which God ordained for His own. Our aim, goal and heart desire is resolution of this tragedy, using The Bible and historical fact for proper solution, inasmuch as in my long life, divisions within The Church have accelerated, not declined!

Every person gives account for ourselves; and, for our influence on all of God's creatures and creation! God knows everything about every person! Each human, from the age of accountability, makes their own decision as to whom they will choose to follow, God and our Savior; or, Satan. Man is a morally accountable agent, responsible to make wise decisions for building his or her own life for personal, eternal good. Therefore, we are wise to learn all truths that will build our personal life for time and eternity. Nosiness, relative to other believers is forbidden! John 21:21,22.

IN THE CHURCH founded on one Foundation (I Corinthians 3:11), Satan is still at his destroying work, as Apolyon, or, 'the destroyer', having begun his treacherous activity by attempting to cast doubt on The Holy

Person of The Eternal Son of God, Messiah of Israel and Savior of all humanity; and, relative to His Infinite, Holy Work as The Incarnate God! Satan's work, as the wicked one, has severely scarred and scattered Israel to the ends of the earth. In the same manner, from the time of the Apostles in Acts 4; and, from the days of Saul of Tarsus, Acts 8:1-3, Satan has made havoc of The Church in every way open to him. He has slaughtered and massacred hundreds of thousands of God's most faithful saints.

Please allow me to state here that "the gifts and calling of God are without repentance" Romans 11:29. What God has given Israel shall be Israel's forever! Nor, has God taken from Israel's Eternal Covenant and transferred it to The Church. This error of belief in a so-called 'transfer of calling', labeled Covenant Theology, is not accurate at all! Israel's Covenant, given to Abraham, is eternal; and, as the Church Age ends, Israel's Covenant will be activated once more; first, into the crisis time of Jacob's Trouble; then, into the Millennial Kingdom; followed by Israel's leadership over the nations in The New Earth! Israel shall be the Eternal Administrator, with Messiah Prince, on David's Throne as Absolute Lord of All.

Today, God's Own division of the human race remains: The Jew, The Gentile, and The Church of God, I Corinthians 10:32; and each of us is responsible before God to be extremely careful, lest we offend God with wrong attitudes toward any, but, particularly, in regard to The Nation of Israel and her people!!

The "wise men from the east" led by the star to Bethlehem, worshipped the Child newly "born King of the Jews"; presenting to Him "gifts, gold and frankincense and myrrh", and "departed into their own country another way" (Matthew 2), where they doubtless related what they had seen and heard.

The Jews are not Christ haters! The original Church consisted of Jews and proselytes only. Horribly wicked abuses have been heaped on their heads by blaming them, even though some obeyed God, in the generous extension of His Salvation's Work. Converted Jewish Apostles and people were *very* slow to respond; and, Paul was drafted to carry the message. Persecution drove them to their task. They were broken hearted that the

Jewish people, in large measure, rejected the savior; and they were radically disobedient often brother and sister, brother against sister, and brother against brother, broke their heart! With the radical beliefs they held (much like the Muslims of today) it was heart-wrenching, and gut wrenching to make the break.

Eusebius writing of events which took place in the second century relates that many of the disciples at that time "whose souls were inflamed by the Divine Word and were with a more ardent desire of wisdom, first fulfilled our Saviour's commandment by distributing their substance to those that were needy.

Then after that, travelling abroad, they performed the work of evangelists to those who had not yet at all heard the word of faith, being very ambitious to preach Christ and to deliver the books of the Divine Gospels. And these persons, having only laid the foundations of faith in remote and barbarous places and constituted other pastors, committed to them the culture of those they had perfectly introduced to the faith, and departed again to other regions. Thus churches were founded and the evangelists pressed further onward, preaching the Word and baptizing, throughout the Persian Empire and beyond.

Studies show the Word spread by the Meads, Persians, and Phrygians; on into Achaia and Macedonia, to Epirus, spreading widely even in the islands and the provinces of the Roman Empire. Churches spread rapidly and it seems they were shielded against some of the influences that affected the Western Peoples, therefore they were kept in a purer state than the Western provinces. They had both Books and Godly Traditions to keep their hearts warm, rather than debates about the Person of Christ. The awe and reverence of these protected their doctrines, and the sacred reverence in which their baptism was held kept them true to their profession.

"Early in the fourth century Papa ben Aggai propounded a scheme for the federation of all the churches in Persia, including those in Syria and Mesopotamia, under the rule of the bishop of the capital city, Seleucia-Ctesiphon, a position which he himself then occupied. The proposition was strenuously opposed but continued to be pressed, and the bishop came to be called the *Catholikos,* and in time (498) the title Patriarch of the East was adopted." THE PILGRIM CHURCH, E H. Broadbent, p. 68, 69.

The Christian bears an overwhelming debt, both to God and to The Nation of Israel who was used of God to provide the world's Savior; and, who obeyed His Direction in sharing His Eternal Gospel of Salvation with the world, as these disciples had done, they knew first hand so much of how the Apostle Paul had witnessed and worked. Much had been taught, also, of The Twelve Apostles who had laid down their lives for the Name of The Lord Jesus; and, as John had been treated brutally and incarcerated on the Ilse of Patmos, where he completed The Revelation of God before being released to die at Ephesus; also, there were those who carried the message among the scattered Jewish believers, and in the Synagogues which were scattered everywhere, as they preached the Word!!

WITH THESE FACTS BEFORE US, may we proceed now with true candor in evaluating the urgent need for experiencing the Oneness of God's people, as we appear to be confronted soon with a larger, more open opposition in our great nation to God's Church; and, particularly in caring for His Mission for which He Agonized in the sweating of great drops of blood in Gethsemane. Every member of Adam's guilty, fallen race, for whom He shed His Blood on the beastly cruel Cross on Calvary's Hill, on Golgotha's brow invited, is invited to come in these word "whosoever shall call upon the Name of The Lord shall be saved." (Romans 10:13) (Hebrews 2:9 "tasting death for every man"). It does seem to me that a more specific look at our subject of Bible Baptism could be helpful: as to the mode and meaning of baptism; and, properly conveying the significance of its proper teachings; also, as to how it is to be specifically practiced through this age, based on its tenets as it has been explained in Scripture, to serve during The Church Age as the distinct Ordinance of God!

From the Day of Pentecost until modern times, Satan has used his distortions in every realm of proper Church Teaching, far more efficiently, it would seem, than has our Lord's Church, because His Church has not had a better understanding of God's Purpose, Plan, Power and Principles,

His Holy Spirit, The Lord of The Harvest, has sought to teach His people, who have not to this day, learned how to listen to and obey Him Who is in charge of The Church, sent from The Head of The Church, as He was placed in command on earth.

It seems from existing evidences within Christ's shattered Church, that we are too preoccupied with trying to pull weeds, (Matthew 13:24-30), with Satan's wicked plants getting into His professed church to cause havoc, hatred, and harmony loss, within the church, with his treachery, having been highly effective in accomplishing his goal. We are to be, in Truth, The Solid, Unified, Efficient Body of Christ we are supposed to be, in fulfilling His Mission as The Holy Spirit yearns to see properly done! This calls for true servants who have hearing ears, to listen carefully and prayerfully to The Holy Spirit; and, obey Him!

As our Savior came, taught, Suffered, Died, and Arose in Eternal Triumph, Satan's gnostic philosophies cast doubts into the minds of both Jew and Gentile as to Who Our Holy Redeemer, Son of David, Son of God really is in His Incarnation, as well as to significance and meanings of prophetic Truth!

False teachers, arising out of the church's drift from God, and from the gentile world, distorted every aspect of His Redeeming Work. Diversification of attacks grew in number, kinds and distortions! Those wretched seeds of doubts, so well portrayed in our Lord's Teachings in Matthew 13:24 – 43, continue to undermine Bible Truth to the present hour, along with their perverted concepts and multiplied additional heresies with twisted, endless philosophies that mock God and His Redeemer.

ALL OF THIS requires understanding that 'every Word of God is pure', that 'one jot or one title' shall not pass from it, 'till all shall be fulfilled!' that 'every Scripture is God-breathed, *Theopneustos';* and, that every individual believer urgently needs the very purest teachings from The Holy Spirit, as we are yoked together with our Lord (Matthew 11:28-31) for a life filled with effectiveness and growing capabilities for enlarging His harvest returns.

Satan still harbors his dreams to exalt his throne above the stars of God. (Isaiah 14:12-15). Ezekiel 28:12 -19 goes far beyond Nimrod and the king of Tyre or Tyrus, to the church of Laodicea (Revelation 3:i5, i6.) Gentile beginnings of rebellious defiance of Truth and Righteousness, which The Bible declares will climax in The Beast and Antichrist, at the end of this age. Isaiah 14:12-15, introduces the evil one who pursues his dream by mangling The Church of God; and, blinding the human race to the realities of God's Eternal Truth.

WITH THE SIGNIFICANT SPECIFICS of our Wonderful Lord's Great Commission laid out and Biblically supported, as I understand them to be, it is time to quote from another recognized, broadly approved, document:

Patrick Fairbairn's BIBLE ENCYCLOPEDIA, Vol. 1, p.260: "The Reformed churches concur in holding this doctrine of baptism. They regard it, when received in respect to its original Institution and doctrinal character, not as the efficient cause of faith and spiritual life, but, like circumcision,

Ro. iv., the sign and seal of these to the believing participant, pledging through an established ordinance in his church all the grace connected with faith and life; and on the part of the baptized, ratifying as by a solemn act of adhesion and surrender of himself to God, his belief in the gospel, and obligation to comply with its precepts. But for these ends the virtue of the ordinance hangs, not on the ritual administration (as Romanists, and in part also as Lutherans hold), but on the working of God's Spirit, and the exercise of faith in the subjects of the ordinance.

"4. The *conditions of baptism,* or the amount of religious knowledge and state of spiritual attainment required of those who were recognized as proper subjects of the ordinance, are not fully and categorically exhibited in New Testament scripture; they are rather implied in the nature of the ordinance, and left to be inferred from attendant circumstances, than formally and distinctly enunciated."

Our Call of God demands incisive discernment and rigid adherence to Holy Scripture, proceeding on the clear Premises of The Infinite, Holy

Word of God, The Volume of the Book, The Bible! This and this alone is our Guide Book, our Compass, our Shield! To depart from these in any measure is not to be countenanced on penalty of paying a most tragic price. The History of His Church proves my point! Please, let us be open and candid in turning to our God, to become once more His obedient Church, sowing His Word alone; and, reaping 100-fold!

Baptism. Christian baptism is the immersion of a believer in water as a symbol of death to sin and resurrection to newness of life. Jesus himself required baptism at the hands of John the Baptist, meeting his remonstrance with the remark that "thus it becometh us to fulfill all righteousness," and it was on this occasion that His Divine Character as The Son, was proclaimed from heaven by The Voice of God; along with this fact, God's Holy Spirit descended, visibly, and rested on Him! The Holy Spirit's singular, visible descent to rest upon His Church came on The Day of Pentecost. The fact that, thereafter, as in Samaria, in Acts 8, in the house of Cornelius, in Acts 10; and, in relation to the disciples of John the Baptist (or, the baptizer), in Acts 19, The Holy Spirit's entry into the lives of new converts had been committed from The Day of Pentecost, to the hands of believers, to share His Gospel, His Good News with every person on earth!

Baptism, Christian baptism is the immersion of a believer in water as a symbol of death to sin and resurrection to newness of life. Jesus himself required baptism at the hands of John, the Baptist, meeting his remonstrance with the remark that "thus it becometh us to fulfill all righteousness," and it was on this occasion that his Divine Sonship was proclaimed from heaven and that the Spirit rested upon him.

The meaning of the word, the description of the act in individual cases, and the symbolism (burial and resurrection) all seem to fix the outward form of the ordinance as immersion.

"Our Lord's own direction regarding baptism makes it follow faith, and the very nature of the ordinance renders it exclusively to those capable of repentance and faith." – A MANUAL OF CHURCH HISTORY, Vol. 1, p. 136 – Albert Henry Newman, D. D., LL. D.

A straightforward obedience to The Bible gives no room for today's utter church confusion, not only now relative to baptism, but, to a genuine bold belief in the infinite infallibility of Scripture, or the total scope of our Redeemer's Victory!

The modern lack of obedience to The Word of God, as professed believers, continues to weaken the professed church in 2013, with her lost her vision of perishing humanity that faces an everlasting Hell. Unless The Church is won to a true, life-transforming change of vision and purpose the apostasy will become complete! What His Church can't deliver, perishing humanity is helpless to receive! Where must we go to find a resolute readiness to face the true call of God; or to embrace The Whole Counsel of God that God could use to start that urgent, long overdue passion to live in true obedience to The Bible for the Glory of God, as faithful children!

CHAPTER VI
THE POTENTIAL CRISIS AND BAPTISM

The horrible carnage and war over baptism caused millions to forsake the church. London was filled with orphans! Misery, death, doubt and delusion filled the earth! I want you to see what a little love will do!

George Mueller, born into a German tax collector's family, was often in trouble. He learned early to steal and gamble and drink. As a teenager he learned how to stay in expensive hotels, then, sneak out without paying the bill. But at length he was caught and jailed. Prisons did him little good, for upon release he continued his crime spree until on a Saturday night in 1825 he met the Lord Jesus Christ.

Mueller married and settled down in Bristol, England, growing daily in faith and developing a burden for the homeless children running wild and ragged through the streets. At a public meeting in Bristol on December 9, 1835, he presented a plan for an orphanage. Several contributions came in. Mueller rented Number 6 Wilson street, and on April 11, 1836 the doors of the orphanage opened. Twenty six children were immediately taken in. A second house soon opened, then a third.

From the beginning Mueller refused to ask for funds or even to speak of the financial needs. He believed in praying earnestly and trusting the Lord to provide. And the Lord did provide, though sometimes at the last moment. The best-known story involves a morning when the plates and bowls and cups were set on the tables, but there was no food or milk. The children sat waiting for breakfast while Mueller led in prayer for their daily bread. A knock sounded at the door. It was the baker. "Mr. Mueller," he said, "I couldn't sleep last night. Somehow I felt you didn't have bread for breakfast, so I got up at 2 A.M. and baked some fresh bread." A second knock sounded. The milkman had broken down right in front of the orphanage. And he wanted to give the children his milk so he could empty his wagon and repair it. There were over 50,000 answers to prayer!

Such stories became the norm for Mueller's work. During the course of his 93 years, Mueller housed more than 10,000 orphans! Please pray! Pray!

WHEN THE PENNSYLVANIA WEST BOUND train on which C.E. McCartney was traveling stopped at Altoona before beginning the ascent of the mountains, he noticed there many powerful engines, their bunkers filled with coal, steam up, smoke issuing from the stacks, fires glowing under the boilers, and engineer and firemen at their posts. The engines were ready to go into action. They had been fueled and fired and manned for action...and they DID GO INTO ACTION, PULLING THE LONG TRAINS OVER THE MOUNTAINS. WHY IS IT that The Church under Almighty God with ALL POWER moves like the toy trains in the store window? THEY FORGOT TO PRAY!!

Think not that I am come to send peace on earth; I came not to send peace, but a sword.

For I am come to set a man at variance against his father and the daughter against her mother and the daughter-in-law against her mother-in-law. And a man's foes shall be they of his own household. Matthew 10:34-36

WERE THERE THE PASSION, Prayer and caring of the Lord Jesus present in His Church, an overnight change would be seen in America and throughout the world! Can't we see? Do we care?

One of the most beautiful examples I have ever known in my ministry comes to mind: The father said: "We were headed for total disaster! The wife, Catholic! The husband, Lutheran! Their lives were transformed by the Word of God! But in the process of ministry, when they wished I would stop coming around; but, I longed to see them saved and their young children, but I gently persisted and it thrills my heart to see every member of the family serving: two pastors, two missionaries, one youth worker, ministry captain, and the mother just led a young man to a living faith! They are great blessing to me.

In the 4th century heretical baptism was generally regarded as valid, if performed in the name of the triune God. The Roman view prevailed over the Cyprianic, at least in the Western Church; except among Donatists, who entirely rejected heretical baptism (as well s the catholic baptism), and made the efficacy of the sacrament depend not only on the ecclesiastical, but also on the personal piety of the officiating priest.

We "let the beauty of the Lord our God be upon us...." Psalm 90:17. "Let this Mind be in you, which was also in Christ Jesus, Who Being in the Form of God, thought it not robbery to be equal with God: but made Himself of no reputation, and took upon Him the Form of a Servant, and was Made in the Likeness of men:" Philippians 2:5-7.

TO SUBSTITUTE for Baptism ANYTHING which excludes all symbolic reference to the Death of Christ, and, THE BLOOD ATONEMENT, which was to be presented "to My father and your Father' is to be very strongly opposed! His broken body, 'whose form was marred more than that of any man', with every drop of His Atoning Blood causes me to stand in awe! The ultimate Sacrifice is worthy of the ultimate devotion, even as it was presented to the Father, in absolute holiness! "When I consider thy heavens, the work of thy fingers, the moon and the stars, which thou hast ordained, what is man, that thou art mindful of him? And the son of man, that thou visitest him?" Psalm 8:3,4.

Regeneration and baptism, are both regarded in the New Testament as proper for the restoration of man's right relations to God and to his people in the proper obedience to God, when permissible. They properly constitute parts of one whole, and are not to be unnecessarily separated. Baptism should follow regeneration without delay, after the candidate and the church have gained evidence that a spiritual change has transformed the individual into a new creation. No other duty and no other ordinance can be required of the individual. (II Cor. 5:17).

FOR CENTURIES WE HAVE WAITED FOR HIS RETURN, BUT PERHAPS THE TIME WILL BE EXTENDED: "At midnight the sailors slipped excitedly up the ladder changing the watch on the turret guns. It was mid-August on the West Pacific. We had left Europe and its wreckage behind in early July. With Sherman tanks and combat engineers aboard we were headed for what we thought was another war. At midnight the sailors cried, "We dropped an atomic bomb!" Technically, the war was over!

The Japanese emperor was paralyzed with fear! He signed immediately! His deity suddenly ended! But it was months before the war ended! For more than a year, the unbelieving, bewildered soldiers came out of hiding, surrendering their weapons! But, wars have continued! The troubles in the world mirror the experience of the Church! Satan, in all of his viciousness continues to create problems. All of the horrible violence, turmoil and chaos continues to trouble the human race! We wait! Will the Lord come today?? Therefore, we labor night and day with the *urgent cry:* "PRAY FOR THE PEACE OF JERUSALEM!"

WE ASK THE QUESTION, WHY? "Baptists had much influence in The Toleration Act of May 24, 1689, for the relief of Dissenters, and marks the transition to better things. "For this change of public sentiment the chief merit is due to English Non-conformists, who in the school of persecution became advocates of toleration, especially the Baptists and Quakers" CREEDS OF CHRISTENDOM, Philip Schaff, VOL. I, P.802.

Every Reformer worthy of the name acknowledged the unquestionable meaning of *Baptizo. Why* does the haggling go on? I consider it a disgrace!

IT IS INEVITABLE that there would be potential crisis in Baptism because of all it represented! I believe that persecution stems from extreme jealousy, undiscerned for what it is!! Cain killed Abel (Abel's sacrifice was accepted, Cain's was not!) When there is disobedience, passion rages. Read the Record of Saul and David! How many times did Saul Vow not to kill David? It seems to have been continuous for more than twenty years. The Scribes, Pharisees, and all the rest were livid with jealousy!! The Reformers chose to get along with authorities under 'the god of this world' and snuggled in!! They devised a mode of 'baptism' seen as a compromise, which brought the thirty years war to an embarrassing conclusion and left the church under the control of the state. We are 'born crucified'. Man-made laws united toward stamping out the Immersion that was the emblem of radical conversion, even seeing it was done with murder and torture! Zwingli set 'Capital Punishment' in order and, they proceeded with passion.

RESPECTING AUGUSTINE'S doctrine of infant baptism, Wall's History of Infant Baptism, Vol.1, p. 173ff (Oxford ed. Of 1862), gives his view of the slight condemnation of un-baptized children contains the germ of the 'scholastic fancy' of the *limbus infantum* ad the *paena damni,* as disfinct from the lower regions of Hell and the *paena sensus.* Augustine's view of baptism stems from the belief that baptism is necessary for Salvation, but this is the very factor that has corrupted Covenant Theology the most tragically. When you study the life of Augustine, he had very few years to prepare properly for the enormous influence he carried. I consider that a tragedy; but, the lack of real foundation in learning is always disaster!

The persistence in contrary positions, which cannot be justified, stubbornly resisting real obedience to The Living God; and, to His Infinitely Holy, explicit Word, places the professed church in a position of total uselessness! As our Wonderful Lord said to the very last representation of His Church in this age, in Revelation 3:14-22."**And unto the angel of the church of the laodiceans, wrote: These things saith the Amen, the beginning (*the protokos, The Originator*) of the creation of God;**

"**I know thy works, that thou art neither cold nor hot: I would thou wert cold or hot. So then because thou art lukewarm, and neither cold nor hot, I will spue thee out of my mouth. Because thou sayest, i am rich and increased with goodsand have need of nothing; and knowest not that thou art wretched, and miserable, and poor, and blind, and naked:**

"**I counsel thee to buy of me gold tried in the fire, that thou mayest be rich; and white raiment thou thou mayest be clothed, and that the**

shame of thy nakedness do not appear;and anoint thine eyes with eye-salve, that thou mayest see.

"As many as I love, I rebuke and chasten: be zealous therefore and repent. Behold, I stand at the door and knock; if any man hear my voice, and open the door, I will come in to him, and will sup with him and he with me. To him that overcometh will I grant to sit with me in my throne, even as I also overcame, and am set down with my Father in His Throne. He that hath an ear, let him hear what the Spirit saith unto the churches."

I AM DEEPLY CONCERNED with what has happened to the Church in those centuries when it went into apostasy, revamped, and came out as a system of apostates. There is no grounds whatever for the teaching of false doctrines; and, of Covenant Theology in particular!! To usurp the doctrines given to Israel is incredible to say the least and with all the warnings of apostasy repeatedly given, there is not a single excuse for inventing a new Faith and order Bible believers by the hundreds of thousands would choose to be roasted, anathematized, and executed in the most wretched ways, if they realized what had occurred? God help us!

I found it quite stunning to find the following statement in a Catholic high school textbook in regard to baptism: "Now about baptism: this is how to baptize. Give public instruction on all these points, and then "baptise" in running water, "in the name of the Father and of the Son and of the Holy Spirit" (Matt. 28:19). If you do not have running water, baptize in some other. If you cannot in cold, then in warm. If you have neither, then pour water on the head three times in the name of the Father, Son, and Holy Spirit" (Matt. 28:19). Before the baptism, moreover, the one who baptizes and the one being baptized must fast, and any others who can. And you must tell the one being baptized to fast for one or two days beforehand...." (How do infants do that?) READINGS in the HISTORY of (Catholic)

CHRISTIAN THEOLOGY, VOLUME 1, P 23, William C. Placher. *Petilian, a Donatist bishop, had written a letter to his followers defending the Donatist position: Baptisms performed by the Catholic party Augustine represented were often invalid, for they were performed by priests ordained by corrupt bishops who had betrayed the church in the time of persecution. Somewhere shortly after 400 Augustine responded in this treatise.* READINGS in the HISTORY of CHRISTIAN THEOLOGY, VOLUME 1, P. 23, William C. Placher. (In a lengthy debate with the Donatists 'p.111-113' I am shocked to say the least that sprinkling isn't mentioned one time, for they would have been laughed out of school!)

Seneca writes of the savagery, immorality and vileness of the human heart, following the crucifixion and in the years of turmoil that followed: the barbarians, the sacking of Rome, the wars that raged, What a remarkable setting, which The Church of God wrestled with! Miracle of miracles, even The Catholic System, from which Protestantism emerged, must be fruit even from the Dark Ages! Those who carried The Torch of Salvation, baptism and the standard of ethics which we have should be deeply cherished. When the Slavs came on the European scene is unknown, but Latin and Greek writers of the 6th Century, Procopius, Jornandes;, Agathias, the emperor Mauritius and others who lived on the frontiers of the Roman Empire, mention them in their writings, but in the era of Charlemagne (768-814 A.D.) the Slavic peoples occupied the entire region of Eastern Europe, from the Baltic to the Balkan and were fertile ground for evangelism, subdued and converted by Charlemagne, from 79i to 796, disappeared from history in the Ninth Century! The Moravians, Bulgarians, Bohemians and the peoples of Poland and Russia emerged from that background, in customs and habits, but not in language. The Magyars, settling near Theiss and the Danube became the ruling class of Hungary. I speak of this to show the restlessness of the human heart, savage of action and keeping little to no records of conduct "SYSTEMATIC SLAUGHTER, beheading, burning, drowning, began afresh under the Empress Theodora's orders, and continued many years, but it failed to shake the stedfastness of the believers. It was claimed that between the years 842 and 867 the zeal of Theodora and her inquisitors had brought about the death of 100,000 persons. This time is described by Gregory Magistros, who 200 years later, was in charge of the persecution of similar people in the same district. He writes "Prior to us many generals and magistrates have given them over to the sword and without pity, have

J. Clarence Ford, LittD

spared neither old men nor children, and quite rightly. What is more, our patriarchs have branded their foreheads and burned into them the image of a fox....others again have put their eyes out, saying, 'you are blind to spiritual things therefore you shall not look on sensible things'." THE PILGRIM CHURCH, E. H. Broadbent, p. 52,53

The 9th Century to the 11th Century were filled with violence and practices of those called Paulicans of Thonrak; although there were doubtless many differences in the numerous scattered churches, yet this authentic account given by one of themselves, is applicable to most of them. The author is unknown, but writes with power and eloquence as well as with deep feeling and earnestness. He writes to give to the new born children (converts) children of the Universal and Apostolic Church of our Lord Jesus Christ the holy milk whereby they may be nourished in the faith. "Our Lord", he says, "asks first for repentance and faith and then baptism, so we must follow Him and not do after the deceitful arguments of others, who baptize the unbelieving, the reasonless, and the unrepentant. When a child is born, the elders of the church should give counsel to the parents that they may train the child in godliness and faith. This should be accompanied by prayer, the reading of the Scriptures and giving the child a name. When anyone is baptized it should be at his or her earnest request. Baptism should be in rivers, or other water in the open air. The one to be baptized should, on his knees in the midst of the water, confess his faith before the congregation present, with great love and tears. The one who baptizes should be of blameless character. Prayer and the reading of Scripture should accompany the act." (*The Key of Truth" translated and edited by F. C. Conybeare, this document was found by the translator in 1891 in the library of the Holy Synod at Edjmiatzin, and has added valuable annotations).

By taking a strong, prayerful, obedient stand as our God requires, for His Unified Teaching of His Church, God's Holy Spirit would have a force that He could use to evangelize our world in a single week! It is in such effort toward being truly obedient and Biblically uniform in One Faith and One Baptism, that this writing is purposed in design to serve Him! I believe it to be an effort with which God will be in some measure, pleased;

and, hopefully, will seem proper and right to all who love Him; also, above all, one upon which He may be pleased to place His Blessing to assist in unifying His people in heart, mind, spirit, purpose, form and efficiency!

May I illustrate that our God is not pleased with substitutes for obedience? When God commands, "Enter by The Door", He doesn't mean it is acceptable to crawl in a window. He says in John 10:1... "He that entereth not by The Door into the sheepfold, but climbeth up some other way, the same is a thief and a robber."

Not that water baptism brings us into His Kingdom; but, it is God's first-step command to every believer; and, should surely help to eliminate some measure of internal strife within His Church. God's design is, that following our being born of God by The Holy Sprit; and, following our having been baptized by His Holy Spirit into Christ's One Body of spiritual members, I Corinthians 12:13; each individual, upon having believed and thus receiving The Lord Jesus Christ, instantly, at that point, having become a member of His Spiritual Body, The Church, having experienced water baptism, by our immersion in water, which becomes our first act of obedience to Him as His child. Surely all true believers want to be obedient children, and, not be seen as devious, self-servers, putting our family and tradition ahead of God's clear command in His Holy Scriptures! There is no obedience to God without conformity to His Command.

ALL FOUR GOSPELS, after The Resurrection of our Lord Jesus Christ, provide us with records of our Risen Savior's visible, Personal fellowship with His faithful followers. The first three relay His Divine Commission to His Church in His Own Words, directing His Apostles and followers to our singular mission to reach and teach believers in the world with God's Holy Counsel of Truth; then, the practical Apostle John sets out his Record of The Truth, with a beautiful visual of the work involved in His Great Commission to His Own, who are to serve as fishers of men. John 21:3-11.

As each previous Gospel set out His Command, now John in John 21:6 uses The Call that our Lord Jesus Christ had extended to them: Matthew

4:19: "Follow me; and, I will make you fishers of men", are His Command: "Cast the net on the 'right side' of the ship, and ye shall find. They cast therefore; and, now they were not able to draw it for the multitude of fishes."

This is obviously done to teach his disciples that not only was self-effort of the unsent fruitless; but, obedience to their Lord brought more blessing and fruit than they were unable to handle alone! It was in obedience to His Command that the fish harvest was granted to them; and, they united forces to do the work. Their call now was to 'the other side', to the Gentile world where millions waited for His Word.

"THIS IS A DAY of apostasy in creed, conduct, doctrine and duty! The man who ignores it or minimizes it becomes a party to it!! Anarchy in the world, apostasy in the professing church, apathy, listlessness, smug complacency, resting at ease in Zion; luke-warmness—'neither hot nor cold'." Vance Havner said it! Think about it!! I tremble to think of the awful hour of quibbling giving answer to our God, seated on His Infinite Throne of Glory, surrounded by His Holy Angels!!

MATTHEW'S RECORD of His Great Commission follows the disciples' obeying His command to meet Him in Galilee. His Commission was given to His obedient followers: "Then the eleven disciples went away into Galilee, into a mountain where Jesus had appointed them. And when they saw Him, they worshipped Him; but some doubted. And Jesus spoke the infinite command! This is an order!! UNTO THE END OF THE AGE *(AIONIOS)*!!

"ALL POWER IS GIVEN UNTO ME in Heaven and in earth. Go ye therefore, and make disciples of all nations, baptizing them in the Name of The Father, and of The Son, and of The Holy Spirit: Teaching them to observe all things whatsoever I have commanded you: and, lo, I am with you always, even unto the end of the world (or, age). *(aionios)*."

His Church's obedience and progress are to be learned from the single Inspired History found in te Book of Acts. Beyond This Open-ended Book that leaves The Church's obedience to be followed from that point by study of faithful records kept by His devout servants and followers who have left for us known continued reports of The Church's advance through the centuries that have intervened.

The brilliant scholar, Dr. Philip Schaff, born with Reformation heritage in Europe, (1819-1893), son of a Swiss carpenter, with outstanding career of a scholar in Tubingen, Halle, and Berlin, on his way to a very bright future in Germany was persuaded to join the faculty of the theological seminary of the German Reformed Church in Mercersburg, Pennsylvania. His achievements leave with us his massive, eight volume History of The Christian Church, recognized by The Church at large as certainly one of the most efficient works on Church History that has been produced in modern times. I wish to present here an extended quote from that massive work:

"THE IDEA OF BAPTISM. It was solemnly instituted by Christ shortly before his ascension, to be performed in the name of the Father, the Son, and the Holy Spirit.... 2. The usual FORM of baptism was immersion. This is inferred from the original meaning of the Greek *Baptizein* and *Baptismos;* from the analogy of John's baptism in the Jordan (Matt. 3:1-3; from the apostles' comparison of the sacred rite with the miraculous passage of the Red Sea (I Cor.10:1-4) with the escape of the ark from the flood, with a cleansing and refreshing bath, and with burial and resurrection; finally, from the general custom of the ancient church, which prevails in the East to this day." HISTORY OF THE CHRISTIAN CHURCH, VOL. 1, p. 467-468.

"True, the New Testament contains no express command to baptize infants; such a command would not agree with the free spirit of The Gospel. Nor was there any compulsory or general infant baptism before the union of church and state;"! HISTORY OF THE CHRISTIAN CHURCH, VOL.1, P. 470. (This volume covers the first one hundred years of Church History.)

Doctor Schaff has already proceeded with a lengthy apology of justification for sprinkling and for infant baptism, before having made the above candid statement. The union of church and state did not occur until 315 A.D. The above acknowledgment negates his pro-infant baptism stance, based on assumptions of ancient practices without either Bible Text; or, provable historical incidence of practice during the first (as he declares) 315 years of The Church Age;. This in no way casts reflection on a brilliant scholarship; but, it does say volumes relative to fallen man's tragic inability (even after being Born Again) to be unbiased in our views of facts that cut across the grain of our own personal experience, practice and classic position. Also, such individuals shrink from conflict with equals.

If the very word '*Baptizein*' and the word '*Baptismos*' mean immersion, (and, they certainly do), as the Eastern Greek Church continues the practice, on what ground under Heaven can sprinkling and pouring be 'obedience'? Also, on what basis are untaught infants to be baptized, when Christ's Great Commission places baptism after the preaching of The Gospel and the making of disciples!?

I Corinthians 14:40 confirms that God expects proper order to be observed by His Church as His Own Requirement in obeying The Holy Scriptures.

"Water is essential to baptism. The Schoolmen agreed that wine, oil, or other liquid will not do. Duns Scotus said in regard to baptism in beer that its validity would depend upon a scientific test whether the beer continued to be a species of water or not. The Lombards declared without qualification for immersion as the proper mode. Thomas Aquinas refers to it as the more general practice of his day and prefers it as the safer mode, as did also Bonaventura and Duns Scotus. At any rate the water must be applied to the head, for this is the most important part of man, standing as it does for the immortal agent. Both trine immersion, the custom of the Greek Church, and single immersion are valid. Trine immersion symbolizes the three persons of the Trinity and the three days of the Lord's burial; single immersion the unity of the Deity and the uniqueness of Christ's death. Synods, as late as the synod of Tarragona, 1391, spoke of the submersion of children in baptism." HISTORY OF THE CHRISTIAN CHURCH, Vol. V, p.711,712. The Middle Ages, (A.D. 1049 – 1294).

While Calvin, very obviously, believed that baptism was by immersion, it was a time of strong turmoil. Israel had abandoned the faith and was violent in their rejection of Christ. They hated the Name! Many became agnostic, looking for answers in philosophy and natural wisdom. It was this setting of reaching and searching that gave rise to a new era of religious philosophy answering to the need. Aristotle made such an inroad with his version of philosophy that out of this, the evolutionary movement could spring! The last 200 years has left the church in total chaos!

What an hour for selecting a spiritualizing of Old Testament philosophy which would answer the need. The 8th day would do for baptism! This would provide for the heritage of Israel to be transferred to the Church! The promise of Abraham was to Christians! He was the father of all who believe! Whatever promises of Abraham to his heritage was spiritualized to the Church, so, Canaan was The Promised Land to Christians; the Covenants were to the Church, and Prophecy could be spiritualized, and there really was a great future to the Church, and the world would be converted to all Christendom, and then Eternity would begin. It made perfect sense and all would be well! But, then, World War I came! It was time for Philosophy again!

Evolution was the perfect answer! Those unable to accept this were naive and other philosophies of arrogant idealism were put forward as fulfilling all righteousness. They have fabricated a complete system for which they have absolutely NO foundation, other than a sweet idealism of philosophy! What a playhouse to spawn every concept that natural science could comprehend. They have stolen the heredity of Israel, canceling ¼ of the Old Testament: (1) There is No Millennium; (2) There is no heritage for Israel; (3) There is No Circumcision for Israel. However, The Gospel is to go "to the Jew first." Romans 1:16! "God was not willing that any should perish, but that ALL SHOULD COME TO REPENTANCE. Therefore, the Gospel is to go to "every man" Mark 16:15; John 3:16,17; II Pet. 3:9; If Israel had received the message the way they should have, the world would have been reached long ago!!

Instead of having the heart of Paul and seeking the Salvation of Israel: the complete repentance of that great nation, they have chosen this single verse to unload forever on Israel! Therefore, there is thirty five

million Americans, as well as all of Europe that would shed no tears if Israel were destroyed today!!

PLEASE NOTICE: There is NO conversion experience that is advocated in the following experiences:

"Let it be regarded as the goal towards which we are to run. For you cannot divide the matter with God, undertaking part of what his word enjoins, and omitting part at pleasure. For, in the first place, God uniformly recommends integrity as the principal part of his worship, meaning by integrity real singleness of mind; as if it had been said that the spiritual commencement of a good life is when the internal affections are sincerely devoted to God, in the cultivation of holiness and justice. But seeing that in this earthly prison of the body, no man is supplied with strength sufficient to hasten in his course with due alacrity, while the greater number are so oppressed with weakness, that hesitating, and halting, and even crawling on the ground, they make little progress, let every one of us go as far a his as his humble ability enables him, and prosecute the journey once begun, no one will travel so badly as not daily to make some degree of progress."This, therefore, let us never cease to do, that we may daily advance in the way of the lord; and let us not despair because of the slender measure of success. How little soever the success may correspond with your wish, our labor is not lost when today is better than yesterday, provided with true singleness of mind we keep our aim, and aspire to the goal, not speaking flattering things to ourselves, nor indulging our vices, but making it our constant endeavor to become better, until we attain to goodness itself. If during the whole course of our life we seek and follow, we shall at length attain it, when relieved from the infirmity of the flesh we are admitted to full fellowship with God," INSTITUTES OF THE CHRISTIAN RELIGION by John Calvin Vol. 1, p. 5.

An eleven year old girl was dying of leukemia. She had been baptized in infancy. She was terror stricken. The pastor brusquely had told them all was well that she had been baptized and there was nothing to fear. Not knowing how to deal with the matter, the parents called me. I went and talked with the child. She asked the Lord Jesus to be her Savior. It was a beautiful experience, as I spoke with her about God's wonderful Love, how the Savior had gone to the cross and died for her sin. She was overjoyed and began to ask me questions about heaven. I read to her, and sought to explain the beauties of Heaven as best I could, her heart was thrilled! She continued asking her Mother questions that she answered to the best of her ability, a few days later she was swept into eternity in a glory that radiated from her. Her Parents were blessed and rested in the beautiful experience.

If you wish to know why I have a passion for reaching people with God's Love, it was football evening and one of the players had gotten an automobile, so to show it off, he crowded his car with players to drive a mile for a coke before the game. It was dusk and enthusiastic boys were talking of the game and the car, but a two ton truck, loaded heavily with milow, had stalled on the road and the driver had abandoned it, leaving it on the road unattended and unlighted....the rear corner caught the auto at the hood level and sheared the corner of the top, curling it down and broke the neck of a Catholic sophomore.

No priest came. No comfort for broken hearts of parents was forthcoming, I went to the home, spoke as tenderly as I knew how to the parents, reading to them portions of Scripture, and then I said, "let's pray.

They fell on their knees before me, and I gently knelt beside them and prayed. They were Spanish, seemingly unable to understand English and I never knew how well I reached them but they knew I loved them. My heart still aches for those sweet parents, whom I never saw again. They vanished from the community and I could only guess where the funeral was held. I have no doubt God is able to speak well to the human heart so there is understanding, and reveal His Love to the heart of a dear Catholic child. My God is beautiful!

MARTIN LUTHER'S VIEWS ON BAPTISM: "As to the *mode* of baptism, he gives here, as elsewhere, his preference for immersion, which then still prevailed in England and in some parts of the Continent, and which was not a point of dispute either between Romanists and Protestants, or between Protestants and Anabaptists;... "Baptism," he says,

"is that dipping into water whence it takes its name. For, in Greek to baptize signifies to dip, and baptism is a dipping." "Baptism signifies two things,--death and resurrection; that is, full and complete justification."..
He proceeds from this point into the matter of the immersion of babies.
HISTORY OF THE CHRISTIAN CHURCH, Vol. V, p.218,

CHAPTER VII
THE PROBLEMS OF INFANT BAPTISM

"INFANT BAPTISM has led in the Greek church to infant communion, this course seems logically consistent. If baptism is administered to unconscious babes, they should partake in the Lord's Supper also. But if confirmation of any intelligent profession of faith is thought necessary before communion, why should not such confirmation or profession be thought necessary before baptism? On Jonathan Edwards and the Halfway covenant, see New Englander, Sept. 1884: 601-614; G. L. Walker, Aspects of religious Life of New England, 61-82; Dexter, Congregationalism, 487, note – "It has been often intimated that President Edwards opposed and destroyed the Halfway Covenant. He did oppose Stoddardism, or the doctrine that the Lord's Supper is a converting ordinance, and that unconverted men, because they are such should be encouraged to partake of it." SYSTEMAATIC THEOLOGY, A.H. Strong,

"AND THESE WORDS, which I command thee this day, shall be in thine heart; and thou shalt teach them diligently unto thy children, and shall talk of them when thou sittest in thine house, and when thou walkest by the way and when thou liest down, and when thou risest up." Deuteronomy 6:6-7.

We believe that this sort of discipline is the most adequate for little children to be formally entrenchedin the Word of God; and, that it should under no circumstances be neglected. This would properly call believers to their post and give the strictest adherence to Bible Truth!

Luther had seen the Divine pattern for the churches, and it was not without an inward struggle that he abandoned the New Testament teaching of independent assemblies of real believers, in favour of the National or state system which outward circumstances pressed upon him. The irreconcilable differences between these two ideals was the essential ground of conflict.

"John the Baptist appeared suddenly on the banks of the Jordan with an urgent message, 'Repent! for the Kingdom of Heaven is coming!' He had emerged from the desert region beyond the Jordan, where he had been meditating on what appeared to him the crisis of the hour." MAN'S RELIGIONS, John B. Noss, p. 433.

"Now about that time, Herod, the king stretched forth his hands to vex certain of the church. And he killed James, the brother of John, with the sword. And because he saw it pleased the Jews, he proceeded further to take Peter also." (Then were the days of unleavened bread.) Acts 12:1-3 It is evident that The Church faced the constant power of evil. Chapter 13 begins the era and saga of Paul. The remainder of the book of acts is occupied with the drama of Paul's mission. Stephen had been stoned and it was obvious that Peter and Paul passed off the scene in 67 A.D. Then, came the scattering of the Jewish Nation in 70 A. D. This was to be a harbinger of the next three hundred years! The Roman Empire spelled its doom for meddling with the destruction of Israel.

"Baptism was performed WITH EXORCISM in Lutheranism churches, and it was counted one of the chief crimes of the Cypto-Calvinists that they abolished this rite. A Saxon pastor who baptized without exorcism gave great offense to the peasants, who cried after him: 'The naughty priest has not expelled the devil.'

"IT IS ALMOST INCREDIBLE to what extent the Lutheranism bigotry of those days carried its hatred of Zwinglianism and Calvinism. Schlussburg ((Superintendent of Ratzeburg) one of the most learned champions of Lutheran orthodoxy, in his *Theologia Calvinistroaum Libri Tres,* Franco Forti ad Moenum, i592, tries to prove that the Calvinists are unsound in almost every article of the Christian Faith ((*'sacramentearios de nullo fere doctrinoe Christianoe articulo recte sentire'),* and has special chapter to show that the Calvinistic writings overflow with *mendaaciis, calumniuuis*

conviciis, maledictuis et contumeliis. He regards many of their doctrines as
d ownright blasphemy. Philip Nikolai, a pious Lutheran pastor at Unna o\,
afterwards at Hamburg, and author of two of the finest Christian hymns
('*Wie scon leuchtetder Morgenstern and Wachetauf! Ruf runsdie Stimme*')
called the God of the Calvinists 'a roaring bull' (*Wucherstier and Brullocks)*
a bloodthirsty moloch, a hellish Behemoth and Leviathan, a fiend of men!'
KurtzerBeiricht von der Calvinisten Gott und ihrer Religion, frkf. 15970; *die
erst i'ctgoria, triumph and freudenjubel uber des Calvin. Geistes Niederlag,
1600; Calvinischer Vitzliputsli, etc.* See Frank, Vol. 1. p.346

"Provost Magirus, of Stutgart, thought that the Calvinists imitated at times
the language of Luther, as the hyena the human voice, for the destruction of
men. John Modest wrote a book to prove that the Sacramentarians are no
Christians, but baptized Jews and Mohammedans *('beweis aus der heiligen
Schrift dass die Sacramentirer nict Christen Sind, sondern getafte Juden und
Mahometisten, etc.* Jena, 1586). John Pratorius in a satire *(Calvinisch Gasthaus
zue Narfrekauffen, etc.),* distinguishes open Calvinists, who have no more
sense than a horse or an ass; secret Calvinists, who fish in the dark; and several
other classes (see Frank, Vol. 1 p. 282 sq,) The second Psalm, speaking of the
rebellion against Jehovah and his Anointed, was applied to the Calvinists,
and their condemnation was embodied in catechisms, hymns and popular
rhymes,...) THE CREEDS OF CHRISTENDOM, Vol.1, p.346-347.

"DOGMATIC THEOLOGY, Vol. II., p. 574 "That baptism is not a
means of regeneration but only the sign and seal of it, is evident from its
relation to faith. It presupposes faith, and faith presupposes regeneration
Philip said to the eunuch, "if thou believest with all thy heart thou mayest
(be baptized") (Acts 8:37). No faith, no baptism. Christ's command for
the church in all time is, "He that (First) believeth and is baptized (in
profession and sign of his faith) shall be saved" (Mark 16:16).

The apostle Peter (i Pet. 3:21) declares that "baptism doth save us by the
resurrection of Jesus Christ." Not by its own efficacy, therefore, but as the
emblem of what has been done by Christ's redemption, whose "resurrection"
is one of the constituent factors in it." DOGMATIC THEOLOGY, Wm.
G.T. Shedd, p. 468

Zwingly was the first to emancipate the Salvation of children dying in infancy from the supposed Indispensable condition of water-baptism, and to extend it beyond the boundaries of the visible Church. This is a matter of enormous interest (and of some, intense agony) since the un-baptized children far outnumber the baptized, and constitute nearly one half of the race.

He teachces repeatedly, that all elect children are saved whether baptized or not, whether of Christian or heathen parentage, not on the ground of their innocence (which would be Pelagian), but on the ground of Christ's atonement. (It took a long time to realize that children are more important than birds, bees, flowers and shrubs, even the groundwork of empires.!) He is inclined to the belief that all children dying in infancy belong to the elect; their early death being a token of God's mercy, and hence of their election. A part of the elect are led to Salvation by a holy life (Titus 3:5; Epesians 2:8,9); and another part by an early death. (I believe both are saved by Grace).! THE CREEDS OF CHRISTENDOM, Philip Schaff, Vol. 1, p. 378.

The Roman Catholic Church. In keeping whth her doctrine of original sin and guilt, and the necessity of water-baptism for salvation (based upon mark xvi, 16 and John 3:5) teaches the salvation of all baptized, and the *condemnation* of all *un-baptized* children; assigning the latter to the *limbus infantum* on the border of hell, where they suffer the mildest kind of punishment, namely, the negative penalty of loss (*poena damni* or *carentia bearificoe visionis*) but not the positive pain of feeling (*poena sensus*).

"St Augustine first clearly introduced this wholesale exclusion of all unbaptized infants from heaven—though Christ expressly says that to children emphatically belongs the kingdom of Heaven. He ought consistently to have made the salvation of infants, like that of adults, depend upon their election; but the churchly and sacramental principle checked and moderated his predestination theory, and his Christian heart induced him to soften the frightful dogma as much as possible.

"As he did not extend election beyond the boundaries of the Catholic Church (although he could not help seeing the significance of such holy outsiders as Melchizedek and Job under the old dispensation), he secured at least, by his high view of the regenerative efficacy of water baptism, the salvation of all infants dying in infancy. To harmonize this view with his system, he must have counted them all among the elect." THE CREEDS OF CHRISTENDOM, Vol. 1, p. 379.

"AND IN ORDER TO PRECLUDE THE NOTION THAT THE MERE APPLICATION OF WATER HAS ANY SPIRITUAL EFFECT LIKE THAT OF REGENERATING THE SOUL, THE APOSTLE EXPLAINS THAT BAPTISM DOES NOT "SAVE BY THE PUTTING AWAY OF THE FILTH OF THE FLESH, BUT BY "THE ANSWER OF A GOOD CONSCIENCE TOWARD GOD." THE ANSWER OF A GOOD CONSCIENCE" IS ITS PACIFICATION THROUGH THE ATONEMENT OF CHRIST FOR SIN, TO WHICH BAPTISM HAS REFERENCE. FOR, AS ST. PAUL SAYS, "AS MANY OF US AS WERE BAPTIZED WITH REFERENCE TO *(EIS) JESUS CHRIST WERE BAPTTIZED WITH REFERENCE TO (EIS) HIS (ATONING) DEATH," DOGNATUC THEOLOGY, WILLIAM G.T. SHEDD, P. 469,469.*

BY EARLY IN THE 4ᵀᴴ CENTURY, many troubling heresies had laid hold on the Church; and, Augustine, who had spent some years in vain, even corrupt living, was ill prepared for his role, but his charm appears to be lasting in nature. However the statement is made: "In Augustine we already find all the germs of the Scholastic and Catholic doctrine of baptism, though they hardly agree properly with his doctrine of predestination, the absolute sovereignty of divine grace and the perseverance of saints." HISTORY OF THE CHRISTIAN CHURCH, Philip Schaff, Vol 111, p. 482.

We do not have the works of Augustine before us, but Philip Schaff states: "Augustine, in his anti-Donatistic writings, defends the validity of heretical baptism by the following course of argument: Baptism is an institution of Christ, in the administration of which the minister is only an agent; the grace or virtue of the sacrament is entirely dependent on Christ, and not on the moral character of the administering agent; the unbeliever receives not the power, but the form of the sacrament, which indeed is of no use to the baptized as long as he is outside of the saving catholic communion, but becomes available as soon as he enters it on profession of faith; baptism, whenever performed, imparts an indelible character, or as he calls it a 'character dominicus' 'regius.' He compares it often to the 'not a militaris' which marks the soldier once for all whether it was branded on his body by the legitimate captain or by a rebel, and binds him to the service, and exposes him to punishment for disobedience." (That an infant makes a 'profession of faith', is not possible; and, most certainly he has branded on his brain the eternal nature of the transaction, which is absent from most pedo-baptists)" THE HISTORY OF THE CHRISTIAN CHURCH, Philip Schaff, p. 484-485.

"The Lutheran Creed retains substantially the Catholic view of baptismal regeneration, and hence limits infant salvation to those who enjoy this means of grace; allowing, however, some exceptions within the sphere of the Christian Church, and making the damnation of un-baptized infants as mild as the case will permit. At present, however, there is scarcely a Lutheran divine of weight who would be willing to confine salvation to *baptized* infants." THE CREEDS OF CHRISTENDOM, Vol. I, p 379,380.

The Church, sometime after the merger of Church and State, has multiple errors which became widespread, creating controversy and calling for the convening of Church Councils, Infant baptism, needing a basis for justification, used human logic for justification (not Holy Scripture). Problems were already rising, due to the waiting until near death, (sometimes too near), to care for the matter of baptism. But Constantine (with whom the problem began) and Augustine (354-430 A.D.), arose in The Church Age from the false assumption that God is finished with The Nation of Israel; and, that baptism of infants is a proper replacement for God's Command to Israel to circumcise their infants on the eighth day of life. No Scripture justifies 'trading this for that'! God's Church is no bargain basement; and we need to abandon every false premise and rest our obedience to Him, on His Clear COMMANDS!

What God gave to Israel is Israel's! God's Church possesses, or is responsible to possess, both the gifts and calling God (which are without repentance) since He has provided them! His assignments should be carried out meticulously and all deviation from duty is to drift from the Truth into apostasy. Three beautiful Truths of God are:

1.   ALL infants belong to Christ by full and Absolute Purchase, The Incarnate Jehovah Elohim repossessed every vestige of His property, in His Death, Burial, Resurrection and Ascension! (John 1:1-4). Not only did He taste death for every man, but he retains Absolute authority over every creature, including Satan! He is The One who breathed into the human nostrils the breath of life; lit. *'the breath of lives'* (In Fact, the 'lives' which he breathed into man were a *plurality!)* and, he has a perfect right to reclaim infants as His Own, at will, as He does every particle of His Creation! His Eternal Ownership, certainly values human infants highly and far ahead of His vegetable, animal and mineral creation! They are His Due eternally! Please let it rest with that! Let us please bear in mind that baptism is no basis for anyone's salvation. Rather, it is a witness to a salvation already received! Every human to the age of accountability (whatever that is, in His Church Age, another of His secrets in this age), leaving all parents challenged to help their babies to know Him at the earliest possible age!

2.   Israel, God's chosen Nation, has an eternity that is just as secure as that of The Church, but 'they are not all Israel that are of Israel'; and, they, likewise, are indebted to their children, equally with Christians. Let us also keep clearly in mind that His original Church began exclusively with Israel; and, had elements of Heavenly Love that even the Jewish redeemed heart had real difficulty with. (Acts 6:1-2) The Divine Command has extended its full sweep of love and hope to the entire Gentile World. Furthermore, His Design for Israel's National Future in His New Earth has specific ramifications.

His Church is not at liberty to 'replace', mix and match, laying title to any of Israel's promises, but they need to claim every solitary thing He has not promised to (and for) His Church. His promises to His Church outshine in the supernatural realm, everything God ever gave to His Eternal Nation, Israel, without The Church having to steal a thing. "THE IDEA OF BAPTISM. It was solemnly instituted by Christ, shortly before his ascension, to be performed in the name of the Father, the Son, and the Holy Spirit. It took the place of circumcision as a sign and seal of church membership." HISTORY OF THE CHRISTIAN CHURCH; Vol.1, p. 466.

There is no indication that "it took the place of circumcision", none whatsoever! The building of a fabrication for infant baptism is 'assumed', without any evidence. If baptism had "taken the place of circumcision" it would have been so declared! There is nothing to this effect to be found in the Holy Scriptures. Nothing is stated or implied to this effect.

Infant 'baptism', as Doctor Schaff tells us, is not directed in The New Testament, or practiced by The Church in the first 315 years of The Church Age; as mentioned earlier in this writing. To ignore God's Foundation for His Church and Its Ordered Method of Construction, I Corinthians 3:11; or, making changes in Its Structure more than 300 years after the fact, is ridiculous to the point of total absurdity.

His Church is formed by man's supernatural New Birth from sinful humans, into "the sons of God", I John 3:2, Regenerated by The Holy Spirit, by means of the Living, Eternal Word of God. In that same Infinite, Eternal Process, each Spiritually Reborn person is Baptized into The Body of Christ (I Corinthians 12:13); and, is given a specific place in That Body, "as it hath pleased Him." (I Corinthians 12:1-31, v.18).

The child of God then grows by earnest obedience, through proper teaching, as God's Spirit, alone, is God's Personal, Efficient Agent in the process of both rebirth, growth and development as He leads, teaching every man, developing believers into specific vessels from faith to faith. He is not only our Regenerator and our Instructer, He is our Keeper, constantly at work, conforming us to The Image of God's Dear Son.

The Church's responsibility is to provide nurturing for development and growth, by absorbing Bible Truth. Whatever is not clearly and specifically stated in Holy Scripture may be wisely passed on as 'opinion'; but MUST not be passed on as Church Dogma, without the clear statements of Holy Scripture. Conversion in Spiritual Transformation is exclusively the work of the Holy Spirit under sound teachers of The Word. Baptism should be followed by strong teaching of Holy Scriptures. Baptism is the first act of obedience for all believers.

In CALVIN'S INSTITUTE of the CHRISTIAN RELIGION, he proceeds with "BAPTISM (*baptisw*) is the initiatory sign by which we are admitted to the fellowship of the Church, that being ingrafted into Christ we may be accounted children of God." CALVIN'S INSTITUTE of the CHRISTIAN RELIGION, Vol. IV, P. 513 There certainly is no need for mothers to die with broken hearts because they failed to get their children baptized.

THEN HE PROCEEDS, Vol. IV on p. 524 to say: "How much better, therefore is it to lay aside all theatrical pomp, which dazzles the eyes of the simple, and dulls their minds, and when any one is to be baptized to bring him forward and present him to God, the whole Church looking on as witnesses, and pray over him; to recite the Confession of Faith in which the catechumen has been instructed, explains the promises which are given in baptism, then baptize them in the name of the Father and the Son, and the Holy Spirit, and conclude with prayer and thanksgiving." CALVIN'S INSTITUTES of the CHRISTIAN RELIGION, Vol. IV p. 524

THEN, "Whether the person baptized is to be wholly immersed, and whether once or thrice, or whether he is only to be sprinkled with water, is not of the least consequence: churches should be at liberty to adopt either, according to the diversity of climates, although it is evident that the term *baptize* means to immerse, and that this was the form used by the primitive Church." CALVIN'S INSTITUTES of the CHRISTIAN RELIGION, Vol. IV, P.524.

I find this to be totally absurd, considering the fact that The Word of God makes no exception. The Russian Church certainly makes no exception! And, if "it is evident that the term *baptise* means to immerse, and that this was the form used by the primitive Church" WHY is it needful to spend fourteen pages to say nothing?

"I am finding, pg 520 "These things, I say, we ought to feel as truly and certainly in our minds as we see our body washed, immersed, and surrounded with water." This is enfolded in the text!

"This is inferred from the original meaning of the Greek *Baptizein* and *"Baptismos;* from the analogy of John's baptism in the Jordan; from the apostles' comparison of the sacred rite with the miraculous passage of the Red Sea, with the escape of the ark from the flood, with a cleansing and refreshing bath, and with burial and resurrection; finally, from the general custom of the ancient church, which prevails in the east to this day." HISTORY OF THE CHRISTIAN CHURCH, Vol. 1, p. 468. (Without hesitation or missing a beat, He proceeds.) "But sprinkling, also, or copious pouring rather, was practiced at an early day with sick and dying persons...."

Nevertheless, the first step gives life its initial direction, therefore, proper obedience in baptism is vital to nurtured growth. We have no reason or justification for disobedience in this matter. The Eternal Word of God is absolute in its clarity on the matter. Nor does the stature of anyone within His Church who has acted otherwise, justify diverse action! God is no respecter of persons.

Also, as history bears horrible witness, baptismal form has been a divider of His Church, particularly in the past 500 years, leading even to wars and hatred within His Body! Simple obedience in baptism would at least solve The Church's great need for practice of that correct doctrine in a critical area where division continues to cause friction, create confusion; and, complicate the process of harvest. Lost souls are confused; and, many believe The Church to be as confused as they. We can put a stop to this problem by living according to The Eternal Word of God.

"Love works no ill to his neighbor: therefore love is the fulfilling of the law. And that, knowing the time, that now it is high time to awake out of sleep: for now is our salvation nearer than when we believed. The night is far spent, the day is at hand: let us therefore cast off the works of darkness, and let us put on the armor of light. Let us walk honestly, as in the day;.. ThBut, put ye on the Lord Jesus Christ..." Romans 13:10-14.

The Professing Church of The Lord Jesus Christ has done far greater damage to Itself than what has been done by the ten emperors of Rome in their Great Persecutions during the first three hundred years of The Church Age. "Every Scripture is God-breathed*!" (Theopneustos)!* The Inspired Text of Holy Scripture does not permit trifling with its Infinite, Lucid, Writing! Biblical Writing is True! I pray God you will assist me in heralding its Truth!!

Faithful Gospel preachers in modern times have brought hundreds of thousands, perhaps millions, to saving faith in The Lord Jesus Christ, in enormous rallies of multiplied thousands, where great numbers were saved and millions more heard God's Good News of The Gospel. Graham ministry rallies, with use of personal workers partially overcame some of the difficulty with personal workers, continued teaching by radio; and, printed materials that enabled converts to grow into more mature status. Every true believer has a heart that desires to please God; and, this provides an open field, in my opinion, for helping many to strong development and service.

God's Church in 2014 A.D. stands in a condition much like that caused by a devastating, all-consuming war or tornado that hits any region. Rebuilding Europe after World War II was accomplished in some measure at costs that amounted to billions upon billions of dollars, yet scars remain. But it was vital that it be rebuilt! It would have been much simpler to have built it with finesse originally, than to re-build it with its remaining scars. Rebuilding after either a war or tornado, requires that the litter first be removed before building can start!

The continuing chaos of The Church's disobedience to God is Its greatest stumbling block to reaching lost, confused, baffled humanity, as it asks, "Which church saves? Which church is right?..coming to their humanly logical conclusion, "These folk are as confused as I...so what should I do?" Therefore, they continue to be blinded by Satan in their lost state! The historian, Gibbon, mocks The Church because of It's seeming chaos! Confusion in The Church created a climate where evolution and cultism have found rich breeding grounds!!

The Church at Corinth was commanded to allow no man to despise Timothy, the young servant of Christ. (I Corinthians 16:11) The Holy Spirit was grieved at the conduct of the Corinthian Church. (I Corinthians 11:22) On what ground do we dare allow our own continued disobedience to clear commands, as those entrusted with The Eternal Truth of God? It is time we obey God; reconsolidate our unified Bible Premise of action; and, revitalize His Own Passion in us, restoring a sweet Unity of The Holy Spirit, founded on The Word of God, to better complete The Church's obedient service to Him!!

WHY should Christian Baptism cause division among earnest, devout church members of churches, where it is impossible for any person to know who truly loves God, since it is "The answer of a good conscience toward God!"? I Peter 3:21. The Mystery aspect of the Christian Faith will not allow any man to analyze His Sovereignty! But, obedience to the faith is the forthright command of God!

"For there is One God, and One Mediator between God and men, the Man, Christ Jesus." I Timothy 2:65. That God-Man also is The One Way to Heaven; and, **obedience to HIM** is Orders from God the Father! John 14:6. The Apostles said, "We ought to obey God rather than men." Acts 4:19; 5:29

"Hauk, referring to New Testament baptism, remarks: "Baptism probably always took place through immersion in flowing water." As regards the subjects of baptism he has the following: 'That in the New Testament is found no direct trace of infant baptism must be regarded as firmly established; Attempts to prove its necessity from the manner of its institution, its practice from such passages as Acts 2:39; I Cor. 1: 16, suffer from the defect that the thing to be proved is presupposed." From the defect that the thing to suffer that the thing to be proved is presupposed." In relation to the introduction of infant baptism Loots remarks: "Infant baptism first provable in Irenaeus, still combated by Tertullian, was to Origen an apostolic usage." Alfred Henry Newman, A MANUAL OF CHURCH HISTORY, Vol. 1, p.136.

If there was ever a time when our youth needed to stand on the solid Rock of Truth's Foundation (I Corinthians 3:11) to face the chaos of today's social structure, ravaged by drink, drugs, evil entertainment and wickedness of every stripe that complicate an already agnostic culture, it is in today! To stand is to obey! May God help us to at least be His obedient children in such a wicked hour as we live in today! God is obviously angry enough to speak radically and frequently through His creation; and, the reason for this is stated clearly in Luke 19:40 as our Lord declares, "I tell you that, if these should hold their peace, the stones would immediately cry out!" The professing church of today has this generation confused to the ultimate!

Many modern youth come from homes where God is ignored, except where cursing is the spoken language; and, debates rage between parents. These youth, in far too many homes, endure a warfare between parents, usually waged in stony silence regarding God, that frequently ends in their divorce! Children are likely to blame God or themselves (almost never their parents) for existing problems. This is only one of the reasons our record suicide rate in our younger generation exceeds that of any in our history.

World War II robbed American homes of fathers and sons. Yet, 78% of American homes were still two parent homes at the end of that war. In 2011, the 2010 Census records show that two parent homes in America stands at 48%. If existing parents choose to try to raise their families together, lack of tender love and enraged silence on personal faith gets frustrating to the point in the lives of the youth, that they in far too many cases decide they hate both home and their church that at an accelerated rate, not only divides their two parents, but confuses children to the ultimate, making our youth the most fertile breeding ground on earth for the agnostic culture that is present today in our culture!!

In the early 20th Century, it was estimated that ninety percent of the underworld was made up of people who had attended Sunday school quite regularly in their childhood, even youth! Our own American culture, as we have moved into the 21st Century, has spawned almost countless religious bodies that have scrambled to find new names for their organization. An elderly lady in the 1970's, born at the end of the 1800's, still bore mental and spiritual scars because a church officer, in his fine church, sent her back 'across the tracks' to meet with 'her kind'! This was not racial. She had delicately white skin. Their society-first membership was highly embarrassed by this child 'from the other side of the tracks', doubtless dressed differently from their own, bringing her pennies to their great Sunday school.

The Methodist minister who immersed my parents raged at their insistence on immersion! He considered them just too stubborn to be sprinkled! I have no doubt the reason my father who was leading the Methodist Church choir, instead of attending a church in their small city, and, couldn't afford the kind of clothing worn by folk at the Baptist Church in town! Be that as it may, I suspect it was because of the preacher that my parents dropped out of church. My father was silent on the matter! He always encouraged our attendance as his sons. I have no doubt my father's heart was broken. Baptist church practice of refusing to accept a baptism administered by others as my mother did, simply didn't attend. I have no doubt my father's heart was broken. In my opinion, it makes no difference who does the baptizing! The faith of the baptized is what counts! A baptism is a baptism and the issue is between the baptized and God, alone, as long as the matter has been settled between the individual and God, and, as long as the Death, Burial, and Resurrection of our Holy Redeemer has been recognized and the individual was immersed!

An officer in a Lutheran church that regularly counted the congregation's offerings with another officer, on one occasion at least, mentioned the matter of personal salvation; and, raised questions about baptism. The other, resting comfortably on such questions, because his parents had him baptized in infancy, was highly offended at such discussion, commenting, "I wish you would just go somewhere else to worship." He did. He also understood why he should be immersed and accepted the Baptism.

OUR LORD ORDERED that His Church observe two clear commands (Ordinances) which were to express unity and solidarity (Baptism and The Lord's Table). There should be set before the world a unified declaration at all times!! His Church is ONE: heart, mind, spirit and body!! The observance should be unified under one Triune God: The Father, The Son and The Holy Spirit. As One Body of believers, it should serve with its singular purpose of harmony, evangelizing, bringing its humanity to God, baptizing, teaching, and encouraging human hearts with diligent study of The Holy Scriptures; and, stop the insanity of questioning The Holy Scriptures, as to The Body of Christ and people of God in Christ!! I Corinthians 12:13!

Through the centuries, The Communion Table had been observed in all churches with a similarity that was at least significantly recognizable as to its purpose. America knew a strength that had formed around the Bible. It gave a courage and fearlessness that produced an invincibility. In World war II, men stood like granite with the Holy Scriptures kept where they could be read. But the war was devastating! There was strong defection and deterioration, with the vicious attack within the educational system and the strength of America was gone! No longer were Infants and little children brought up to believe the Bible; but, the educational system did its evil work in producing a degenerate society! It's unbiblical and false premise is due the Judgment of Almighty God! What had been a mighty nation is drowning in debt and has become weak. (Hebrews 2:1 "Therefore, we ought to give the more earnest heed to the things which we have heard, lest at any time ***we should drift from them!*** I suspect we are going the way of the ancient Roman Empire! This nation is headed for the Judgment of God.!

The 'danger of drifting' is made multiple times worse by the chaotic teaching that sprinkling is baptism. It is highly significant that the 2200 voices which are sounding in the current culture stem largely from the infant baptism source to which they may be traced. You will notice that the immersionist bodies stay reasonably close to the Scriptures. At least they are willing to learn from Scripture. It's very interesting that John Wesley traveled 40,000 miles on horseback, spreading the Holy Scriptures intact that God might call whom He would to believe ALL of it. Heresies were to spread, increase, distorting and twisting Holy Scripture!! You have to read diligently to discern 'the Way of Life.' You will notice that strong anamosity can be traced, usually, to a sprinkling background.

"The Reformers, having suffered from attacks by The Catholic Church, that had suffered divisions of its own, through the centuries; and, knowing there were great doctrinal issues, stood prepared to protect itself from destruction with tactics modern Christians would hardly defend as 'God pleasing.' And self preservation, even like the concerns of America's Pilgrims, made use of severe methods. They inherited the doctrine of persecution from their mother Church, and practiced it as far as they had the power. They fought intolerance with intolerance.... The Protestant governments in Germany and Switzerland excluded, within the limits of their jurisdiction, the Roman Catholics from all religious and civil rights, and took exclusive possession of their churches, convents, and other property. They banished, imprisoned drowned, beheaded, hanged, and burned Anabaptists, Antitrinitarians, Schwenkfeldians, and other dissenters.

"In Saxony, Sweden, Norway, and Denmark no religion and public worship was allowed but the Lutheran. The Synod of Dort deposed and expatriated all Arminian ministers and school-teachers. The penal code of Queen Elizabeth and the successive acts of Uniformity aimed at the complete extermination of all dissent, whether papal or protestant, and made it a crime for an Englishman to be anything else than an Episcopalian.

"The Puritans when in power ejected two thousand ministers from their benefices for non-conformity; and the Episcopalians paid them back in the same coin when they returned to power (proceeding to sprinkle infants). 'The Reformers' says Gibbon, with sarcastic severity, 'were ambitious of succeeding the tyrants whom they had dethroned. They imposed with equal rigor their creeds and confessions; they asserted the right to the magistrate to punish heretics with death. The nature of the tiger was the same, but he was gradually deprived of his teeth and fangs.'" HISTORY OF THE CHRISTIAN CHURCH, Philip Schaff, Vol. VIII, P. 700-1,000.

ALL MAINLINE CHURCHES agree as to the form used in baptizing by The Church as it began, based on the only word used by either our Lord or Holy Scripture, the Greek word, *baptizo,* (correctly pronounced in English as *baptidzo*), meaning always to "plunge into" or "immerse", and stated so by every leader of every historic division of the church as each began in earlier ages (THEN turned and sprinkled!! WHY? There is no justification for change, as we shall see as we arrive at statements from each originator of every segment of the church in historical times!! Centuries of disobedience is the major hindrance to The Church's unified efforts; and, is a most striking major factor in its membership's failures; and, MOST of the drifting into apostasy.

The major purpose of this effort is to strengthen the bonds of the Love of Christ in the hearts of His people for each other, appreciate the contributions to our Lord's purposes by each segment of His Church; and, help believers to return to a deeper understanding and appreciation for The Bible as God's verbal and plenary Inspired Book of Truth, because each major division of His Church has made great and continuing contributions to His cause in the world, in spite of the 42 efforts in mistranslation effort!! Surely greater harmony among His Own would produce results that would amaze even our lost world itself, opening opportunities each part of His Church is in need of!

The real problem with most folk isn't that they can't understand the Scriptures. They really don't want to 'get it'! They would feel just a little better if part of what it plainly says could be slightly 'modified'. God doesn't happen to stutter; but, 'the old King James' perhaps needs a little 'explaining'! I really think it might be good for folk to go to prayer and let Him explain it! There is power and authority in prayer! Please remember 60% of the preachers pretending to give it out, don't believe in The Verbal Plenary Accuracy of The Word of God. I Peter 1:10,11. II Peter 1:21; II Timothy 3:1

I really think that when people get everything mastered perfectly, they will doubtless be in Heaven! But the Word is explicit enough to obtain a very satisfying comprehension, where people are given to prayer.

CHAPTER VIII
THE PERIL OF DOUBT
IN BAPTISM

AUGUSTINE WAS BAPIZED by Ambrose in Milan in 387, was made bishop of Hippo in North Africa in 395, living in the time of the breaking up of the Western Roman Empire, a barbarian army was besieging his city of Hippo when he passed away! There was great turmoil! Briton and Saxon refused to meet at the same communion table; the Germanic invaders and plunderers, pressed by the Mongol hordes from the east, who were drawn by the dream of wealth, into northern Italy, settled, tilling the soil, as the fifth century came with the Visigoths under Alaric arriving from the Balkans to Northern Italy, sacking Rome in 410. Jerome was in Bethlehem writing a commentary on Ezekiel when word came of the carnage and the stabling of horses in churches, as the Alps were drenched in blood. The *vandals* moved in 406 into Gaul, over the Pyrenees into Spain, then across the Straits of Gibraltar into North Africa, founding an empire with its Capitol City of Carthage in 429. They obliterated and crushed all that was in their path. The amazing thing is that The Church survived the crisis, but the violence of rebellion against the Name of God created enormous conflict that was to continue to the end of the age. The limitless challenge of the mission fields of the world has claimed the lives and labors of the Missionaries of the Cross" AND THIS IS THE RECORD that God hath given to us eternal life, and this life is in His Son. He that hath the Son hath life: and he that hath not the Son of God hah not life." I John 5:11,12.

THE WESTMINISTER CONFESSION (XIV.ii) defines *Faith* in Jesus Christ as "a saving grace whereby we receive and rest upon Him for salvation."

But Dr. Wm. G.T. Shedd states "There is a difference between belief (assensus), and faith (fiducia)." Then proceeds with the attempt to distinguish a difference that becomes very confusing (in my opinion) and by the time I have read the paragraph through repeatedly I get very foggy, blurred, and totally uncertain state of mind that would raise doubts about the personal relationship with Christ, which (in my opinion) has left millions with a great uncertainty whether they have Faith or belief; and if they are 'in' or 'out', whether they 'believe' or just give an assent and will go to an eternal hell. They have no real clue whether they are saved or lost!! I've talked with hundreds of them.

"THE VIEWS OF THE ANTE-NICENE FATHERS concerning baptism and baptismal regeneration were in this period more copiously embellished in the rhetorical style by Basil the Great and the two Gregories, who wrote special treatises on this sacrament, and were more clearly and logically developed by Augustine. The Patristic and Roman Catholic view on regeneration, however, differs considerably from the one which now prevails among puritanical types, in that it signifies not so much a subjective change of heart, which is more properly called conversion, but a change in the objective condition and relation of the sinner, namely his translation from the kingdom of Satan into the kingdom of Christ. Some modern divines make a distinction between baptismal and moral regeneration, in order to reconcile the doctrine of the fathers with the fact that the evidences of a new life are wholly wanting in so many who are baptized. But we cannot enter here into a discussion of the difficulties or confine ourselves to a historical statement." HISTORY OF THE CHRISTIAN CHURCH, Philip Schaff, Vol. 111, p. 481.

Lets get Back to the Bible!! Read it! Heed it! *Baptidzo doesn't mean "sprinkle"; Rantidzo does!* It doesn't mean "pour" *"ekXew"*; It means to "plunge into" and, it has meant that for two millenniums! I rather believe it still does!! Furthermore, there is nothing "difficult" about it! Nor is it a 'sacrament'! "Much ado about nothing", simply read the Eternal Word of God! Simply read the facts of 900 years of Church practice! 1600 years of building church baptistries, Catholic confession by placing an immersion tank in a modern Catholic Church, and, a simple study the Catholic dictionary will prove my point. Let modern parents of still-born children be at peace!

"THE NECESSITY OF BAPTISM, **in order to salvation,** is the principal point of difference between Augustine and Calvin, and explains the sacramentarianism, together with the double sense of regeneration, which are formed in the system of the former but not in that of the latter. The following passages express it: "Take the cause of any infant you please If he is already in Christ, why is he baptized? If, however he is baptized that he may be with Christ, it certainly follows that he who is not baptized is not with Christ; and because he is not 'with' Christ he is 'against' Christ" If, however, he is baptized that he may be with Christ it certainly follows that he who is not baptized is not with Christ; and he *that* is not 'with' Christ is 'against' Christ; and because he is not 'with' Christ he is 'against' Christ." DOGMATICTHEOLOGY, Wm. G. T. Shedd, p. 431-432.

THEREFORE, the agonizing belief that 'maybe' your un-baptized baby went to Hell! Such folly is unacceptable, even unjust! God is a Righteous, Infinite, Holy Redeemer; and, any injustice toward those who have no capacity to act, is an unjust act.

Would you please give me ONE VERSE OF SCRIPTURE??? The Lord didn't say 'Suffer little elected children to come unto me.' The Covenant Theologian has MANY problems. None of his theology is built on the Holy Scriptures of God, of "Thus saith the Lord!"

VERY EARLY in the Church Age great questions relative to the Person of Christ and His work became a broad field in which Satan could sow his seeds of doubt. Was Christ really the Son of God; how infinite was His work; were infants saved; how efficient was His Work; what about Christians sinning; what about election and regeneration? Leading theologians struggled with their faith. In the meantime people died, hearing the horrible clamor of confusion. However, God has power to remove fog and give peace! We have no wish to perpetuate this awful darkness. It certainly is not of God.

"**BUT WE SEE JESUS,** who was made a little lower than the angels for the suffering of death, **crowned with glory and honor; that he by the grace of God should taste death for every man.**" Heb. 2:9.

"AND HAVING MADE PEACE thorough the Blood of His Cross, BY HIM to reconcile ALLTHINGS unto Himself; By Him, I say, whether they be things ON EARTH or THINGS IN HEAVEN.

AND you, that were sometime alienated and enemies in your mind by wicked works, (You notice that it was 'by wicked works' they were alienated) yet now hath he reconciled in the body of His flesh through death, to present you holy and un-blamable and un-reprovable in His sight:

If ye continue in the faith grounded and settled, and be not moved away from the hope of the Gospel, which ye have heard and which was preached to every creature which is under heaven; whereof I, Paul, am made a minister." Col. 1:20-23. (Phil. 1:6)

"for when we were without strength, in due time Christ died for the ungodly." Rom. 5:6

"For by one offering he hath perfected for ever them that are sanctified." Heb. 10:14.

"**AND THIS IS THE RECORD,** that God hath given to us eternal life, and this life is in his Son. He that hath the Son hath life; and he that hath not the son of God hath not life. "These things have i written unto you that believe on the name of the Son of God: that **ye may know that ye have eternal life, and that ye may believe on the name of the Son of God.**" I John 5:11-13

GIVEN THE VARIABLE of the human personality with his struggles of perseverance in the deep things of God, the clear, vivid and strong mastery of *knowing* the eternal, sovereign God NEVER changes His Mind!! "He is able to save them to the utter-most that come unto God by Him, seeing He ever liveth to make intercession for them" Heb. 7:25. "For by one offering he hath perfected for ever them that are sanctified." Heb. 10:14. This is why love, tenderness, infinite care, gentleness, all the loving features of the New Birth are so vital!!

There would never be expressions of arrogant infidelity were it not for harsh words! By all means, cultivate a gentle spirit of love! Let your heart be filled with overflowing love in the absolute! This Love of Christ will not 'fry' or 'roast' their enemies. I think the Bible says to 'pray for them.'

The pious nonsense of a 'common and effectual call' radically and totally confuses the issue! "Whom He did predestinate, Them He also called." His call is to "whosoever will"! Are you willing? Then let us move forward with the investigation! Believe God! Romans 8:26-39.

"VOL. II., P.486 Augustine distinguishes the common from the effectual call (which I consider nonsense) in the following passage: "God calls many predestinated children of his to make them members of his only predestined Son, not with that calling with which they were called who would not come to the marriage, since with that calling were called also the Jews, to whom Christ crucified is an offense, and the Gentiles, to whom Christ crucified is foolishness; but with that calling he calls the predestinated which the apostle distinguished when he said that he preached Christ, the wisdom of God, and the power of God, to them that were called, Jews as well as Greeks." DOGMATIC THEOLOGY, Wm. G. T. Shedd, VOL. III, P.427

"VOL III., P. 491. The two uses of "regeneration," in a wide and narrow sense, by the Reformers and seventeenth century divines, are different from those in the Patristic church, (Why is this so?) which grew out of the patristic view of the sacraments. Augustine, for example, employs the term to denote, both the apparently and professedly regenerate, and the really such. The former are members of the visible church, but not the invisible; the latter belong to the invisible church also. (Why is this so?) The former may therefore fall away, the latter may not. He remarks as follows in perseverance, Ch. 21: "Of two (professedly) pious (pius) men, why to one should be given perseverance unto the end, and to the other it should not be given is an unsearchable judgment of God. Yet to believers it ought to be a most certain fact that the former is of the predestinated, and the latter is not" DOGMATIC THEOLOGY, Wm. G. T. Shedd, VOL. III, P. 429

I call your attention to the comment "the two uses of 'regeneration' in a narrow sense, by the Reformers and seventeenth century Church leaders, different from those of the Patristic church, which grew out of the patristic view of the sacraments." I am a bit stunned at the frank statement by Doctor Shedd. This is the key to the fact that the Reformed Church has closed the door to the 'Patristic Church' and has become a law unto themselves. Evidently, the Reformers can readily acknowledge the habits of the early church and can, with a straight face, proceed right on with the doctrinal statement that violates historical fact. You may, therefore, accept the revamped theology or not.

The 'Ninety-five Theses' had a *very* strong purpose! They were to spell out the vast scope of troubling heresies which were practiced by the church that had an improper and distorted Biblical base ! These practices had blinded the multitudes to Holy Scripture Truth, leaving the church to drift in a morass of evil and uncertainty; and, creating a completely chaotic state. There was no way whereby pure doctrine could possibly be achieved. Had the church been flexible enough to move beyond this, perhaps to a unity of spirit and a true Oneness might have been achieved. Inasmuch as all the Reformers were united on the matter of baptism, there might have been a working out of the difficulties. The heads of the churches were iron clad in their firmness; and Luther chose even to compromise on this point, but the "indulgences" were not readily given up, because of their highly lucrative and indulgent nature, the appeal was there.

It was the Bible which had the first place in enlightening and developing Luther; he was helped by Stampitz also, and found in the writings of Tauler and some of the more Biblical doctrine, He said, than all the Universities and teachings of the schoolmen; nothing was sounder and corresponded more with the Gospel. He soon became active as a writer and his early pamphlets (1517-1520) were written in the spirit of the brethren;

showing how salvation is not through the intervention of the Church, but that every man has direct access to God and finds Salvation through faith in Christ and obedience to His Word. He was laid hold of by the teaching of Scripture that salvation is of the grace of God, through faith in Jesus Christ, and not obtained by our own works. The ability and zeal with which Luther preached these truths not only awakened hope and expectation in the circles where they were already known, but powerfully affected others who had hitherto been ignorant of them.

he papal indulgences sold by Tetzel, showed a shamelessness buffoonery in his business which, more perhaps than anything else, impressed on people its inherent charlatanry. When he came to Wittenberg, Luther, failing to arouse the Elector of Saxonry to action, he was encouraged by Staupitz, himself, nailed on the church door the Ninety-five Theses which set Europe in a blaze, as men realized that a voice had at last been raised to utter what most felt—that the whole system of indulgences was a fraud and had no place in the Gospel.

Martin Luther faced and fought the whole vast Papal power, he was a master of arts in his culture, dynamics and strong personality, as he addressed the nobility of the German Nation on the liberty of the Christian Man" and his 'Babylonian Captivity of the Church' in Europe. The Pope was enraged and issued a Bull excommunicating him; but the man whose heart almighty God had touched burned the Bull publicly at Wittenberg (1520). Summoned to Worms before the Papal authorities, he braved all dangers and went, and none was able to harm him.

Luther knew the total treachery of the pope and his hirelings, having observed how the pope had dealt with faithful men, including John Huss! His life being threatened, and while the pope had supplied conveyance to Worms, he was constantly on the alert. His friends carried him off secretly to a castle, the Wartburg, and let it be supposed that he was dead. There he translated the New Testament into German, following it later by the Old Testament. The effect of increased regarding of the Scriptures, and that in a time when questions of religion were violently agitating masses of the population, that was to change the whole aspect of Christendom. The dull hopelessness with which men had seen the ever increasing corruption and rapacity of the Church, was exchanged for a vivid hope that now at last, the time of revival had come, the time of a return to Apostolic, primitive Christianity; Christ Himself was seen afresh, revealed in the Scriptures as the Redeemer and immediate Saviour of sinners and the Way to God for suffering humanity.

Martin Luther's very large band of sympathizers grew enormously, but the old system of Roman Church, as the vicious lion that it had become, was not at all to be trusted and would not be changed without a struggle. There were some who with Erasmus who hoped for compromise and peace, being very tired of conflict! The monks, who saw their position and privileges vanishing, were violent beyond measure, and the Papal authorities decided to use the old weapons of cursing and killing to crush the new movement, but Martin Luther had come to be as dogmatic as the pope. This, Friend, is what occurs when two irresistible forces meet! There was violent stalemate and each went their way!

The Holy Scriptures, which were forbidden to the laity of the church because of 'their inability to understand', has kept the Roman Catholic membership in darkness even to recent history. A crisis was coming, in which Political rivalries made the situation very dangerous. Oppression of the land workers lead to the Peasants' War (1525), for which Luther and his party were blamed by the pope. A general conflagration threatened the nations. Erasmus, who was of much milder character, wrote in 1520) "I wish Luther.. would be quiet for a while....what he says may be true, but there are seasons."

Luther struggled with his convictions! Had circumstances permitted, he would have accepted immersion and would very likely have been a Fundamentalist. He had been sprinkled at the behest of devout parents, and this is extremely difficult to renounce! The State Church would not be obedient, but would rebel; and, control would be lost!

It was not without an inward struggle that he abandoned the New Testament teaching of independent assemblies, immersion, which the Catholic Encyclopedia acknowledges to be the original stance of The Church of real believers, but favored the National or State church system

25

which outward circumstances pressed upon him. The irreconcilable difference between these two ideals was the essential ground of conflict. Baptism and the Lord's Supper took on great importance in the fight, only because in the true church they mark the gulf dividing the Church! Whereas in a National Church they are the only logical action, since birth and baptism, must be consolidated into one action to be efficient! Infant baptism and the general administration of the Lord's Supper does away with the necessity for personal faith in the recipients. Moreover, the powers arrogated to a priesthood, were alone, competent in performing requirements.

It is not at all surprising, that the Roman Catholic Church, with the perception of the infallibility of the pope might proceed with the Holy Scriptures in any manner they should choose, allowing its clergy to express disbelief of the Word of God, choosing to tolerate freely those of every deviation from the Bible, but can hunt down those who are careful to keep and treasure God's Word. The State Church, perhaps emboldened by this example, to follow the pattern of the Mother Church in martyring those who resist their authority.

With unprecedented power and courage Luther had brought to light the Scripture truths as to the individual salvation of the sinner by faith, but failed when he might have shown the way to a return to Scripture in all things, including its teaching as to the church.

The tragedy of yielding in crisis immediately drew the sword upon dissenters and placed the church under cannon law, giving to the church the sword of persecution! No doubt, Luther, had a violent struggle, and even though he 'preferred immersion', he was tired of the struggle and thought perhaps there could be peace made with the Vatican. It achieved nothing. You don't compromise with sin without continuing to compromise until you totally capitulate! This is the horrible danger of drifting!

BECAUSE OF THE ISSUE of baptism in water, the communities of believers faithfully holding the traditions of the fathers, were persecuted, but largely for the immersion tradition and the Holy Scriptures, they held the common thread of Unity in the Spirit, they were called Paulicans, Anabaptists, Waldenses, Etc. but communities of believers seemed to spring up like living fire that refused to be put out.

In 1463, in the mountains of Reichenan, and again in 1467 at Lhota, there were general gatherings of brethren, at which many persons of rank and influence were present, where they considered afresh the principles of the church. One of the things they did was to baptize those present for the baptism of believers by immersion which was common to the Waldenses and to most of the brethren in different parts, though it had been interrupted by pressure of persecution." THE PILGRIM CHURCH, E. H. Broadbent, P. 130

THE BIBLE is The Constitution of The Church and contains every valid bylaw to be practiced by His Bride, The Church. The Lord Jesus Christ is God's Living Word. (John 1:1-14; Revelation 19:13). The Inspired Written Word (II Timothy 3:16,17; II Peter 1:21) is given in Two Testaments: The Old Testament, consisting of The Law, The Prophets, and The Writings; and, The New Testament, consisting of It's 27 books: The Four Gospels, Acts, The Epistles of Paul, Peter and John; The Books of James and Jude; and The Book of Revelation. (No one has ever disproved that The Book of Hebrews was written by The Apostle Paul.)

Further, no one else who has been suggested was truly prepared in heart, mind and spirit for that task, or has left evidence of possessing such required intellect as that which we see employed by The Apostle Paul on every occasion of testing, after Stephen passed off the scene! Heb. 13:22-25.)

1. Because baptism is the first of the defining ordinances for Our Lord's 'One Church', it is to be observed with the same uniformity as that of the Communion Table. These began at The Last Supper on the night He was crucified.
2. And has obtained with amazing uniformity throughout the professing church! No body of believers is a law to itself; and, inasmuch as the Word, Baptidzo, warrants no deviation from

it's Biblically defined meaning and significance, can there be justification for today's careless handling of the topic of baptism?! In fact, the premise on which such change stands is totally false; and, therefore should cease.

3.   Because baptism is public witness to 'One Church.'
4.   Because baptism is commanded by our Lord.
5.   Because baptism has one meaning; and, one only.
6.   Because baptism is to be sought by the one baptized.
7.   Because baptism is designed to declare identity with our Lord in His Death, Burial and Resurrection; and, inasmuch as His Church is to be seen as seated with Christ in Heaven. Colossians 3:1-4.
8.   Because baptism declares the believer's intent in life.
9.   Because baptism is the believer's first act of obedience to The Lord Jesus Christ.

For these just and totally valid reasons, let us return to Holy Scripture for support of our practice.

Perishing humankind has stumbled into Hell, lost eternally, for EONS OF TIME, largely because God's people do not speak with one voice of true love as a convincing witness for God in accord with His Word. God's commands are clear.

His One Church's failure to simply conform to orders is the largest reason for division, a problem we also have. We are not sent to criticize our ancestors; but to thank God for every one of them; and, for the Holy Inspired Scriptures, passed to us in proper form for our own direct obedience to them.

During a visit to Brussels, we had the privilege of visiting an ancient convent. The types of cages and places of confinement which we witnessed were hideous. It is beyond belief where those who disobeyed the church were confined, in cramped holes which were dug, with iron bars placed over them, until one could scarcely move at all; to be helplessly confined, with a hole through which a crust of bread or bowl of soup could be thrust, without provision for relieving one's self! Beyond any question, great numbers of these who were abused by the church were devout believers! True converts were often placed in such abominable places! Converts, brought to believe in immersion for baptism were targets. Many hymns of Baptists were written in prison and were included in the collection of the Brethren.

Baptism and The Lord's Table stirred much very harsh controversy and anger. The Word of God was so often ignored but the Infinite Truth of God is to be esteemed to be far more deeply precious than opinion!

We are responsible to receive these Holy Scriptures, in trust, with thanksgiving to God and appreciation for our ancestors, prayerful interpreting Holy Scripture with real discernment for ourselves; and, obeying those Scriptures above every human opinion!

For 1450 years, our ancestors did not have personal copies of Scripture, except what they could obtain of hand written copy of Scripture Portions, and these were very expensive. It is such an enormous privilege to have our printed copy of Holy Scripture. The Catholic Church did everything in her power to keep their people from getting copies and then did all they could to discourage personal reading, claiming the people could not understand, without these writing being "interpreted"!

Is it not extremely interesting that the universal emblems of memorial in Church Communion are the bread and the cup, even though there are twists in their observances? Still, The Body and The Blood of Christ set forth a common testimony. Why, then, was it not so with baptism, to "keeping the unity of the Spirit in the bonds of peace?"

Our God of Love can only acknowledge a people of Love!! ***"He that loveth not, knoweth not God, for God is LOVE." I John 4:8***

"Love never fails.. and now abides faith, hope, love, these three; but the greatest of these is Love." – I Corinthians 13.

For God so loved the world, that He gave His Only Begotten Son, that whoever believes in Him, should not perish, but have everlasting life. John 3:16. ***The Love of God, and Prayer are man's True Liberators.***

It becomes a very awesome thing when men begin to play games with the word of God! A Jewish man told me how he and fellow Jewish youth made their fabulous interpretations of Holy Scripture in an attempt to outdo each other. But, when church leaders engineer a system of theology that twists Holy Scripture to invent interpretations, it should send chills down our spine!

The great harlot of Revelation 17 is under the Judgment of God, and why she is called 'the mother of harlots?!' It is great cause for prayer! Please listen carefully to Revelation 17:3-5 "So he carried me away in the Spirit into the wilderness: and I saw a woman sit upon a scarlet colored beast, full of the names of blasphemy.

"And the woman was arrayed in purple and scarlet colour, and decked with gold and precious stones and pearls, having a golden cup in her hand full of abominations and filthiness of her fornication.

"And upon her forehead was a name written, MYSTERY, BABYLON THE GREAT, THE MOTHER OF HARLOTS AND ABOMINATIONS OF THE EARTH."

Water Baptism is our profession of identification with our crucified, risen, ascended Redeemer, addressing also our full access to The Eternal Throne of God.

"Farrel published at Neuchatel in 1533, and introduced at Geneva in 1537, the first French Reformed liturgy... Calvin's s liturgy was published twice in 1542. It was introduced at Lausanne in the same year, and gradually passed into other Reformed churches.

"Calvin built his form of worship on the foundation of Zwingli and Farrel and the services already in use in Swiss Reformed Churches...Calvin prepared also liturgical forms for baptism and the Holy Communion...

Baptism also was performed before the congregation at the close of the service, and in the simplest manner..

"The English and American Baptists have inherited some of the principles without the eccentricities and excesses of the Continental Anabaptists and Mennonites. They are radical but not revolutionary in politics and religion, and as sober, orderly, peaceful, zealous, and devoted as any other class of Christians. They rose simultaneously in England and America during the Puritan conflict, and have become, next to the Methodists, the strongest denomination in the United States.

"The great body of **Baptists** are called Regular or Particular, or Calvinistic **Baptists, in distinction from the smaller body of General or** Armenian or Free-Will Baptists. They are Calvinists in doctrine and Independents in Church polity, but differ from both in their views on the subjects and mode of baptism. They teach that believers only ought to be baptized, that is, dipped, or immersed, on a voluntary confession of their faith. They reject infant baptism as an unscriptural innovation and profanation of the sacrament, since an infant can not hear the gospel, nor repent and make a profession of faith. They believe, however, in the salvation of all children before the age of responsibility. Baptism in their system has no regenerative and saving efficacy: it is simply an outward sign of grace already bestowed, a public profession of faith in Christ to the world, and an entrance into the privileges and duties of church membership. They also opposed from the start national church establishments, and the union of Church and State, which one of their great writers (Robert Hall) calls 'little more than a compact between the priest and the magistrate to betray the liberties of mankind, both civil and religious.' They advocate volunteerism, and make the doctrine of religious freedom, as an inherent and universal right of man, and, a part of their creed." THE CREEDS OF CHRISTENDOM, Philip Schaff, Vol.1, p. 845, 846.

The healing of the lame man in Acts 3:11, demonstrated to all who were present that Peter and John had direct access to God's throne.

It is the Presence of God in the life behind the baptism that validates this public witness, as the Works of our Lord validated His, in the eyes of man. God spoke publicly to the crowd by His followers, demonstrating they had real access to His Throne; and, were not acting by self-motivation! Acts 1:8! Baptism, therefore, is an ordered principle of God.

Matthew 28:18-20 gives us the Absolute Command of our Holy Redeemer; and, this opens the door to a life of full obedience to our Eternal Triune God, under the Holy Spirit, Who directs all proper activities of His Church! One of God's Principles appears to be that any act of disobedience halts growth and progress until it is confessed, removed by The Sovereign Act of God; and, progress may continue.

A true return to Biblical Truth in obedience to it; and, the strong proclamation of it, will do much to heal His Church of problem divisions; and, restore a true practice of the all Biblical principles that gave His Church the full daily blessing of God in the true joy and power of the Holy Spirit.

Satan has defiled, divided; and, destroyed in horrible ways! Sadly, thousands of ministers profess to speak God's truth, then proceed to speak on all sides of the Truth; yet, refuse to preach The Bible, the Word of God, as it is written! (Get honest, specific answers from ministers today, for yourself! Demand honesty! Truth is stealthily avoided in practice constantly in professed pulpit preaching!)

Adam and Eve's beautiful Garden of Eden was entered by Satan! His lies have brought death to humanity through the ages! But, when his lies are told as the Gospel, far more radical issues must be faced for what they are!! It is a thousand fold more serious to invent untrue teachings that are absolute lies! Baptism by sprinkling is only one!!

An infinite number of things occurred! First, false security, then, having no Biblical basis for baptism, doubts, then questions, then false teachings that multiplied like wild fire, then, the strong Greek Philosophy influence, atheism, then came Evolution, then uncertainty of the existence of God, and what he like!.

In the Chronicles of the Anaaptists in Austria-Hungary one of them writes: "The foundation of the Christian faith were laid by the Apostles here and there in different countries but through tyranny and false teaching suffered many a blow and hindrance to the Church being often so diminished that it could scarcely be seen whether a church existed at all. As Elias said the altars were broken down the prophets slain and he remained alone; but God did not let His Church disappear altogether. Otherwise this article of the Christian faith would have been proven false: 'I believe there is one Christian Church one fellowship of the saints.

"But what things were gain to me, those I counted loss for Christ. Yea doubtless, and I count all things but loss for the excellency of the knowledge of Christ Jesus my Lord: for whom I have suffered the loss of all things do count them but dung, that I may win Christ,

"And be found in him, not having mine own righteousness, which is of the law, but that which is through the faith of Christ, the righteousness which is of God by faith: That I may know him, and the power of his resurrection, and the fellowship of his sufferings, being made conformable unto his death:

"If by any means I might attain unto the 'out' resurrection out from among the dead." Philippians 3:7-10. ('Blessed and Holy is he that has part in the FIRST resurrection' Rev. 20:6)

The he spreading of agnosticism, doubts, and 'evil beasts' Titus 1:12 has left us adrift! Strong seeds of divisions erupted into tares among the wheat, but those divisions continue to exist in 2010 A.D. Our Lord indicated these would continue until The Harvest. Recent records are said to indicate 2,280 divisions. II Timothy 4:6-8. I John 5:11-15. The many warnings of our God against these divisions should drive us to prayer!

BUT again we note the faithfulness of our wonderful God. The struggle has been intense and those who were strong in their faith brought hope and peace and love overflowing to hungry hearts until another sweep of violent resistance was revealed of the great power of Satan in his hideous passion to destroy the Church!

The Anabaptist log states "in other lands a good beginning was made and sometimes a good end, when the witnesses laid down their lives, but the tyranny of the Romish Church blotted out almost everything. The Picards, Waldenses and numerous others, kept something of the truth of God."

CHAPTER IX
PATIENCE AND PASSION
IN BAPTISM

"**A** MAN'S FOES shall be they of his own household.

"He that loveth father or mother more than me, is not worthy of me; and he that loveth son or daghter more than me, is not worthy of me.

"And he that taketh not his cross and followeth me, is not worthy of me." Mattew 10:36-38

We, seemingly, are nearing the end of this age and it is more difficult in our time to believe and follow the truth. One of the very difficult decisions is "to renounce the hidden things of dishonesty" II Corinthians 4:2. There is an enormous struggle with having been sprinkled as a child (and millions have been) and being faced with the facts of baptism. But the person who decisively follows the Lord in ALL THINGS will be a much stronger and faithful individual, faithful to follow the Lord!

"For ye have need of patience, that, after ye have done the will of God, ye might receive the promise." Hebrews 10:36

"Knowing this, that the trying of your faith worketh patience,

"But let patience have her perfect work, that ye may be perfect and entire, wanting nothing." James 1:3,4.

DR. G.W. LASHER, in the Journal and Messenger holds in regard to Matt. 3:11: "I indeed baptize you in water unto *(eis) repentance* does not imply that baptism effects the repentance; the baptism was *because* of the repentance, for John refused to baptize those who did not give evidence of repentance before baptism." Baptism was con-joined with believing as a first act of obedience for believers, a step forward in faith, to begin to obey. It is the surrender of the way of the flesh.

PERHAPS it was unavoidable! My father was brought up in difficult years, traveling across Texas and Oklahoma, following the cotton fields, along with a brood of five other fledglings, struggling with long hours, weariness, and total fatigue!

My father was firm. When Saturday and Sunday came, it was time to 'rest and enjoy' that we might be prepared for the coming week. It was harvest time! The crew of harvesters, without warning, gathered to harvest Mr. Ford's crop on Sunday Morning. As I recall it was with a rifle, he stood between the harvesters and the gate, and calmly stated, "There will be no harvest on the Ford farm today. This is Sunday!" Fuming, the harvesters turned their equipment and went to another farm. They respectfully returned to harvest my dad's grain the next day. Certainly he heard the Word of God with strong preaching until the Gospel was deeply imbedded in his mind! He always saw to it that we, too, heard the Word of life!

My Dad had led the Methodist choir, they had a revival and my father and mother went forward for baptism, which they insisted would be by immersion. The Methodist minister pleaded, but to no avail! They were immersed. My father stopped attending the country Methodist church, likely because of the attitude of the minister.

The reason we were not attending the Southern Baptist Church in the town five miles away was because my father could not dress his five boys as the city folk. I remember cousins' dressing proudly in a suit!! My Grandfather had given land also for a Southern Baptist Church near Noel, Missouri.

Grandfather told me of Christ's Death for my sin. I, there, sensed my absolute sinfulness, feeling as dirty as filth, itself, when I was three years of age. But what he had told me was ingrained in my being! I was awed by the graphic telling of my Lord Jesus' horrible experience of being nailed to a rough wooden cross by evil men! This would register with me so early in life, very strikingly; but my grandfather died before I was 3 ½, letting me also know God can do anything He wants to do, any way He chooses to do it!! My Mother, too, taught me many things before I was school age for I spent most days just asking questions. God wanted my grandfather, a Baptist minister, to have that privilege of introducing me to The Savior! I am eternally thankful! Yet it was some years before my baptism occurred.

At age 11, walking in a field of harvested corn, to bring home milk cows for evening milking, Satan challenged my mind with the idea of evolution. Within ½ hour, God had sealed to my heart that, "In the beginning, God" was the only logical possibility for all the miracles of nature.

WHICH CHURCH SAVES? None of them! God's Holy Son is The Savior: "The Way, The Truth and The Life! No one comes to The Father, but by Him!" John 14:6

Israel's Messiah, The Christ of God, God's Holy, Eternal Son is Head of The Church. He said, of Himself, in Matthew 16:18: "Upon This Rock will I build My Church." (NOT "churches."). Here, he indicated to the apostle Peter, "Thou art *petros*, (a little rock—same essence, much, much smaller significance.) But, upon This Rock (*petra* – He, Himself, The Stone cut out of the mountain without hands, Daniel 2:44, 45.)

The Church consists of all redeemed sinners who receive The Savior, The Lord Jesus Christ, as Savior and Lord. He is The Builder of It "Upon this Rock I will build My Church. And the gates of Hell shall not prevail against it." Matt. 16:18. Christ is the Head of the Church. To help His people understand, He uses illustrations. Old Testament Truth, in Its Entirety, is graphic, as well as righteous truth, I Corinthians 10:1-11.

To understand The Relationship, Order and Activity, He gave us I Corinthians 12:1-31. The Banner under which we are to operate is clear. I Corinthians 13 is the classic provision for the totally gentle and harmless way we are to live and witness. The Reformers were like Peter and John, who said, "Lord, wilt thou that we command fire to come down from Heaven, and consume them, even as Elias did?" Luke 9:54-56.

May I call your attention to our Lord's Answer, "ye know not what manner of Spirit ye are of. For the Son of Man is not come to destroy men's lives, but to save them."

To emphasize His Church is a singular Structure, with every stone having an assigned place; and, an order of conduct that is Absolute in its performance. He gave us I Peter 2:1-12, giving us both our place in the structure; and, as believer-priests our Command; our passionate assigned ministry that every believer is to be consumed with a living fire of passion for Him!

Our life is to be like an artesian well, always flowing with witness, gently, kindly, and graciously, opening this fountain for other lives. I am convinced that there is never a moment when there is to be anger, wrath, malice or envy. We are to ever walk in the light, even as He is in the light. When we see Him, we will be clothed in His Glory as His Bride! Revelation 21:2,9; 22:17.

MOST PEOPLE live their entire lifetime with less than 10% of their God-designed brain power actively engaged! This is a scientifically provable fact! Yet, God, our Creator, challenges us to live beautifully and to the very fullest extent of its abundant, potential richness!

ALL deviations are devastating robbers! my passionate heart cry to God is that He shall give His people such a burning desire to serve God with heart, soul and being that the true flame of The Holy Spirit's power shall burn again in us in such a way that God's Presence and Power will blaze once more in His Own, like that final passionate heart cry of Samson that brought down the Philistines' play house!! No wonder God concludes: "He that trusts in his own heart is a fool!" Prov. 28:26. But The Word of our God endures forever! I Peter 1:25

THIS KIND OF LIVING CAN ONLY BE DONE when the help of our loving God is upon us! God is tenderly reaching and pleading with His Full and Infinite Embrace as our Loving Heavenly Father. NOR, CAN THIS BEGIN until we, with our whole heart, RESPOND to that Beautiful Embrace!

II Corinthians 5:19,20. "To wit, that God was in Christ, reconciling the world unto Himself, not imputing their trespasses unto them; and hath committed unto us the Word of Reconciliation.

Now then we are ambassadors for Christ, as though God did beseech you by us: we pray you in Christ's stead, be ye reconciled to God"

What The Lord Jesus Christ did on the cross was to blot out sin forever, in every facet and aspect of it; three days later, He arose in Triumph over sin, death and hell eternally; then after forty days, He ascended to the Right Hand of The Father, and through the ages of time, He is Present There, with The Father, as Proof of Triumph in the Absolute, until every one of His Purposes in time is completed!

His Own, who remain imperfect in activities and in fact, can demonstrate to the universe that we love Him more than life itself; and, do so by CHOICE and by PERSONAL DECISION, in the face of Satan's wiles and deceptions, facing temptation through an earthly life, making use of God's provided weapons; and, making constant choice to walk as obedient children, II Corinthians 10:4, until He chooses to call us unto Himself!

This is absolute and immediate when one has received Christ by faith, and has told Him so! God, the Father, Loves each one with perfect Love. We will not be perfect until we see Him; but, when we fail, we confess it to Him; and, tell Him so. I John 1:9. Our Heavenly Father is a forgiving Father; and, we live to please Him, by choice, when there is every opportunity to do otherwise.

That declaration by each believer is The Father's good pleasure; and, a special cause of Satan's rage that is directed against us, constantly and continually, because we are accessible to him! Case in point; and, for illustration: the man, Job! Job's decision: "Though He slay me, yet will I trust Him!"

This position, we assume decisively, declaring the same, openly and publicly in water baptism as our testimony before angels, demons, Satan and humanity!! Such action must involve the decisive action of the Christian, personally, in the same manner all obedience is rendered in serving Him!

MODERN 'SCIENCE' POSES as man's highest, ultimate scholarly intellectualism, rudely ridiculing The Bible, The Eternal, Infinite, Plenary, Inspired Word of Our Eternal God, with men labeling it mere superstition!! The Bible and its truth hold both man's justification and man's judgment. Existence demands Origin and Infinity of Being!

Obviously man had an origin; and, he was designed by a Being superior to himself. Science has never produced life, animate or inanimate, vegetable or animal! Nor can man or his science create true chemicals. It can only be worked with what already has existence!

Science, therefore, is inferior to existence; hence, can contribute nothing other than opinion, making use of what exists! Matter was originally designed to be compatible by its designer; or, have the result be destructive! Case in point: The splitting of the Atom!! Responding to an article in Journal World, July 12, 2012, on discovery of the "God particle," Carl Burkhead, ironically commented, "If you or anyone wants to discover the author of life, discover Jesus! If anyone wants to understand the origin of the universe, look to the One who spoke it into existence."

HOWEVER, leading professed atheists, like Joseph Stalin, began his pre-Hell, anguished torments of remorse, as witnessed by his closest associate in the final days of his horrible life, is *a classic illustration* of the total bankruptcy of humanism and agnosticism! (Remember Judas!!) Genuine atheists are nonexistent in non-prejudiced intelligent circles!

Stalin's successor, Nikita Khruschef, betrayed many times over, that the Bible verses he had learned, for pennies in Sunday school, mocked his phony, professed atheism over and over again, in his open conversations with others in our own country, on American radio, during his visits here. Nikita Kruschev was no atheist, for he KNEW in his heart and soul that God is the Real Person the Bible declares Him to Be! Both his wife; and, that of Joseph Stalin made the sign of the cross over their caskets, at their death, to no avail. Folk with no courage to place their life in God's Hands and stand for The Truth of God, have no claim on the God of the Bible, or of His Heaven!!

THE FEAR OF THE LORD is the beginning of wisdom: a good understanding have all they that do His commandments: His praise endureth for ever. Psalm 111:10.

YET, BIBLE BELIEVERS are destined to face enemies of The Cross; and, NEED TO BE FORTIFIED WITH FACTS when The Faith of Christ is embraced as based upon God's Eternal Infinite Holy Word, The Bible:

"Every Scripture is given by inspiration of God. (God-breathed: Gr. *Theopneustos*); and, is profitable for doctrine, for reproof, for correction, for instruction in righteousness: that the man of God may be perfect, (fully mature, Gr. *Artios, completely-fully furnished*) unto all good works." II Tim. 3:16,17.

"For the prophecy came not in old time by the will of man: but, holy men of God spake as they were moved (lit: borne along, implying "being full possession of": "Pneumatos hagiios pheromenoi" – "were carried along" by the Holy Spirit." II Pet. 1:21.)

The Bible declares itself to be the Infinite, Absolute, Eternal Word of The Living God, in all of its parts, words and phrases (in the original Hebrew, Greek and Aramaic.) The Greek Text has eight (8) tenses, making what is said much more vivid; the English has only 3. In the Hebrew Text, noun and verb forms help our understanding: singular (1), dual (2); (3) plural, and (4) neuter) are consistently and purposefully employed. This is VERY important! When in use for The Triune God, with His Primary Names used in very meaningful and important ways.

God's Spiritual Breath of Lives, as He breathes lives into US (triune, as signifying plurality) which He Breathes into His Own as His or her Very Own, New Life In Christ has enormous significance! All who Name The Name of Christ, being baptized in open declaration of Faith, enter a totally new experience!

They have real experiences as sons and daughters of God, into a new exposure to spiritual warfare that has raged in the spiritual realm since the rebellion of Satan, who has taken with him a third of the angelic host. Though Satan is a defeated foe, he will not cease to war with God and His angels until he is cast into The Lake of Fire and Brimstone, when God's purpose in allowing him to range through his universe is complete.

"For we wrestle not against flesh and blood; but, against principalities, against powers, against wicked spirits in high places." Ephesians 6:12: LET'S STAND! Not wobble, flinch or fumble!

"BUT THE NATURAL MAN receives not the things of The Spirit of God: for they are foolishness unto him:

neither can he know them, because they are spiritually

discerned." I Corinthians 2:14. Weep for them; but, BEWARE of allowing empathy!

Chapter X

PERSECUTIONS STIRRED BY BAPTISM

"BLESSED ARE THEY who are persecuted for righteousness' sake; for theirs is the kingdom of heaven.

"Blessed are ye when men shall revile you, and persecute you, and shall say all manner of evil against you falsely, for my sake.

Rejoice and be exceedingly glad; for great is your reward in heaven; for so persecuted they the prophets who were before you." Matthew 5:10-12

"Wycliffe doctrines show that the unity of the truth held in these various circles was recognized by their enemies. After a solemn service of degradation Huss was burned. A fortnight before he had written: 'I am greatly consoled by that saying of Christ, 'blessed are ye when men shall revile you'...a good, nay the best of greetings, but difficult, I do not say to understand, but to live up to, for it bids us rejoice in these tribulations...It is easy to read it aloud and expound it, but difficult to live out. Even that bravest Soldier, though He knew that He should rise again on the third day, after supper was depressed in spirit........ On this account the soldiers of Christ, looking to their leader, the King of Glory have had a great fight.

"My dress," the young girl murmured, her words were slurred through swollen lips. "Please give me my dress. I want to hold it."

The Christians surrounding the girl's bed were crushed! Because of her extensive injuries, the doctors could do nothing for her. Weeks ago, the believers had baptized her in her beautiful contrition, having received the Lord Jesus, loving him with all of her heart, they had bought her a white dress to celebrate her new life and pure heart in Christ Jesus.

Her father had not been pleased with his daughter's decision to follow Christ. One night, in a drunken rage, he attacked his daughter, beating and kicking her mercilessly. He left her lying in the muddy street to die. When she did not show up for church, her Christian friends went looking for her and found her unconscious, lying in a heap, her formerly snow white dress now covered in blood and mud. She was brought to a doctor, but her injuries were too severe.

With the simple faith of a ten-year-old, she whispered, "please, I want to show my dress to Jesus. He was willing to bleed for me, I just want Jesus to know that I was willing to bleed for Him," She said and moved into eternity, holding her dress! Her beautiful robe of Righteousness transformed her as she moved into His Presence! Nameless, Her story lives on!

Mark 13:13 "And ye shall be hated of all men for My Name's sake;"

John 15:18 "If the world hate you, ye know that it hated me before it hated you

John 17:14 "I have given them Thy word; and the world hath hated them, because they are not of the world, even as I am not of the world."

The early Church was a stranger in the world and the Conversion of Constantine seemed a welcome relief from the blood and gore of the Roman theatre and the Catacombs. But when heathen brothels were turned into 'churches' and the bishops became magistrates with power, and the unconverted heathen made members of the church, ultimately the true church became the hunted, mocked and ridiculed, just as the Lord Jesus warned.

In a shipping disaster at Samoa, the way in which the British man-of-war *calliope* escaped is suggestive. Her machinery was very powerful, and just as she was about to strike the reef, she raised her anchors, and in the face of the terrible storm, steamed out of the harbor and into the open sea, where she safely out rode the storm. And so in the Christian life, there are times when safety is only to be found in like decisiveness and boldness. Strengthened with might by His Spirit in the inner man, the believer should 'stand', and must bravely go forth to meet its spiritual foes, attacking them with the Love of Christ; and, not be afraid.

The doctrinal statement of the Anabaptists is given at a later time. For all practical purposes it is quite complete and it is very interesting that the records of the Anabaptists were searched out and seized!

"The Anabaptist leaders, Hubmaier, Denck, Hetzer, and Hut, likewise appeared in Augsburg, and gathered a congregation of eleven hundred members. They held a general synod in 1527. They understood the Word of God, they knew the meaning of being taught of God, reading the Holy Scriptures, keeping records, prayer, understanding the importance of BAPTIZO which seems to give real comprehension! The Covenant Theologians fiercely sought to find their records to destroy them. But they taught their children, and were firm in conviction!! Hegis stirred up the magistrate against them: the leaders were imprisoned, and some executed.

"The confusion and strife among the Protestants strengthened the Roman party. The people did not know what to believe, and the magistrate hesitated. The moral condition of the city, as described by Rhegius, Musculus, and other preachers, was deplorable, and worse than under the papal rule." THE HISTORY OF THE CHRISTIAN CHURCH, Philip Schaff, Vol. Vii, p. 578

THE POWER OF GOD, given to the Church in Acts 1:8, is a dynamic to be ever sought! It is available! Perhaps there is a variable in the Church's perfection that requires much prayer and diligent search. II Tim. 2:15.

THE *CATHOLIC* SYSTEM, anticipating the merger of church and state aroused strong controversy which never ceased during the church age. Controversy raged! And, Constantine, anticipated full control that gradually came to be the iron fisted force, using political means to maintain control. Once control was established, even in times of weakness, they dominated the scene.

Yet through blood, tears and violent deaths, the strong dominance of truth and righteousness was extended onward for well over one thousand years, as the Waldenses maintained strong statistics and firm Biblical information. God saw that the truth of the Word of God was maintained. The Dead Sea scrolls fanned the flames of knowledge and discernment far into the distant past.

It was during 596 A,D. that forty Benedictine monks, under Augustine (Name-sake of the original Augustine) were commissioned by Pope Gregory Ist, and they went to England, landing at Kent. The results were amazing because of the abundant fruit. The British and the newer Roman ministry came into conflict, so Augustine, Arch-bishop of Canterbury, was given supremacy over England. The British order continued and was absorbed, in the 13th Century into the Lollard movement. Already, the Scottish and Irish missions were wide spread and were attacked by the Roman system under Boniface, who compelled the people to submit, at least outwardly or be destroyed, receiving state aid for his purposes.

BAPTISTERIES or Photisteries with chapels were designed exclusively for the administration of baptism; these are in the form of church buildings, standing alone. In the first centuries baptism was performed in streams, or in private houses. But after the public exercise of Christian worship became lawful, in the fourth century, special buildings for baptizing believers were constructed, either separately or connected to the main building by a covered walk. The baptismal pools, like the basilicas, were round and often covered with a dome. They were approached by steps. A colonnade stood with a circular, or hexagon gallery for spectators to watch the proceedings, with a spacious vestibule inside a walled hexagon or a rectangular enclosure. Generally, the baptisteries had separate enclosures for the two sexes, with the interior elaborately ornate with flowered designs.

The earliest baptisteries in the Constantinian church of St. Peters in Rome, were constructed, having a rich supply of moving waters supplied by the Vatican fountain and adorned with gorgeous mosaic, designed in green, gold, and purple, where reflections in the water were fabulous. The celebrated baptistery that was of the Lateran church at Rome was quite awesome.

In the Roman Church, adult baptisms became extremely rare, and infant baptism was begun in earnest, it became customary to place a baptismal basin in the porch of the church. I question whether it began this early, but at least by the 9ᵗʰ Century, it was quite common.

When baptism was no longer performed by the bishop alone, every pastor, and each parish performed the rite. Every pastor performed the baptism, with each parish providing baptisteries, which continued in use, even in the later middle ages and new ones were occasionally erected even in the 16ᵗʰ Century.

"Few assume greatness by themselves. Behind the scenes often lies an older mentor, watching with pride. John Calvin exists as a hero in church history because of Guillaume Farel. "Farel was a traveling evangelist in France, full of fire and fury. He was likened to Elijah and was the "Scourge of priests." He considered the pope the Antichrist and viewed the Mass as nothing but idolatry. Priests, wishing him dead, l carried weapons under their cloaks to assassinate him. After one attempt onh his life, he whirled around and faced the priest who had fired the errant bullet. "I am not afraid of your shouts," he roared.

He was small, sunburned, fiery, l and powerful. His sermons were cannon blasts, and his oratory captivated the nation. He often said too much, and one friend cautioned him Your mission is to evangelizel not to curse."

"On April 12, 1523, Farel was forbidden to preach in France. He fled to Switzerland and wandered from town to town, turning stumps and stones into pulpits. When he entered Geneva, the city fathers and priests tried to make him leave. "Who invited you? They demanded. Farel replied: "I have been baptized in the name of the Father, the Son and the Holy Ghost, and am not a devil. I go about preaching Christ, Who died for our sins and rose for Justification. Whoever believes in him will be saved.

Unbelievers will be lost. I am bound to preach to all who will hear. I am ready to dispute with you, to give an account of my faith and ministry. Elijah said to King Ahab, "It is thou, and not I who disturbest Israel." So I say, it is you and yours, who trouble the world by your traditions, Your human inventions, l and your dissolute lies. "He was ridiculed, beaten, but would not give up, but wouldn't give up Geneva. Several years later when young John Calvin came passing through, farel spotted him and gave him a place to minister—and, as it turns out, a place in church history. ON THIS DAY, by Robert J. Moran

The Lutheran baptisms were performed with exorcism. Calvin and Zwingly at first performed exorcisms but they ceased that aspect of the ritual, arousing the anger of the Lutherans. This is totally unBiblical and I trust you are alert to, and aware of, just how essential it is to see that the Living Word of God become the basis of that proper and correct observance of baptism.

..Luther and Zwingly destroyed as with thunderbolts the Babylonian evil, but they set up nothing better, for when they came to power they trusted more in man than in God. (Just beware that the harlot of Revelation 17 has daughters, for she is the "mother of harlots!") When you consider how the Protestant has divided into multiple bodies that have sub-divided into more than 2200 distinct groups,... it is sad.! Then he describes the conflicts with Zwingli on the subject of baptism, and how Zwingli, though he had proved by the clear word of God from the Holy Scriptures, to be by immersion, yet afterwards taught from the pulpit that the baptism of adults and believers is wrong and should not be endured; and how it was enacted that whoever in Zurich and the districts should be immersed should be drowned in water. He shows how this persecution led to the scattering of many of Christ's servants and some came to Austria, preaching the Word.

"the spread of the churches in Austria and the surrounding states was marvelous; the accounts of the numbers put to death and of their sufferings are terrible, yet there never failed to be men willing to take up the dangerous work of evangelists and elders. Of some it is recorded "they went full of joy to their death. While some were being drowned and put to death, the others who were waiting their turn, sang and waited with joy the death which was theirs when the executioner took them in hand.

"They were firm in the truth which they knew; and, fortified in the faith which they had from God, **such stedfastness constantly aroused** astonishment and inquiry as to the source of their strength. Many were won by it to the faith, but the religious leaders of the Roman Catholic and Reformed Churches were adamant; it was generally attributed to Satan.

The believers themselves said: 'they have drunk of the water that flows from the Sanctuary of God, from the well of life, and from this have obtained a heart that cannot be comprehended by the human mind or understanding. They have found that God helped them to bear the cross and they have overcome the bitterness of death.'

"The fire of God burned in them. Their tabernacle was not here on the earth but was pitched in eternity and they had foundation and certainty for their faith.

"Their faith blossomed like as a lily their faithfulness as a rose, their piety and uprightness as flowers of God's planting, The angel of the Lord had swung his spear before them, so that the helmet of Salvation, the golden shield of David, could not be wrested from them. They have heard the horn blown in Zion and have understood it—and on that account they have cast down all pain and martyrdom and not feared.

The Bohemian Brethren were aggressive evangelicals from the Hussite movement. The moderate Hussites felt that something must be done for the conservation and expansion of the evangelical life that had been developed for over fifty years in Bohemia and Moravia because the evangelical teachings of Wycliffe and Huss had been scattered throughout Bohemia and they had also gone into Austria with their teachings and evangelical practices.

(I suspect the hideous attacks by Satan, even using the legal 'christianized' system to do his filthy work would leave God's people too stunned to know if they were coming or going)

The warfare of the ages is continually being waged! With our soldiers returning from the Afghanistan's more than ten year war, minus limbs and in so many cases experiencing unspeakable trauma which needs council and prayer, it reminds me so much of the spiritual warfare that is being fought. Satanic forces are working day and night; torment the folk who for one reason or another are casualties of the spiritual warfare that we face continually and are forced out of the fight!

It is deeply refreshing to know that a Hymn book published in Ulm in 1538 shows the provision made for praise and worship in the congregations of the brethren. So much blessing is gleaned from the ministry of music. The end of its long title states that it was for "the Christian Brotherhood, the Picards, What we have to know is that what was given to us as the martyrdom of 'Heretics' was in reality very devout believers, until now considered as Unchristian and Heretics, used and sung daily to the honor of God. (142). This miss-information is stunning.

The blood of Martyrs is the seed of the Church! While Melanchthon spoke of the Protestant Princes as "chief members of the Church", Luther called them "makeshift Bishops" and frequently expressed his regret for the lost liberty of the Christian man and independence of the Christian congregation that had once been his aim. Without a doubt, Luther grieved over the required adjustments which even included the matter of immersing the believer to fulfill the commands of Christ.

AS THE FOREMOST FIELD OF FRONTAL ATTACK on your faith, in Satan's effort to lay claim to mastery of every field of knowledge, modern science has become his tool, in the hands of his most respected accomplices among men, in the gaining of Satan's own goals! His foremost goal is the silencing of Christian Witness and the ridicule of Christian Faith, even the mocking of Scripture Itself; and, beyond this, the driving of Christians from all effective service to The Eternal God. BEWARE! His goal is to break and mock every Christian and his Testimony! `

"And the Lord God said, It is not good that man should be alone: I will make him an help meet for him" Genesis 2:18. It seems there are scandals that have erupted from the priesthood that have caused

much sorrow through the ages, which could well have been avoided by reading Scripture. Monasticism has been the deeply troubling issue that has been foisted upon the Church and upon the priesthood.

"In the beginning of the fourth century, monasticism appears in the history of the church; and, thenceforth occupies a distinguished place. Beginning in Egypt, it spread in an irresistible tide over the East and West, continued to be the chief repository of the Christian life down to the times of the Reformation, and still remains in the Greek and Roman churches an indispensable institution and the most productive seminary of saints, priests and missionaries." HISTORY OF THE CHRISTIAN CHURCH, Philip Schaff, Vol.III, p. 149.

It is without question that every disobedience has resulted in a multitude of Satanic activity that has made the professed church unfruitful!

SCHOOLASTICISM is the term given to the theology of The Middle (or, dark) Ages. "The chief feeders of Scholasticism were the writings of Augustine and Aristotle... Aristotle was regarded as a forerunner of Christian truth, a John the Baptist in method and knowledge." History of the Christian Church, Vol. V. Ch. 12, p. 591.

THE DARK AGES were impacted heavily by Aristotle's teachings. This Greek philosopher and personal teacher of Alexander The Great, through his ideas and broad influences in The Church was permitted to weaken the firm statements of Scripture.

TODAY, that Trojan Horse, at work within The Church, largely through it's own seminaries, has robbed the church's ministers of a strong Faith in a Verbally, Plenary Inspired Bible! The goal of Satan is to turn out every light! He is the Prince of Darkness!

AS WE TAKE AN OPEN AND PUBLIC STAND FOR CHRIST, *IN BAPTISM,* God's Holy Spirit takes Personal Command to whatever extent *we yield* ourselves to Him! This is God's Order! *Until that arrangement is initiated, baptism and all professed service to God is not in order!!*

167

However, water baptism is the appointed, open testimony to the world of the unseen, Spiritual Baptism in which Regeneration and new life have already been experienced by true believers. I Corinthians 12:13; Romans 8:16,17.

PLEASE LET IT BE UNDERSTOOD we believers are on The Solid Rock, The Lord Jesus Christ! Matthew 16:18. *FEAR HAS NO PART IN CHRISTIAN EXPERIENCE.*

"For God hath not given us the spirit of fear; but of power, and of love, and of a sound mind." II Timothy 1:7. Spirit Control follows our full submission to Him!

For your eternal safety and mine, we must not trust human leadership, but, The Eternal Word of God alone. "Remember now thy Creator in the days of thy youth, while the evil days come not, nor the years draw nigh, when thou shalt say, I have no pleasure in them." Ecclesiastes 12:20.

AS INDICATED EARLIER, the modern community of sciences which advocate the evolutionary process, professes, *without sustainable proofs*, to be scientific in hypotheses in regard to proposed origins, 'assumed processes', 'past activities' within the universe and in 'pre-human advances' to man's appearance on the scene, having *chosen* to build on Charles Darwin's *proposals*, in violation of his own personal pleas, as he, in a personal fear of God, renounced his own previous works in the last years of his life!

Nor, will you ever hear that FACT from the lips of modern mockers! But it is an historical fact! Even his hypothetical possibility of concepts and imaginary drawings of how 'missing links' *could* have looked as set forth in his writing, *The Origin of Species,* ALL of this, he acknowledged to be mere *figments of his imagination*! Folk, eagerly searching for means to promote concepts that would counter The Scriptures, used Darwin's writings and ideas as FACTS, *in violation of his own personal pleas.*

NOTHING has been found that supports and gives credence to evolutionary thought, but the hypotheses have been; and, are today, treated and taught as facts!! This is just another of the devious stunts of Satan, preying upon the minds of humanity, by which he continues his incessant, hideous mockeries! Hear his laughter echo!

FURTHERMORE, 250 years of study, research, exploration and archeological digs have not produced one single proof of the modern, bold claims of evolutionary origins. It must be assigned to total idiocy!! The capstone of idiocy is the fact that science cannot give life to a FLEA.

IN AUGUST of 1957, under the International Union of Biochemistry, and with the collaboration of the Academy of Sciences of the U.S.S.R., a symposium on the "Origin of Life on the Earth" was held at Moscow, with the specific purpose of determining the vital question of the origin of life on the earth. Scientists from 17 countries, most of them outstanding investigators of the various disciplines connected with the problem of biogenesis on the earth.

The first speaker, Professor A.I. Oparin declared that a meeting of scientists at the end of the 19th century "had proved that the spontaneous generation of life from nonliving matter did not take place today under any known laboratory conditions." This fact, however, only animated the writhing serpent; and, imaginary bridges were formed in order to go deeper into anti-Biblical fields by *assumption and hypotheses.*

Let it suffice to say that the brilliant minds present in Moscow in 1959 delved diligently into all facets of biogenesis, embryology, paleontology, etc. without providing us with one single antithesis to Genesis 1:1 - "IN THE BEGINNING, God created the heavens and the earth." (Heb. Shami'im, heavens, pl.) (and).v.27 "So God created man in His Own Image, in the Image of God created He him; male and female created He them."

THE EUROPEAN CHURCH and MUCH OF THE AMERICAN CHRISTIAN PROFESSION has been robbed of The Power of The Holy Spirit by the presence within it of agnosticism, Greek mythology, philosophy, natural science; and, an open ridicule of The Infinite, Eternal Inspired Word of God! Some attempt was made to reconcile humanism with Deity; and, the result is spiritual disaster for all who attempt that stance.

When ten million volts of electricity becomes grounded, it is powerless to perform. There is a positive and a negative, both in the natural; and, in the spiritual field, that we, as believers, must understand the lethal position of attempting to be both an active sinner and a saint.

Matthew 6:24 -*"No man can serve two masters: for either he will hate the one, and love the other; or else he will hold to the one, and despise the other. Ye cannot serve God and mammon."*

THOSE WHO SEE MOST CLEARLY are those who live, walking in The Holy Spirit, led and taught of Him. These are the persons God has chosen to use with greatest effectiveness as He maintains His Position in a Power-filled life that radiates His Own Presence in witness to a lost world.

Dr. A.E. Wilder Smith, one of the world's most highly developed scientific minds in human history, in his classic book, "Man's Origin, Man's Destiny", Which is a critical survey of the principles of evolution and Christianity, was a graduate of Oxford University, received his first Ph.D. in organic chemistry from Reading University. He followed cancer research under the Countess of Lisburne Memorial Fellowship at London's Middlesex Hospital Medical School, at the University of London. From 1951-55 he held the position of Chief of Research at Geistlich Soehne Pharmaceuticals, Ltd., at Lucerne.

In 1964 he was granted the Doctor of Science degree from the University of Geneva. During the same year he received his third doctorate at the E.T.M. in Zurich, Switzerland. He is the author and co-author of 50 scientific publications, has been a world traveler as guest speaker at medical schools throughout the western world. At the School of Medicine in Geneva he was honored with the "Golden Apple" award for "the best course in five years of college life", for three consecutive years. In the three years 1966-67-68 received "Instructor of the Year" award, citation for the best senior year course.

In a cover letter students commented, "He made us not only better scientists, but better men"! This writer concludes his 313 pages of condensed focus on the foibles and fancies of conflicting, confusing, constantly changing theses of hypotheses, from the realm of natural science, relative to concepts, beliefs and assumptions required to present naturalistic, logical theories of man's origin and history, when The Eternal Word of God is rejected, reinterpreted or revised, by stating, p. 312, 313:

"The experience of many Christians has been that serious study and daily application of the Scriptures brings with them the promise mentioned in Psalm 119:97-99 "O how I love Thy Law! It is my meditation all the day. Thou through Thy Commandments hast made me wiser than mine enemies: for th ey are ever with me. I have more understanding than all my teachers: for thy testimonies are my meditation." He might well have added v.100 "I understand more than the ancients, because I keep Thy Precepts." Man's Origin, Man's Destiny, p.312,313 – A.E. Wilder Smith

The most dead, 'hand-me-down' commodity on earth, is a second-hand religion. "For there is One God and ONE MEDIATOR between God and men, the Man, Christ Jesus." – I Timothy 2:5

OUR FAITH RESTS ON THE BIBLE AND THE BIBLE ALONE The ONE Teacher of Scripture today is God's Holy Spirit, Who gave it! Our Lord Jesus Christ, God The Son, said:

> "I have yet many things to say unto you, but ye cannot bear Them now. Howbeit when He, The Spirit of Truth, is come, He will guide you into all Truth for He shall not speak from Himself; but, whatsoever He shall hear, that shall He speak: and He will show you things to come. He shall glorify Me: for He shall receive of Mine, and shall show it unto you." - John 16:12-14

It is the writer's prayer that God's Spirit shall lead us, through His Eternal Word to a thorough and accurate setting forth of the fullest significance and purpose of baptism, in a concise, clear manner.

Both life and death touch infinity; and, demand the supernatural!! Dag Hammarskjhold, former Secretary-General of the U.N., died in a plane crash; and beside his casket stood a wreath of daffodils and two red roses.

It was from the Hammarskjold family. The wreath bore one word—*why? Infinity and eternity* stand both in the birthing room and beside the casket of every person with the question: "Why"? "How"?!! The dramatics of the question *essentially are*: "When its over, its eternity!! Isn't it fascinating how we got here?!! Think about it! Just one more lost sinner in eternity in hell or a saint has gone to Glory!! BUT HOW DO WE KNOW?? "Through faith we understand!! We're really doing SO LITTLE about it!! Perishing humanity is LOST FOREVER!!

> *Mystery surrounds many things in human experience, while simple reality causes others to stand in BOLD RELIEF: RESURRECTION is the LIVING HOPE of the Church. Baptism is a visual of Truth. Deuteronomy 29:29 "The secret things belong unto the Lord our God: but those things which are revealed belong unto US AND TO OUR CHILDREN FOREVER!!."*   -Deuteronomy 29:29

Chapter X1
PRAYER, THE HEART
OF BAPTISM

" **F**INALLY, MY BRETHREN be strong in the lord, and in the power of His Might. Put on the whole armour of God, that ye may be able to stand against the wiles of the devil. For we wrestle not against flesh and blood, against principalities, against powers, against the rulers of the darkness of this world, against spiritual wickedness in high places." Ephesians 6:10-12.

(FOR THE WEAPONS of our warfare are not carnal, but mighty through God for the pulling down of strongholds) 5. "Casting down imaginations, and every high thing that exalteth itself against the knowledge of God, and bringing into captivity every thought to the obedience of Christ. II Corinthians 10:4,5.

IT IS EVIDENT that God knew the path of His Church lay through ten violent persecutions; and, that for over one thousand years of heavy violence within the Church there would be a Satanic delusion working within the professed church that would bring deep confusion and chaos; first, between the east and the west, creating a radical division; and, then, the Reformation Chaos that has shattered!

THE RADICAL MYSTERY of the bringing forward of a fully formed Covenant Theology, was a system of belief that had to be made to stand on its own feet, raising issues that would not stand in harmony with the Christian Faith as it was once delivered to the saints..

The numerous tragedies of Covenant Theology are: (1) It formulates a system of belief that the world is to: (a). be converted gradually; and, thus would provide one thousand years of peace; (b) or, there will not be one thousand years of peace, but, the world will end suddenly and dramatically. (2) Baptism should be administered to children (it was first taught that unbaptized children were lost, putting forward baptismal regeneration), then that children had an uncertain future, then, that children dying in infancy, unbaptized, had a salvation but of an uncertain type. The uncertainty generated by the false premise has degenerated into doubt of Holy Scripture, fostering an agnostic theology that has become 'the habitation of demons, and a cage of every unclean and hateful bird.' Rev. 18:3.

THERE IS NOT TO BE heavy condemnation of the dear people who were troubled, hundreds of millions of them, crying out to God for peace and knowledge that needs to come to modern minds. Many of these precious people cried out to God, lived a beautiful life, and will be present in Heaven. Bibles were forbidden to people in other lands, where the leadership controlled and the poor and the deprived were sternly told "they could not understand the Bible." It is interesting that their Latin jargon has been pressed right back into the understandable languages. Now they hear!

IT IS TRAGIC that the formulation of Covenant Theology seems to have grown out of the violent hatred between the Eastern Church of Constantinople and the Western Church of Rome. Yet the Eastern Church seems to have already developed points of belief that caused the Anabaptists and others of like faith not to unite with them; and, division continues.

"THE AUGSBURG CONFESSION, at first modestly called an *Apology,* after the manner of the early Church in the ages of persecution, was occasioned by the German Emperor Charles V., who commanded the Lutheran Princes to present, at the Diet to be held in the Bavarian city of Augsburg, an explicit statement of their faith, that the religious controversy might be settled, and Catholics and Protestants be united in a war against the common enemy, the Turks. Its deeper cause must be sought in the inner necessity and impulse to confess and 'formularize' the evangelical faith, which had been already attempted before.

"It was prepared on the basis of previous drafts, and with conscientious care, by Philip Melanchthon, at the request and in the name of the

Lutheran States, during the months of April, May, and June 1530, at Coburg and Augsburg, with the full approval of Luther. It was signed, August 23, by seven German Princes (the Elector John of Saxony and the Landgrave Philip of Hesse, etc.) and the deputies of two free cities (Nuremberg and Reutlingen). This act required no little moral courage, in view of the immense political and ecclesiastical power of the Roman Church at that time. When warned by Melanchthon of the possible effect of his signature, the Elector John of Saxony nobly replied: 'I will do what is right, unconcerned about my electoral dignity; I will confess my Lord, whose cross I esteem more highly than all the power of the earth.'

"On the 25th of June, 1530, the Confession was read aloud, in the German language, before the assembled representatives of Church and State, and in the hearing of a monarch in whose dominions the sun never set." THE CREEDS OF CHRISTENDOM, Philip Schaff, Vol. I, p.226.

The marvelous beginning of what is to be "To me to live is Christ, and to die is gain" and "Christ liveth in me." Is a deep and awesome challenge that is intensely real!

In the month of November, 1414. a general Council was assembled at Constance, in order, as was pretended, for the sole purpose of determining a dispute then pending between three persons who contended for the papacy; but the real motive was to crush the progress of the Reformation.

"John Huss was summoned to appear at this council; and to encourage him, the emperor sent him a safe-conduct: the civilities, and even reverence, which Huss met with on his journey where beyond imitation. The streets and sometimes the very roads were lined with people, whom respect, rather than curiosity had brought together.

"He was ushered into the town with great acclamations, and it may be said that he passed through Germany in a kind of triumph. He could not help expressing his surprise at the treatment he received: "I thought (said he) I had been an outcast. I now see my worst friends are in Bohemia."

"As soon as Huss arrived at Constance, he immediately took lodging in a remote part of the city. A short time after his arrival, came one Stephen Pletz, who was employed by the clergy at Prague to manage the intended prosecution against him. Paletz was afterwards joined by Michael de Cassia, on the part of the court of Rome. These two declared themselves his accusers, and drew up a set of articles against him, which they presented to the pope and the prelates of the Council.

"While Huss was in confinement, the Council acted the part of inquisitors. They condemned the doctrines of Wickliffe, and ordered his remains to be dug up and burned to ashes; which orders were strictly complied with. The ashes were then thrown into the Thames river. In the meantime, the nobility of Bohemia and Poland strongly interceded for Huss; and so far prevailed as to prevent his being condemned unheard, which had been resolved on by the commissioners appointed to try him.

"When he was brought before the Council, the articles exhibited against him were read: they were upwards of forty in number, and chiefly extracted from his writings.

"John Huss's answer was this: 'I did appeal unto the pope; who being dead, and the cause of my matter remaining undetermined, I appealed likewise unto his successor John XXIII; before whom when, by the space of two years, I could not be admitted by my advocates to defend my cause, I appealed unto the high judge, Christ.'

"When John Huss had spoken these words, it was demanded of him whether he had received absolution of the pope or no? He answered, "No." Whereupon John Huss answered: "Verily I do affirm here before you all, that there is no more just or effectual appeal, than that appeal which is made unto Christ, forasmuch as the law doth determine, that to appeal is no other thing than in a case of grief or wrong done by an inferior judge, to implore and require aid at a higher Judges hand. Who is then a higher Judge than Christ? Who, I say, can know or judge matters more justly, or with more equity? When in Him there is found no deceit, neither can He be deceived; for who can better help the miserable and oppressed than He?" While John Huss, with a devout and sober countenance, was speaking and pronouncing those words, he was derided and mocked by all the whole Council.

"The excellent sentences were esteemed as so many expressions of treason, and tended to inflame his adversaries. Accordingly, the bishops appointed by the Council stripped him of his priestly garments, degraded him, put a paper miter on his head, on which was painted devils, with the inscription, "A ringleader of heretics."

Which, when he saw, he said: "My Lord Jesus Christ, for my sake, did wear a crown of thorns; why should not I then, for His sake, again wear this light crown, be it ever so ignominious? Truly I will do it, and that willingly." When it was set upon his head, the bishop said: "Now we commit thy soul unto the devil." "But I," said John Huss, lifting his eyes towards the heaven, "do commend into thy hands, O Lord Jesus Christ, my spirit, which Thou hast redeemed.

"When the chain was about him at the stake, he said, with a smiling countenance, "My Lord Jesus Christ was bound with a harder chain than this for my sake, and why then should I be ashamed of this rusty one?

"When the fagots were piled up to his very neck, the duke of Bavaria was so officious as to desire him to abjure. "No,"(said Huss) I never preached any doctrine of an evil tendency; and what I taught with my lips I now seal with my blood." He then said to the executioner, "You are now going to burn a goose. (Huss signifying goose in the Bohemian Language:) but in a century you will have a swan which you can neither roast nor boil." If he were prophetic, he must have meant Martin Luther, who shone about a hundred years after, and who had a swan for his arms.

"The flames were now applied to the fagots, when our martyr sung a hymn with so loud and cheerful a voice that he was heard above all the cracklings of the combustibles, and the noise of the multitude.

At length his voice was interrupted by the severity of the flames, which soon closed his existence." FOX'S BOOK OF MARTYRS, Edited by Wm. Brian Forbush, p.141-143,"

What shall we then say to these things? If God be for us, who can be against us?

He that spared not His Own Son, but delivered Him up for us all, how shall He not WITH HIM, also, freely give us all things? Romans 8:31,32.

FOR YEARS the Muslims in the Sudan have spent their cruelty on the inhabitants of the Sudan! James Jeda had received Christ and had witnessed for Christ in baptism! "Collect some wood!" snarled the soldiers. "Young James Jeda assumed that the soldiers were about to cook their dinner. Earlier that day, he had watched, horrified, as the radical Muslim soldiers killed his parents and four siblings in Southern Sudan. They spared James only to use him as a worker."

"Good news for you, young one," said a soldier, "We are going to let you live. But you must join us by becoming a Muslim." "I cannot become a Muslim", James said simply. "I am a Christian."

"Infuriated by the young boy's faith, the soldiers picked him up and hurled him into the fire. They packed up their gear and left the area, assuming James would die. Young James didn't die. He managed to roll out of the fire and find help.

"Doctors were able to save James's life, but he will always carry reminders of that day. His body bears skin grafts and scar tissue, and one arm is partially deformed by the burns. In heaven, those scars will be true honor; and, be as, a reminder of the day when James Jeda refused to turn his back on Christ!" EXTREME DEVOTION, p. 34

MATTHEW 10:22 "And ye shall be hated of all men for my Name's sake: but he that endureth to the end shall be saved."

(Being confident of this very thing, that He which hath BEGUN a good work in you will perform it until the day of Jesus Christ:" Phil. 1:6.)

Because of our precious Savior's Wonderful Love for us, He gave to His Church two ordinances, (commands), to provide for His own a visible teaching means as continual reminders He is with us at all times with His unseen Presence IN OUR HEARTS:

Baptism and the Lord's Table teach the heart! His Kingdom is Spiritual in nature; but, humans need visible and tangible ways for our five physical senses to better grasp clear concepts of His Spiritual Truth. The Ordinances (Commands) are vivid PICTURES of the spiritual truths they are designed to teach, but THE TRUTHS which they communicate to us teach the HEART. They illustrate, helping us to grasp clearly our beautiful relationship with Him, Whose Blood ALONE ACCOMPLISHED this reality in His Own Divine PERSON, on our behalf, ONCE FOR ALL FOREVER!

Wrong decision, action, and stubborn blindness have resulted from Adam's Fall, Isaiah 53:6, and the human *will* has been damaged as tragically by man's Fall as has his *priorities* ; and, God has written "stubbornness is as idolatry." I Samuel 15:23. All humanity stands indicted as being "guilty of sin," Revelation 3:2, 15-17.

The very Words, even letters of the Original Scriptures are inspired of God: Matthew 5:18. The Scriptures are God Breathed (Greek: *Theopneustos*. II Timothy 3:16,17). That which is the very Breath of God is to be treated with the ultimate respect in Its Authority. It was copied with such care, that mistakes by copiers were avoided. Manuscripts of Holy Scripture confirm its Infinite Accuracy. Obviously, we need to understand how to OBEY our Lord's Word of Command. No man or religious body has authority to distort or to withhold God's Truth. Surely the words of Samuel to Saul are a righteous challenge to obedience:

I Samuel 15:22-23 – "..Hath the Lord as great delight in burntofferings and sacrifices, as in obeying the Voice of the Lord? Behold, to obey is better than sacrifice, and to hearken than the fat of rams. For rebellion is as the sin of witchcraft, and stubbornness is as iniquity and idolatry."

The Bible facts concerning baptism are A TRUST FROM GOD, to be treated with genuine reverence; and, infinite care:

"When a man gets in the Straight Way, he finds there is no room for crooked dealings." – *The Presbyterian*

"..It is evident that the term *baptize* means to immerse, and that this was the form used by the primitive Church."- INSTITUTES of the CHRISTIAN RELIGION – By *John Calvin* – Book iv, Chap. xv, Sec. 19

PRAYER is in order at this point that God may guide through His Holy Spirit until a clear discernment of Bible teaching can be gained and properly taught, based upon irrefutable facts, as understood by The Apostles of our Wonderful Lord:

Generations of devoted Bible believers have worshiped God as the leaders of their church led them. Tender family love must have gentle, loving care as God's Truth is held firmly and taught with an understanding insight, prayerfully and unwaveringly. Love for the individual, alone, will give the Truth welcome. That love requires absolute honesty and integrity in conveying GOD'S TRUTH!

LET US GLADLY ACKNOWLEDGE our deep indebtedness to the broad scholarship of devout hearts found in all facets of The Christian Faith, in which are to be found those who have loved our Eternal God: our Heavenly Father, His Son our Christ, and His Holy Spirit, ALL of Whom indwell the hearts of the people of God. CONTROL and UNITY rest with God's Spirit. John. 14:23.

LET US LIKEWISE STAND ALERT: "..there are certain men crept in unawares, who were before of old ordained to this condemnation, ungodly men, turning the grace of our God into lasciviousness, and denying the only Lord God, and our Lord Jesus Christ." - Jude 4.

"Ye therefore, beloved Seeing ye know these things before, beware lest ye also, being led away with the error of the wicked, fall from your own stedfastness." II Peter 3:17

A great passion existed to destroy The Church but the impossibility of blotting out this great heritage, even when it was driven under ground by

The Ten Great Persecutions, was an impossibility! The Church went into the catacombs, the Power of what seemed to be an insignificant effort, yet ¼ to ½ of the Roman Empire bowed to the Name of Jesus! The struggle to baptize infants continued, and Tertullian warned quite severely against that effort! Inasmuch as not before the 9th Century was any significant effort put forward to sprinkle babies.

Far too much effort for the sprinkling of infants was put forward because copies of the Scriptures was so difficult to obtain. Influential leaders waited too long to be safely immersed (with the belief that no sins could be forgiven after baptism). The heresy of 'falling from grace' was considered an awesome peril, again because copies of Holy Scripture were so difficult to obtain. Hebrews 10:14 and many other Scriptures, I John 5:12-13, etc.

"DEAN STANLEY delights in the pictorial exaggeration of the baptismal immersion in patristic times as contrasted with modern sprinkling. "baptism," he says, "was only a bath, a plunge—an entire submersion in the deep water, a leap as into the rolling sea or the rushing river, where for the moment the waves close over the bather's head, and he emerges again from a momentary grave; or it was a shock of a shower-bath—the rush of waters passed over the whole person from capacious vessels, so as to wrap the recipient as within the veil of a splashing cataract. This was the part of the ceremony on which the Apostles laid so much stress. It was to them like a burial of the old former self and the rising up again of the new self." *(Footnote) HISTORY OF THE CHRISTIAN CHURCH, VOL.II, p. 249*

"The Russian Orthodox Catechism defines baptism as 'a sacrament, in which a man who believes, having his body thrice plunged in water in the Name of God the Father, the Son, and the Holy Ghost, dies to the carnal life of sin, and is born again of the Holy Ghost to a life spiritual and holy." *(Footnote) HISTORY OF THE CHRISTIAN CHURCH, VOL. II, P. 249*

"The baptisteries of the Nicene age, of which many remain in Asia, Africa, and Southern Europe were built for immersion, and all Oriental churches still adhere to this mode." *(Footnote) HISTORY OF THE CHRISTIAN CHURCH, VOL II, P.249*

The statement in History of the Christian Church that large baptisteries 'were common in the southern climates' is hardly necessary. The Russian Orthodox Church immerses their infants as a necessity. If you wish an answer to why the Reformers did not make the correction, perhaps you can tell me why those with multiple doctorates ignore the issue when the Catholic encyclopedia declares that the early church immersed.

"Pouring and sprinkling were still exceptional in the ninth century according to Walafried Strabo *(De Rd. Eccl, c. 26)* but they made gradual progress with the spread of infant baptism, as the most convenient mode, especially in Northern climates, and came into common use in the west at the end of the thirteenth century. Thomas Aquinas (A.D..1274) says that although it may be safer to baptize by immersion, yet pouring and sprinkling are also allowable." *(Footnote)* HISTORY OF THE CHRISTIAN CHURCH, VOL. II, P.2

"Luther sought to restore immersion, but without effect. Calvin took a similar view of the subject as Thomas Aquinas, but he went farther and declared the mode of application to be a matter of indifference, *inst. IV. CH. I5, 19*: "Whether the person who is baptized be wholly immersed *(megatur totus)* and whether thrice or once, or whether water be only poured *(infusa)* or sprinkled upon him *(aspergatur)*, is of no importance *(minimum refert)* : but this should be left free to the churches according to the difference of countries, yet the very word *baptize* signifies to immerse *(mergere)*; and it is certain that immersion was the practice of the ancient church." *(Footnote)* HISTORY OF THE CHRISTIAN CHURCH, VOL. II, P. 251.

"MOST Protestants agree with Calvin, except the Baptists, who revived the ancient practice, but only in part (*single* instead of *trine* immersion), and without the patristic ideas of baptismal regeneration, infant baptism, and the necessity of baptism for salvation. They regard baptism as a mere symbol which exhibits the fact that regeneration and conversion have already taken place. *(Footnote)* HISTORY OF THE CHRISTIAN CHURCH, VOL II, P. 251.

There is no indication that the original baptism was by trine immersion. Inasmuch as the Lord Jesus emphasized "I and My Father are One" and the unity of the Church is urged, I sincerely doubt that trine immersion existed in the beginning. Rather: I believe the "The Father, The Son and The Holy Ghost" signified unity and oneness. Oneness and singularity in immersion are to be as firmly defended on the Authority of Ephesians 4:1-12 as every other doctrine of the Word of God! I think you can clearly see the shattering that occurs in trine immersion! Anyone who couldn't get it right about sprinkling in the 15th Century, appears very wrong also in regard to trine immersion. When the Lord Jesus in John 10:30 said, "I and my Father are One" and in John 14:9-11 He emphasizes "oneness", I believe that we must be firm in a singular baptism! Think it through, and stand firm. We have Scripture for our stand.

When the Lord Jesus had said in Matthew 16:18, "Upon THIS ROCK I will build My Church", then He had prayed so earnestly to the Father, in John 17:9—11 "I pray for them: I pray not for the world, but for them which thou hast given me; for they are thine. And all mine are thine, and thine are mine; and I am clarified in hem. Aknd now I am no more in the world, but these are in the world, and I come to thee. Holy Father, keep through thine own name those whom thou hast given me, that they may be one, as we are."

The craft of Satan is shrewd; and, the hearts of believers who want to love all are very tender; but the clever creature, Satan, seeks with near infinite treachery to bring any type of compromise by which he may crush the Church. He was successful from the very start by bringing about compromise. The Conversion of Constantine extended the roof to all heathendom; and Constantine gave his sword to the Church, and the Church never ceased to use it! Believers who chose to remain pure refused to compromise; and, with Holy Scripture confirmed their stand; but, the church used the sword and obedient believers died by the millions!

Zwingli had controversy, first, with Romanism which sprinkled without warrant. They had no shred of Scripture for it. Romanism chose to take away all that belonged to Israel, without warrant. Again the Bible has plenty to say! Now Zwingli labeled the Truth and those who held to it "Radicalism".

It is interesting that each time when compromise meets obedience it indulges in name calling! Now, the obedient are "Radicals"! Yet obedience must retain The Truth! "Every Word of God is pure." Proverbs 30:5. "All Scripture is given by inspiration of God (literally, "EVERY SCRIPTURE IS GOD-BREATHED" (*Theop-neustos, Gr.*) *II Tkimothy 3:16.* "For the prophecy came not in old time by the will of man: but holy men of God spake as they were moved by The Holy Ghost. (*Lit. were borne along by the Holy Spirit*) II Peter 1:21.

Every Scripture will be fulfilled just as God gave it. It is very hard to be firm and Satan makes it as near impossible as he can. Sometimes, it is all an individual can do to hold steady and this is why for a time. The Reformers aimed to reform the old Church by the Bible; the 'Radicals' attempted to bui9ld an new Church from the Bible! Now, the Reformed Church almost straight across the board can adjust that a bit and go on. They refuse to accept what does not fit the mould for them. They become angry when faced with the issues! Let obedience continue! I find many things fascinating, but especially the fact that there was a very large element of the Church in Britain that immersed until the 17th Century! They drowned and burned many.

BAPTISM is an outward witness to an internal experience that has already occurred. It is a voluntary, requested exerience to serve a believer as the testimony of that inward change, which occurred at the moment he or she, by faith, received The Lord Jesus Christ into their heart and life as their personal, Eternal Savior, Acts 2:41, Acts 8:37; 10:44-48 "This ordinance (of baptism) was regarded in the ancient church as the sacrament of the new birth or regeneration and as the solemn rite of initiation into the Christian Church, admitting to all her benefits and committing to all her obligations. It was supposed to be preceded, in the case of adults, by the instruction on the part of the church, and by repentance and faith (i.e. conversion) on the part of the candidate, and to complete and seal the spiritual process of regeneration, the old man being buried, and the new man arising from the watery grave.

Its effect consists in the forgiveness of sins and the communication of the Holy Spirit. Justin calls baptism 'the water-bath for the forgiveness of sins and regeneration,' and 'the the bath of conversion and the knowledge of God.' It is often called also illumination, spiritual circumcision, anointing, sealing, gift of grace, symbol of redemption, death of sins, &c.

"Tertullian describes its effect through thus: 'when the soul comes to faith, and becomes transformed through regeneration by water and power from above, it discovers, after the veil of the old corruption is taken away, its whole light.. It is received into the fellowship of the Holy Spirit; and the soul, which unites itself to the Holy Spirit, is followed by the body."

Real Conversion Changes sinners into deeply devout worshipers, who seek earnestly to know and to do God's Will! Rom. 12:1-2 "I beseech you therefore, brethren, by the mercies of God, that ye present your bodies a living sacrifice, holy, acceptable unto God, which is your reasonable service.

"And be not conformed to this world; but be ye transformed by the renewing of your mind, that ye may prove what is that good, and acceptable, and perfect Will of God;"

John 20:28-29 "Thomas answered and said unto Him, My Lord and my God. Jesus saith unto him, Thomas, because thou hast seen me, thou hast believed: blessed are they that have not seen; and, yet have believed. The Christian's Witness by Life, Word and Work Is God's Will!The Son of God said: "Father...not My Will, but Thine be done." - Luke 22:42

"Behold, WHAT MANNER OF LOVE, the Father hath bestowed upon us, that WE should be CALLED the sons of God: therefore, the world knows us not, because it knew Him not. Beloved, NOW are we the sons of God, and it doth not yet appear what we shall be: but we know that, when He shall appear we shall be like Him, for we shall see Him as He is." I John 3:1-2.

"The Christian is God's Living Illustration of God's Love for Man! Hereby perceive we the Love of God, because He laid down His Life for us; and, we ought to lay down our lives for the brethren." - I John 3:17

"Let not your good be evil spoken of; for The Kingdom of God is not meat and drink, but righteousness, and peace, and joy in the Holy Spirit. For he that in these things serves Christ is acceptable to God, and approved of men. Let us therefore follow after the things which make for peace, and things wherewith one may edify (strengthen) another." Romans 14:16-19

Christian Testimony and Baptism (Romans 6 presents the *spiritual truths* that water baptism was to illustrate for all who say: "Seeing is believing." Remember Thomas, who said, "Except I shall *see*, I will NOT BELIEVE!".. But, when his Lord appeared, he believed. Just remember: "The world has yet to *see* a born again human that has become everything God has called him to become!".....and can make him to be NOW!

Rom. 6:1-12 "What shall we say then? Shall we continue in sin that grace may abound? God forbid! How shall WE, that are dead to sin, live any longer therein?"Know ye not, that so many of us as were baptized into Jesus Christ were baptized into His Death?

"Therefore **WE ARE BURIED** with **HIM** by BAPTISM INTO **DEATH** that like as Christ was raised up from the Dead by The Glory of God The Father, EVEN SO we also SHOULD **WALK** in newness of life. "FOR if we have been planted together IN THE LIKENESS of His DEATH, we shall be also in the LIKENESS of His Resurrection:

"KNOWING this, that our OLD MAN IS CRUCIFIED WITH HIM, that the body of sin might be *(Gr. Maketi douleuein ta harmartia) (no longer be the enslaved servant of sin),* that henceforth we should not SERVE sin. "For he that is dead is freed from sin."Now if we be dead with Christ, we believe that we shall also live with Him:

"Knowing that Christ being raised from the dead, dieth no more; death hath no more dominion over Him."For in that He died, He died unto sin *(all humanity's sin)* ONCE: "But in that He Liveth, He Liveth unto God. "Likewise reckon ye...(count it this way) ye also yourselves to be DEAD INDEED unto sin, but ALIVE UNTO GOD through Jesus Christ our Lord." "Let not sin therefore reign in your mortal body, that ye should obey it in the lusts thereof."

Thus having been convinced of our sinfulness and of the saving work of our Lord Jesus Christ on the cross, and having personally appropriated this work of Christ, brought before us in the preceding Bible Text by receiving Him as Savior and Lord, we become proper subjects for baptism and membership in a local New Testament Church. In our sincere desire to do His Will, we are NOW ready to consider The Plain Meaning of Baptism.

INASMUCH as The Greek Word, *'Baptizo'* is properly pronounced in English as "Baptidzo"; and, my computer keyboard does not even allow the forming of true Greek characters, this is written for reader understanding in usual English form!!

CHRISTIAN BAPTISM rests upon the Personal Command of our Lord Jesus Christ as the first act of obedience on the part of all who have believed in Him and embraced Him as Savior and Lord. This is the believer's public declaration of complete identity with God's Holy Redeemer Who died for our sin and was raised again for our Justification, in this way entering into the proper practices of The New Testament Church that illuminate the acts of obedience to the Gospel of Christ, in vivid witness to HIM!

"Go then and make disciples of all the nations, baptizing them into the Name of The Father and of The Son and of The Holy Spirit; Teaching them to observe everything that I have commanded you, and lo, I AM WITH YOU ALL THE DAYS, -- PERPETUALLY, UNIFORMLY AND ON EVERY OCCASION—to the very close of the age. Amen—SO LET IT BE." AMP. N.T. – Matt. 28:20.

THE PHRASE, "Baptizing into the NAME" sets forth the distinct nature of baptism as a WITNESS of the believer's FAITH in That One Who Died and Arose again, having entered into death in That HOLY SUBSTITUTE Who *IS* the *COMPLETE* PAYMENT for the sin of EVERY MEMBER of Adam's race..*when it is received*!

Paul's witness: "I AM crucified with Christ; nevertheless, I live! yet not I, but Christ liveth IN ME: and the life which I NOW live in the flesh I live by the Faith OF the Son of God, Who loved me and gave Himself for ME." Galatians 2:20

CHAPTER XII
PORTRAYAL OF SPIRIT CONTROL IN BAPTISM

BAPTISM is to BEAR WITNESS to the lost that THE RESURRECTION POWER of our Eternal Christ is at work in His own people; and, that The Mission of His Church is to go with HIS Message of Love for every member of Adam's race. HE is calling ALL HUMANITY to Resurrection Life NOW! "But we see Jesus, Who WAS MADE a little lower than the angels for the SUFFERING of DEATH, *CROWNED* with Glory and Honor; that He by the Grace of God SHOULD taste DEATH for *every man!*" (Every human, every member of Adam's race.) – Hebrews 2:9

God's GIFT of Resurrection Life is His Personal all that believers "should walk in newness of life" (NEW MEN, where are they?) Rom. 6:4; "My children walk in Truth." II John 4 "But IF we walk in The Light, as HE is in the Light, we have fellowship one with another, and The Blood of Jesus Christ, His Son cleanseth (keeps ON cleansing) us from ALL sin."

"I BESEECH you therefore, Brethren, by the Mercies of God, that ye present your bodies a living sacrifice, holy, acceptable unto God which is your REASONABLE SERVICE. AND be not conformed to this world: but be ye transformed by the renewing of your mind, that ye MAY PROVE what is that GOOD and ACCEPTABLE and PERFECT WILL of God." Romans 12:1-2

For those who have held that "sprinkling" better conveys the Holy Spirit's coming UPON the believer, Acts 2:2 is quite clear: "And suddenly there came a sound from Heaven as of a mighty rushing wind, and IT *FILLED ALL* THE *HOUSE* WHERE THEY WERE SITTING." The Infinite

Holy Spirit of God is represented well by the immersion of the believer, as of The Resurrection of our Lord.

"The 'Teaching of the Twelve Apostles' (in ch.7,) enjoins baptism, after catechetical instruction, in these words: 'Baptize into the name of the Father, and of the Son, and of the Holy Ghost in living (running) water. But if thou hast not living water, baptize into other water; and, if thou canst not in cold, then in warm...'"

'Justin Martyr gives the following account of baptism: those who are convinced of the truth of our doctrine, and have promised to live according to it, are exhorted to prayer, fasting and repentance for past sins; we praying and fasting with them. Then they are led by us to a place where is water,... they receive the water-bath in the name of god, the Father and Ruler of all, and of our Redeemer Jesus Christ, and of the Holy Ghost. For Christ says: except ye be born again, ye cannot enter into the kingdom of heaven. (John 3:5),.. from children of necessity and ignorance, we become children of choice and of wisdom, and partakers of the forgiveness of former sins..... The baptismal bath is called also illumination *(psotismos),* because those who receive it are enlightened in the understanding."....

"The *Didache,(The Teaching of The Twelve)* allows pouring in cases of scarcity of water. But afterwards this mode was applied only to infirm or sick persons; hence called *clinical* baptism. The validity of this baptism was even doubted by many in the third century..." *Schaff, History of the Christian Church, Vol.I p247-254.*

(THE DIDACHE or The Teaching of The Twelve Apostles, from the early 2nd Century, **by an unknown writer,** reflects beliefs of that period, affected, itself, by heresies already at work.)

At The Great Schism of the Church, in 1054 A.D., The Roman Catholic Church chose the experience of Constantine as a model (but rejected the fact that he was immersed: NO OTHER thing was CONSIDERED but *immersion* for baptism in those days!!) The Roman Magistrates did whatever pleased them!! They chose sprinkling as the primary form of baptism and retained this form in defiance of the Eastern Church! They sold indulgences for the raising of money. They promoted their priesthood to have power to forgive sins; and their pope to the position of Christ (they fall on their knees in adoration, kissing his hand); and, he had power to change the form of baptism. This, was to be regretted, but, was not corrected in the Reformation, even though the leaders of the Reformation believed in immersion. Some deny this to be true but their unbelief doesn't alter facts. They Deified Mary, even though that was not done until the 18th Century!! Constantine was there and He demanded the best in his belief in the significance of baptism with the passion to go into the presence of his Lord without any failure to mar his record of performance!! His stature as a churchman became a model, made so by church leaders.

The Greek Church retained and followed the true meaning of that Greek Word *baptidzo;* and, continued to immerse! All who were the recipients of membership in their churches, including infants, were immersed! Probably their immersion of infants would have been sufficient to block all Anabaptist participation.

"It was in the early years of the eleventh century, that the first reports of the appearance of heresy were bruited about here and there in Italy and Southern France. About the year 1000 a certain Leuthard, claiming to be inspired, appeared in the diocese of Chalons, destroying crosses and denouncing tithes. In 1012 Manichean separatists appeared for the first time in Germany, at Mainz, and in 1022 at Orleans, where King Robert and his consort.

Constace were present at their trial. Fifteen were tried, and thirteen remained stedfast, and perished in the flames. Constance is said to have struck one of them, her former confessor, with a staff and to have put out one of his eyes. Heretics appeared at Liege in 1025. About the same time a group was discovered in Treves who denied transubstantiation and rejected infant baptism. The castle of Monteforte near Turin became a stronghold for them, and in 1034 Heribert, archbishop of Milan, seized some of their number, including their leader Gerard. They all accepted death in the flames rather than adore a cross. In 1052 they appeared at Goslar, where the guilty were discerned by their refusal to kill a chicken. With these notices, and a few more like them, the rumor of heresy is exhausted for nearly a century." HISTORY OF THE CHRISTIAN CHURCH, Philip Schaff, Vol V, p. 472

The further historical significance of immersion of **BELIEVERS** in water as indication of full release from the judgment of the slavery of sin is drawn from the Old Testament experience of Israel redeemed from Egyptian slavery is richly and vividly set in graphic illustration for believers in I Corinthians 10:1-2 "Moreover, Brethren, I would not that ye should be untaught that all our fathers were under the cloud and all passed through the sea; And were all baptized unto Moses in the cloud and in the sea;"

THE CLOUD AND THE SEA are clearly used here to portray that God's people, in their being set free from slavery as they left Egypt, had the Red Sea opened before them; and, the Cloud of God's own Presence covered them in that Exodus from Egypt. Egypt is used in a very broad way in Scripture to illustrate this present world. No more graphic picture could be printed in The Scripture Text.

PETER CONCLUDED HIS MESSAGE on the Day of Pentecost, by saying: "THEREFORE let all the House of Israel KNOW ASSUREDLY, that God hath made that same Jesus, Whom ye have crucified, both LORD and CHRIST.""NOW WHEN THEY HEARD THIS, they were pricked in their heart, and said unto Peter and to the rest of the Apostles, Men and Brethren, What shall we do?

"Then Peter said unto them, Repent, and be baptized EVERY ONE OF YOU in the Name of Jesus Christ for, (i.e. *as a witness to)* the remission of sins, and ye shall receive the Gift of The Holy Spirit..

"Then, they that gladly RECEIVED HIS WORD were baptized." "... and let each one of you be baptized upon the ground of your confession of belief in the sum total of all that Jesus Christ is in His glorious Person, this baptismal testimony being in relation to the fact that your sins have been put away..." Kenneth Wuest: *An Expanded Translation*

Careful study of The New Testament Church practice dispels any reasonable doubt that water baptism is a clear command of the Lord

Jesus Christ and initiates the Christian into he public profession of Faith in taking our stand for Him before the world in The Church Age. The Gospel of Mark complements The Great Commission text that is given in Matthew 28:18-20.

Mark 16:15, 16 – And He said unto them, Go ye into all the world, and preach the Gospel to every creature. "He that believeth and is baptized shall be saved: but he that BELIEVETH NOT shall be damned."

It is essential that clear comprehension be gained from Scripture, lest we stumble into an ancient heresy that His Ordinances are an Integral *PART* of the FINISHED WORK of our Savior. The Blood of the Cross and in His Glorious Resurrection. NOTHING must EVER blind us to the Eternal Truth that THE LORD JESUS CHRIST, and HE ALONE is THE SAVIOR OF THE WORLD..not works, water, or wisdom of men. His Ordinances (commands) are not to be attached to HIS COMPLETED WORK in His death, burial and Resurrection, as 'Sacraments.' Obedience is obedience, not helping Him SAVE US. Salvation is by FAITH "not of works lest any man should boast." Eph. 2;8-9. (That eliminates 'saving sacraments'.)

"FOR *BY ONE OFFERING, HE* has *PERFECTED FOREVER* them that are sanctified." Heb. 10:14

These *O R D I N A N C E S* for The New Testament Church were practiced as acts of obedience by all believers; and, for proper order in the church. There would be the immersing of believers and the sweet sharing in the Communion Service, not as sacraments but as proper acts of obedience, deep reverence, and true communion with our wonderful Christ and our God! These were ORDAINED TO BE a witness, also, to an unbelieving world. Satan has constantly created turmoil, confusion and chaos, to seek to destroy the church at every turn!

God Ordained Observances, prayers and meditation as we anticipate His Coming, until He returns to take His Church to be forever with Himself! Virtually every division of the professed body of the visible Church on earth so understands this to be our Lord's order and uses water for the immersion of the believer in the receiving of baptism.

THE FALL OF MAN and the resulting death imposed as man's sentence from God for obeying Satan, presupposes Satan's power over the human race; and, anticipates his meddling with all facets of the human experience, both physical and spiritual. In his raging fury Satan marshaled every willing perverted human mind to fight his battles against the Truth of God, that could be deceived into his cause by use of human ego that envisioned personal glory from the attack of EVERY DOCTRINE of The New Testament Faith.

Such attacks by Satan by means of his spiritually blind dupes were vicious and destructive, from the very arrival of Messiah Christ at the Inn in Bethlehem, attacking His Deity, His Saving Work and His Lordship over all; then, the efficacy of His Finished Salvation on behalf of humanity; and, His Ownership of all creation.

The following illustrates Satan's devious, deadly machinations: "The strict Roman Catholic dogma, first clearly enunciated by St. Augustin (though with reluctant heart and in the mildest form), assigns all *unbaptized* infants to hell on the ground of Adam's sin and the absolute necessity of baptism for salvation. A *dogma horrible*, but *falsum*. Christ, who is The Truth, blessed *unbaptized* infants, and declared: "To such belongs the kingdom of heaven." The Augsburg Confession (*Art. IX.*) still teaches against the Anabaptists:

"*quod baptismus sit necessarius ad saluted*, but the leading Lutheran divines reduce the absolute necessity of baptism to a relative or ordinary necessity; and the Reformed churches, under the influence of Calvin's teaching, went further by making salvation depend upon divine election, not upon the sacraments, and now generally hold to the salvation of all infants dying in infancy. The Second Scotch Confession (A.D. 1580) was the first to declare its abhorrence of "the cruel (popish) judgment against infants departing without the sacrament," and the doctrine of "the absolute necessity of baptism." *SCHAFF, Vol. II, p.255, Note.*

This tragic, false, destructive heresy contributes heavily to church division, makes salvation dependent upon use of material means beyond the Redeeming Blood of The Eternal Son of God and, shatters the assurance of believers improperly and unjustly.

Essentially, man as designed is a spiritual being, as every segment of the whole heathen world bears witness. THEREFORE, further clarification of God's teaching is essential to the good health of HIS Church!

A.H. STRONG, Scholar, Theologian and voluminous writer, Author of Strong's Systematic Theology; editor of Strong's Exhaustive Concordance, with its Hebrew and Chaldee Dictionary; and, Greek New Testament Dictionary, covering every facet of Holy Scripture, is without doubt a master linguist. He declares:

THE MODE OF BAPTISM: "This is immersion, and immersion only. This appears from the following considerations:

A. The Command to baptize is a command to immerse. We show this: (a) From the meaning of the original word *baptidzo*. That this is to immerse, appears: FIRST – from the usage of Greek writers...including the Church Fathers,...and the authors of the Greek Version of the Old Testament.LIDDELL AND SCOTT, GREEK LEXICON: "*baptizo*". To dip in or under water; Lat. *Immerge.*"

SOPHOCLES, Lexicon of Greek Usage in the Roman and Byzantine Periods, 140 B.C. to 1,000 A.D. – *baptizo, to dip, to immerse, to sink...* There is no evidence that Luke and Paul and the other writers of the N.T. put upon this verb meanings not recognized by the Greeks."

THAYER, N.T. Lexicon: "*baptidzo*, literally to dip, to dip repeatedly, to submerge,...metaphorically, to overwhelm.... *baptisma* immersion, submersion... a rite of sacred immersion commanded by Christ."

PROF. GOODWIN of Harvard University, Feb. 13, 1895, says: "The classical meaning of *baptizo*, which seldom occurs, and of the more common *bapto,* is to dip, (literally ormetaphorically), and I never heard of its having any other meaning anywhere. Certainly I never saw a lexicon which gives either sprinkle or pour, as meanings of either. I must be allowed to ask why I am so often asked this question, which seems to me to have but one perfectly plain answers. THE INTERNATIONAL CRITICAL COMMENTARY.

PLUMMER, on Luke, p. 86 – "It is only when baptism is administered by immersion that its full significance is seen."

ABBOT on Colossians, p. 251- : "The figure was naturally suggested by the immersion in **baptism**" see GOULD on Mark, p. 127; SANDAY on Romans, p. 154-157. No one of these four Commentaries was written by a Baptist.

Conant, Appendix to Bible Union Version of Matthew, 1-64, has examples "drawn from writers in almost every department of literature and science; from poets, rhetoricians, philosophers, critics, historians, geographers; from writers on husbandry, on medicine, on natural history, on grammar, on theology; from almost every form and style of composition, romances, epistles, orations, fables, odes, epigrams, sermons, narratives: from writers of various nations and religions, Pagan, Jew, and Christian, belonging to many countries and through a long succession of ages. *IN ALL*, *THE WORD* HAS RETAINED ITS GROUND-MEANING WITHOUT CHANGE. FROM THE EARLIEST AGE OF GREEK LITERATURE down to its close, a period of nearly two thousand years, NOT AN EXAMPLE has been found in which the word HAS *ANY OTHER MEANING.* THERE IS NO INSTANCE in which it signifies to make a partial application of water by affusion or sprinkling, or to cleanse, to purify, apart from the *literal act of immersion* as the means of cleansing or purifying." (pointed truth emphasis given here.) See Stuart, in Bib. Reports., 1833L313; See Broadus on Immersion, 57, note. *A.H. Strong – Systematic Theology, p.933, par.9.*

See quotation from Maimonides in Ingham, Handbook of Baptism, 373, "'Whenever in the law washing of the flesh or of the clothes is mentioned, it means nothing else than the dipping of the whole body in a laver; for if any man dip himself all over except the tip of his little finger, he is still in his uncleanness... *"Watson, in Annotated Par. Bible, 1126."*

Cramer, Lexicon of N.T. Greek, *sub voce- "Baptidzo", immersion or submersion for a religious purpose,"* Grimm's ed. Of Wilke – *"baptidzo", 1. Immerse, submerge; 2. wash or bathe, by immersing or submerging...* In the N.T. rite, he says it denotes "an immersion in water, intended as a sign of sins washed away, and received by those who wished to be admitted to the benefits of Messiah's reign."

A.J. Gordon, Ministry of the Spirit, 67 – "The upper room became the Spirit's baptistery. His Presence 'filled all the house where they were sitting' (Acts 2:2)...Baptism in the Holy Spirit was given once for all on the day of Pentecost, when The Paraclete came in Person to make His abode in The Church."

Meyer's Com. On Matt. 3:11 – *"en"* is in accordance with the meaning of *baptidzo* (immerse) not to be interpreted instrumentally, but on the contrary, in the sense of the element in which the immersion takes place."

SURELY THE DEFINITION of the word and the consistency of its usage, the fact that the colorful Greek language is so exact in its meaning, rules out flexibility of interpretation. These by no means stand alone in their providing clear and vivid concepts of the true meaning, as will be noted later, but let us first consider the Scripture Texts, upon which EACH reached their conclusion and conviction, which every scholar thus far noted, has confirmed for us. ACTS 2:41 Greek Text: *"Oi-men.oun 'asnenws apodexamenoi* "Those therefore who gladly welcomed his word *e'Baptisthasan, were baptized."*

DR. A.T. ROBERTSON, in WORD PICTURES IN THE NEW TESTAMENT, says: *Vol.III, p.37 – "Oun* connects with what precedes as the result of Peter's sermon while *men* points toward what is to follow. *Many were baptized (ebaptisthesan).* First aorist passive indicative, constative aorist. Only those who had already received the word were converted, were baptized."

ATHANASIUS, --"The father of orthodoxy, always bases his conclusions upon Scripture, and appeals to the authority of tradition only in proof that he rightly understands and expounds the sacred books. The Catholic faith, says he, is that which the Lord *gave,* the apostles *preached,* and the fathers have *preserved;* upon this the church is founded, and he who departs from this faith can no longer be called a Christian." – *Philip Schaff, HISTORY of the CHRISTIAN CHURCH, Vol. III, p. 606,607.*

MAY WE ALSO CONSIDER that until 1450 A.D., ALL manuscripts of Holy Scripture and Church Records were, by necessity, prepared in manuscript form by hand; and, were not freely available to all of The Church Fathers or to the Church at large, The Proper Biblical Basis for Baptism, The Plain Meaning of Baptism, we now proceed to Chapter XIII, The Prime Elements of **Baptism.**

Chapter XIII

POWER OF CHANGE
BY BAPTISM

T HERE ARE A NUMBER of usages in the old testament of words
which imply a total "dipping" of the finger (having nothing to do
with baptism) but, the nearest experience to dipping the entire body is
found in I Kings 5:14, "Then went he down, and dipped himself seven
times in the Jordan" and it has some connotations of what believer's
baptism bears witness in the New Testament. But in reality seven in the
number of completeness to which every believer bears testimony in the
waters of baptism. Certainly leprosy is the best picture of sin to be found
in the Bible. I think it is quite fascinating.

THE PRIME ELEMENTS of a true experience in baptism that is
according to Holy Scripture, it is needful to show that it includes: Faith
in the Death, Burial, and Resurrection of the Crucified, Living Christ,
believing it was in our place that He died! It was for us! We believe that
He is the Eternal Son of God who cannot lie! That He is as Eternal as the
Father. Just remember that the God we worship is able "of these stones,
to raise up children unto Abraham!" Also, that our Lord said, "Before
Abraham was, I AM!" HE IS "The "Eternal I Am"!

"**THEREFORE WE ARE BURIED** with Him by baptism into death, that
as Christ was raised up from the dead by the glory of the Father, even so we
also should walk in newness of life." Romans 6:4, The Eternal Life to which
even we are given is the "from eternity to eternity" KIND of life! And It is all
because of HIM!! FOREVER, O Lord, THY WORD is settled in Heaven!

"Therefore, if any man be in Christ, he is a new Creation; old things are
passed away; behold, all things are become new." II Corinthians 5:17.

"I HAVE BEEN crucified with Christ: nevertheless I LIVE; yet not I, but CHRIST LIVETH in ME; and the Life which I NOW LIVE in the flesh I live by THE faith of THE SON OF GOD, who loved me and gave HIMSELF for ME!" Galatians 2:20. (*sunestauromai*) 1 pers. Sing.. perf. Ind. Pass. IT IS DONE! And I had nothing to do with it, but accept it and yield myself to HIM! THANK GOD! I DIED in my Perfect Substitute and arose with HIM!

MOREOVER, BRETREN, I would not that ye should be ignorant, that all our fathers were under the cloud, and all passed through the sea, And were all baptized unto Moses in the cloud and in the sea;" I Corinthians 10:1,2.

The element relative to baptism is the figure represented by baptism in the cloud and in the sea! It is classic as a vivid portrayal of baptism, even as deaf mute language underscores the silent message conveyed to all who observe that witness.

"BEING BORN AGAIN, not of corruptible seed, but of incorruptible, by the Word of God, which Liveth and Abideth FOREVER!." I Peter 1:23. As if the sphinx appeared, coming out of the water as a clean creation! In all of the pedo-baptist language used, the figurative resurrection vanishes. Is it not quite strange that there is a rage given vent to in seeking to destroy immersionists; and, that history is filled with their preoccupation with it?

THE HORRIBLE PERSECUTIONS, troubling heresies and false teaching that mushroomed out of the Holy Land, make it extremely difficult to trace what kinds of 'Gospel' spread to the Far East. Surely the chaos that existed leaves Truth in the gracious Hand of God. How much did the hearers understand? When The British made contact with China, they were greeted by the Cross, but significantly the real content of the message was strongly clouded. By the seventh century much of the Far East was reached with the message of Christ.

The Muslim religion copied suitable material from Christian teachings to fabricate a Jesus who will come back for war; Simon the sorcerer developed a great following as a baptized apostate! The Nestorian cult spread like wild fire, teaching that Jesus Christ was two people, one who died; and, One who had risen from the dead!

> "Near singan-fu (Cathay and the Way hither" Col Sir Henry 'Ule, Hakluyt Society) a slab was found containing a long inscription in the Syriac and Chinese, dating from the reign of Te Tsung (780-3). At the top is a cross and the heading "Monument commemorating the introduction and propagation of the noble law of Ta Ts' in the Middle Kingdom. Among other things it records the coming of a missionary, Olopun, from the Empire of Ta Ts' in 635, bringing sacred books and images, tells how the books were translated, the doctrine approved by the imperial authority and permission given to teach it publicly. It describes the spread of the doctrine, and how later, Buddhism made more progress, but, under Hiuan Tsung (713-755) a new missionary Kiho came and the Church was revived.

About the middle of the fifth century, just when the doctrine of the person of Christ reached its formal settlement, the first representations of Christ Himself appeared, even said by tradition to be faithful portraits of the original. (The image-hating Sensorians ascribed the origin of Iconolatry to their hated opponent, Cyril of Alexandria, and put it into connection with the Monophesite heresy (Assem., p.401).

When our Holy Redeemer stated in Matthew 16:18, **"And I say also unto thee, That thou art Peter,** (*Petros,* a pebble) **and upon This Rock (The Infinite Rock of ages) I will build MY church,** *And the gates of Hades shall not prevail against it."* He was stating a principle that would characterize the Church age! It was to be an entire age of conflict. We get tired in the battle...but it continues!! It takes every conceivable form and we are driven to prayer! Our challenge is to rest on The Rock, but we are lured from it! I Corinthians 15:58.

Isaiah 51:14 "As many were astounded at thee His Vissage was so marred more than any man, and his form more than the sons of men"--

His form was marred beyond recognition—Mary, His most devoted follower, didn't recognize him! 300 years of blood in ten hideous persecutions, then came the centuries where they were hunted and murdered! What our Lord wished to prepare His people for is: We have 2000 years of facing every challenge that the forces of Hell can muster! But, thank God we are more than conquerors through Him that loved us and gave HIMSELF for US!!

"And what shall we more say? For the time would fail me to tell of Gideon, and of Barak, and of Samson, and of Jephthah of David also, and Samuel, and of the prophets, who through faith, subdued kingdoms, wrought righteousness, obtained promises, stopped the mouths of lions, quenched the violence of fire, escaped the edge of the sword, out of weakness were made strong, became valiant in fight turned to flight the armies of aliens. Women received their dead raised to life again, and others were tortured, not accepting deliverance, that they might obtain a better resurrection: and others had trial of cruel mockings and scourgings, yea, moreover of bonds and imprisonment; they were stoned, they were sawn asunder, were tested, were slain with the sword; they wandered about in sheepskins and goatskins; being destitute, afflicted, tormented (of whom the world was not worthy) they wandered in deserts and in mountains, and in dens and caves of the earth. And these all received witness through faith, received not the promise, God having provided some better thing for us, that they without us should not be made perfect." Hebrews 11:32-40

IT IS WELL that the Apostles had a teacher like no other, but as strongly and as infinitely worded as the Upper Room discourse was, it is beautiful that we can rest, rejoice and find the Power of God in "all Scripture!" II Tim 3:16,17.

(Matthew 13:24-30); The exhortations and warnings of the New Testament against false doctrine must be constantly heeded because of the deadly peril of Satan's delusions and near infinite attacks. For Centuries true believers protected the Holy Scriptures and refused to reveal where they were hidden, lest they be destroyed. Roman Catholicism deliberately kept their people ignorant of Holy Scripture, preaching in Latin and 'explaining' to their people that they were far too ignorant of divine things to understand so they, therefore, must have them 'explained' in Latin. It was illegal and dangerous to give copies of Scripture to their people. Their vigil was constant! Only when they were forced to do so, the priests forsook Latin; but, did insist their people must have The Scriptures "interpreted" for them.

'1. The Judaizing tendency of the fallen human mind and heart endangered all men, but especially the Jewish mind. With the Jewish Order already in place, it became a perennial threat, being used of Satan to taunt and lure all Christendom; and, alert to the fact that "a little leaven, leaveneth the whole lump,

'2. The opposite extreme is a false Gentile Christianity, which may be called the Paganizing or Gnostic heresy. It is as radical and revolutionary as the other is treacherous and deadly. It violently breaks away from the past, while the Judaizing heresies held tenaciously and stubbornly to ritual.

"3. As attempts had already made, before Christ, by Philo, by the Therapeutae and the Essenes, etc. to blend the Jewish religion with heathen philosophy, especially that of Pythagoras and Plato, so now, under the Christian name, there appeared confused combinations of these opposite systems, forming either a Paganising Judaism, *i.e.* Gnostic Ebionism, or a Judaizing Paganism, *i.e.* Ebionistic Gnosticism, according as the Jewish or the heathen element prevailed." HISTORY OF THE CHRISTIAN CHURCH, Philip Schaff, Vol. 1, p. 555, 556.

"As the great Mohammedan invasion swept over Persia, large numbers of the Chaldeans, or Nestorian, Christians were either scattered or absorbed into Islam, especially to Arabia and southern Persia. When order was restored, however, and the Abbaside Califs were reigning in Baghdad, Syrian Christians became prominent at the court as doctors and teachers of philosopy, science, and literature. In 762 the Catholikos removed from Selucia, which was ruined, to the new capital of the conquerors, at Baghdad.

"The rise of Genghis Khan and his immense conquests, leading (1258) to the capture of Baghdad by the Mongols, did not greatly affect the Syrian

Church. The heathen Mongol rulers were tolerant, and they employed Nestorians in important political negotiations with the western powers, with the object of combining with them for the destruction of Islam. Active in these negotiations was a Chinese Nestorian, Yabh-alaha III, who rose from lowly rank to be Catholikos of the Syrian Church (1281-1317).

"From the seventh century to the thirteenth the Syrian Church was as important in the East as the Roman and Greek Churches were in the West. It covered immense territories and included large populations. From Persia and Syria, it spread it had spread until it became numerous with long established missions in India and China. The majority of the peoples of Turkestan, with their rulers had accepted Christianity, and in the chief centers of Asia the Christian church was to be found along with the heathen temple and the Mohammedan mosque." THE PILGRIM CHURCH, E.H. Broadbent, p. 78-81.

"The only difference between John's baptism, and the baptism of our time, is that John's baptism upon profession of faith in a savior yet to come: baptism is now administered upon profession of faith in a Savior who has actually and already come." DOGMATIC THEOLOGY, p. 932.

THE GREEK TEXT was prepared for classic and refined theology of the New Testament age. Eight tenses with provision for the most refined of meanings that make a difference. The present tense is endless, hence eternal. *Baptizo* leaves no room for posturing, specifically indicating immersion for baptism.

"Centuries before the beginning of the Christian era (660 B.C.-341A.D.) The Greeks had wrought out a civilization that in literature, philosophy, science, and art, greatly surpassed the achievements of all other nations. Their language had been so developed as to constitute the most perfect instrument for the embodiment and conveyance of thought that had ever been known and is still unsurpassed." A MANUAL OF CHURCH HISTORY by Albert, Henry Newman, D.D., LL. D., P.20

IN THE CONSECRATION of the Priesthood of Israel to show the hallowed place of mediation, the high priest was brought before the tabernacle, where great efforts were made to emphasize the holiness of God. Exodus 28:1-46. We speak of "the priesthood of believers", Revelation 1:6; and it is well for every believer to bear in mind that coming before the Throne of Grace in worship and intercession for ourselves and for others, should be one which sets us apart in "holiness to the Lord."

One hundred fifty years before the Christian Era, the Essenes lived in separate communities. Membership was obtained by initiation of sacred rites into the order. After a year's probation and instruction they were to proceed with an initiation quite like believers' baptism. After two full years further testing they were introduced to the common meals and a full communion.

JOHN'S BAPTISM is a 'baptism unto repentance'. It was for Israel and for Israel alone! It was a calling of God to Repentance for that great nation, Malachi 4:6. Many horrible years had passed since Israel had been given freedom by King Cyrus to return to their land. But Syria and Egypt played out their war games there with tragic results! The priesthood was purchased with huge sums from Rome; and, the Levitical Order was maintained. There is, however, bound into the Abrahamic Covenant, eternal blessings for Israel! But it is clearly evident that in the Covenant with Israel, provision was made for "All the families of the earth." "AND in thee shall all the families of the earth be blessed." Genesis 12:3

IT IS VERY TRUE that "They answered and said unto him, Abraham is our father," "BUT, I say unto you, I will not drink HENCEFORTH of this fruit of the vine, until that day when I drink it NEW with YOU in my Father's kingdom!" Matthew 26:29.

This was to have an expanding influence, and also a supernatural development. Twelve Thrones, twelve chosen men, and, His Transformed Body, Supernatural, Complete and Absolute! It will reach into the infinity of the eternal ages! Be not unwise, but understanding what the Will of the Lord is! It will be Absolute. The Church shall have splendor as a Body, a Building, and a Bride. Baptism with fire is symbolic (Matt. 3:11; Acts 2:3), (The reality is Awesome!) built upon the Foundation of the Apostles and Propohets!

MATTHEW 3:5-6 – OF JOHN THE BAPTIST" "Then went out all Jerusalem, and all Judaea, and all the region round about Jordan, and were baptized of him in Jordan, confessing their sins. v. 13-17. "Then cometh Jesus from Galilee to Jordan unto John, to be baptized of him. But John forbade him, saying, I have need to be baptized of thee, and comest Thou to me?

And Jesus answering said unto him, Suffer it to be so now: for thus it becometh us to fulfill all righteousness. Then he suffered him. And Jesus, when he was baptized, went up straight way out of the water: and, lo, the heavens were opened unto him, and he saw the Spirit of God descending like a dove, and lighting upon him: and, lo a Voice from Heaven saying, This is my beloved Son, in Whom I am well pleased."

MARK 1:5 – "And there went out unto him all the land of Judaea, and they of Jerusalem, and were all baptized of John IN Jordan, confessing their sins."

9. "And it came to pass in those days, that Jesus came from Nazareth of Galilee, and was baptized of John IN Jordan." (The first "in" of v.9, is the Greek Word, "*en*", (in); while the second is "*eis*" (into); and, is properly so translated in many places in The King James Version.

Greek Lexicon: "*eis*" – "Of a place ENTERED, or, entrance INTO a place. – *Thayers Greek English Lexicon.*

The evidence that immersion is the original mode of baptism is well summed up by Dr. Marcus Dods, in his article on Baptism in Hastings' Dictionary of Christ and the Apostles.

MARK 1:10-11 – "And straightway COMING UP OUT OF THE WATER, He saw the Heavens opened, and The Spirit like a dove descending upon Him: and there came a Voice from Heaven, saying, Thou art My Beloved Son, in Whom I am well pleased."

JOHN 3:23 "And John also was baptizing in Aenon near to Salim, BECAUSE THERE WAS MUCH WATER THERE: and they came, and were baptized."

ROMANS 6, sets forth the Christian's SPIRITUAL experience of I Corinthians 12:13 "For BY *ONE SPIRIT* are we all *BAPTIZED INTO ONE BODY,* whether we be Jews or Gentiles, whether we be bond or free; and have been ALL made to DRINK *INTO* ONE SPIRIT." Romans 6, explains The Truth taught in water baptism.

ROMANS 6:3 – "Know ye not, that so many of us as were baptized INTO Jesus Christ were baptized INTO *His DEATH?*"

(One of the Church's greater scholars, but a fervent advocate of "sprinkling" objected to the fact that the word, *"baptidzo" is in the Greek Aorist Tense, making it permanent in nature, teaching: "conformity to the WORD baptizo is like saying 'he that believeth and is DROWNED shall be saved."*

ON THE CONTRARY, the graphics are beautiful! Believers by being baptized, testify to their faith: "having died *with* HIM, they (Galatians 2:20), being RISEN WITH HIM, Colossians 3:1-4; and, being CALLED OF GOD, rise to "walk in NEWNESS OF LIFE."

ROMANS 6:4-6, therefore proceeds on to say: "THEREFORE we are BURIED *WITH HIM* by BAPTISM INTO DEATH: that LIKE as Christ WAS RAISED UP from the dead by the Glory of the Father, EVEN SO, we also SHOULD *WALK* in NEWNESS OF LIFE. *(Declaring identity with The Crucified, Risen Christ)*

"For if we have been PLANTED together in the LIKENESS of His Death, we shall be also in the likeness of HIS RESURRECTION:

"Knowing this, that our old man is crucified with Him, that the body of sin might be destroyed, that henceforth we should not serve sin." *"symbol... picture"* – Robertson – *Word Pictures-p362.*

(Verse 5, from the above text implies that baptism is to be like two things: That which is planted AND that which is buried. This designed significance holds throughout The New Testament, a major case in point which well portrays the Christian's reckoning dead their old nature drawn from Adam; and, their received New Nature of Life, as drawn from our Eternal, indwelling Christ through God's Spirit in our Conversion Experience:

Colossians 2:10-15 "And ye are complete in Him, which is The Head of ALL principality and power; In WHOM also ye are circumcised with the circumcision made without hands, in putting off the body of the sins of the flesh by the circumcision of Christ: BURIED with HIM in baptism, (I Corinthians 12:13) wherein also ye are RISEN WITH HIM through the faith of the operation of God, who hath raised Him from the Dead.

"And YOU, being dead in your sins, and the uncircumcision of your flesh, hath He MADE ALIVE, together with Him, having forgiven you ALL TRESPASSES; BLOTTING OUT the handwriting of ordinances THAT WAS against us, which was contrary to us, and took it out of the way, nailing it to His Cross; and having spoiled principalities and powers, he made a shew of them openly, triumphing over them in it."

ACTS 2:41 "Then THEY THAT GLADLY RECEIVED THE WORD were baptized: and the same day there were added unto them about three thousand souls."

Acts 8:12-13 "BUT WHEN THEY BELIEVED PHILIP preaching the things concerning the Kingdom of God, and The Name of Jesus Christ, they were baptized, both men and women. Then Simon himself believed also: and when he was baptized, he continued with Philip, and wondered, beholding the miracles and signs which were done."

Paul, at Ephesus, found those who had been baptized by John, Acts 19:4-5 "WHEN THEY HEARD THIS, they were baptized in The Name of The Lord Jesus."

INASMUCH AS (John 3:22-23) "After these things came Jesus and his disciples unto the land of Judea; and there he tarried with them, and baptized. And John also was baptizing in Aenon near to Salim, because there was much water there."

"It seems that *baptize,* both in the Jewish and Christian context, normally meant immerse and even when it became a technical term for baptism, the thought of immersion remains. The metaphorical uses of the word in the NT appears to take this for granted, such as the prophecy that the Messiah will baptize in Spirit and fire (Matt. 3:11), the "baptism" of the Israelites in the cloud and the sea (I Cor. 10:2), and Jesus' death as a baptism (Mk. 10:38-39: Lk. 12:50). The Pauline representation with Christ is consonant with this view." Dictionary of N.T. Theology. Vol 1. P, 85

THE HURLBUT DICTIONARY seems to make it quite clear that the immersion of converts in the Jordan River is not the absurd matter that pedo-baptists have indicated. In fact, at the time, it was very adequate to accommodate the large number of repent- ants.

"THE JORDAN RIVER varies in width from eighty to one hundred eighty feet, and in depth from five to twelve feet." Or, a channel that was 9 feet in depth and eighty feet wide. Its course travels over 200 miles in covering the distance of sixty miles. By this we may know that there was very abundant water for the immersion of believers.

IT BECOMES VERY CLEAR as we consider The Text of Holy Scripture, that there is no possible way to misconstrue the obvious significance of the immersion of a believer in water. It is The Command of our Lord. It sets forth the believer's witness of personal faith that our Lord's Substitutionary Death for each sinner that trusts His Eternally Atoning Death has received that New Life by Faith, placing that believer INTO a New Way and a New Kind of Life. It is his witness of assurance of The Blessed Hope, that there shall be a resurrection of the physical body; and, that inasmuch as every barrier between our soul and our Savior has been forever removed, we presently find ourselves Converted, to have become New Creatures in Christ, our Resurrected Head, with His having taken us with Himself into The Spiritual Realms to live, walk and work in His Kingdom of Love, liberated from the shackles of sin and to have been Commissioned by our Divine Lord to be a fervent and faithful witness to The Truth of The Glorious Gospel of Christ that has proven Its Power to our own hearts. Also, knowing that when we leave this body in physical death, we shall find ourselves IMMEDIATELY in His Glorious Presence, Who now freely offers Salvation to every person on earth who will receive it. The Trumpet Call of Almighty God to absolute obedience as loving, servants has been heard through the ages!

HOWEVER, the very point of this writing is to be totally objective so we turn our attention next to the church history by moving to the twelveth century:

Let it be understood that the selections which we have chosen from history were radically and outrageously called 'heresy' when the believers have boldly been labeled 'heretic' because of their practice of immersion.

About the middle of the twelfth century, heresy suddenly appeared again at Liege, and prosecutions were begun. In 1145 eight men and their women were burnt at cologne. The firmness of the victims was exemplified in the case of a young woman, who was held back for a time with the promise of marriage, but, on seeing her coreligionists burnt, broke from her keepers and, hiding her face in her dress, threw herself into the flames. And so, Caesar of Heisterbach goes on to say, she descended with her fellow-heretics to hell. At Rheims, 1157, and again at Cologne in 1163 we hear of trials and burnings, but thereafter the Cathari are no more heard of in Germany.

CHAPTER XIV
THE PERSONAL STATEMENTS ON BAPTISM

THE ENGLISH REFORMATIONIST, Wycliffe had so kindled the light of reformation that it began to illumine the darkest corners of popery and ignorance, spreading the light everywhere! "His doctrines spread into Bohemia, and were well received by great numbers of people, but by none so particularly as John Huss, and his zealous friend and fellow martyr, Jerome of Prague." FOX'S BOOK OF MARTYRS, John Fox, (or Foxe), p 144 parag. 3, Edited by: Wm. Byron Forbush.

JEROME OF PRAGUE, companion of Dr. John Huss, a co-martyr of Dr. Huss, born in Prague, educated in that university, where he particularly distinguished himself for his great abilities and learning. He visited several universities and seminaries in Europe, particularly the universities of Paris, Heidelburg, Cologne, and Oxford. At the later place became acquainted with the works of Wickliffe, and being a person of uncommon application, he translated many of them into his native language.

"On his return to Prague, he professed himself an open favorer of Wyckliffe, and finding that his doctrines had made considerable progress in Bohemia, and that Huss was the principal promoter of them. He became an assistant to him in the great work of reformation.

"Finding that his arrival in Constance was publicly known, and that the Council intended to seize him, he thought it most prudent to retire. Accordingly, the next day he went to Iberling, an imperial town, about a mile from Constance.

From this place he wrote to the emperor, and proposed his readiness to appear before the Council, if he would give a safe-conduct; but was refused. He then applied to the Council, but met with an answer no less unfavorable than that from the emperor.

"After this, he set out on his return to Bohemia. He had the precaution to take with him a certificate, signed by several of the Bohemian nobility, then at Constance, testifying that he had used all prudent means in his power to procure a hearing.

"Jerome, however, did not escape. He was seized at Hirsaw by an officer belonging to the duke of Sultsbach, who, though unauthorized to act, made little doubt of obaining thanks from the Council for so acceptable a service.

"The duke of Sultsbach, having Jerome now in his power, wrote to the Council for directions how to proceed. The Council, after expressing their obligations to the duke, desired him to send the prisoner immediately to Constance. The elector Palatine met him on the way, and conducted him into the city, himself riding on horseback, with a numerous retinue, who led Jerome in fetters by a long chain; and immediately on his arrival he was committed to a loathsome dungeon.

"Jerome was treated nearly in the same manner as Huss had been, only that he was much longer confined, and shifted from one prison to another. At length, being brought before the Council, he desired that he might plead his own cause, and exculpate himself: Which being refused him, he broke out into the following exclamation:

"What barbarity is this! For three hundred and forty days I have been confined in a variety of prisons. There is not a misery, there is not a want, that I have not experienced. To my enemies you have allowed the fullest scope of accusation: to me you deny the least opportunity of defense. Not an hour will you indulge me in preparation for my trial. You have swallowed the blackest calumnies against me. You have represented me as a heretic, without knowing my doctrine; as an enemy of the faith, before you knew what faith I professed: as a persecutor of priests before you could have an opportunity of understanding my sentiments on that head. You are a General Council: in you center all this world can communicate of gravity, wisdom, and sanctity: but still you are men, and as men seducible by appearances. The higher your character is for wisdom, the greater ought your care to be not to deviate into folly. The cause i now plead is not my own cause: it is the cause of men, it is the cause of Christians; it is a cause which is to affect the rights of posterity, however the experiment is to be made in my person.

"This speech had not the least effect; Jerome was obliged to hear the charge read, which was reduced under the following head: 1. That he was a derider of the papal dignity. 1. An opposer of the pope. 3. an enemy to the cardinals 4. A persecutor of the prelates 5. a hater of the Christian religion.

"This trial of Jerome was brought on the third day after his accusation and witnesses were examined in support of the charge. The prisoner was prepared for his defense, which appears almost incredible, when we consider he had been three hundred and forty days shut up in loathsome prisons, deprived of daylight, and almost starved for want of common necessities. But his spirit soared above these disadvantages, under which a man less animated would have sunk; nor was he more at a loss of quotations from the fathers and ancient authors than if he had been furnished with the finest library.

"The most bigoted of the assembly were unwilling he should be heard, knowing what effect eloquence is apt to have on the minds of the prejudiced. At length, however, it was carried by the majority that he should have liberty to proceed in his defense, which he began in such an exalted strain of moving elocution that the heart of obdurate zeal was seen to melt, and the mind of superstition seemed to admit a ray of conviction he made an admirable distinction between evidence as resting upon fact, and as supported by malice and calumny. He laid before the assembly the whole tenor of his life and conduct. He observed that the greatest and most holy men, had been known to differ in points of speculation, with a view to distinguish truth, not to keep it concealed. He expressed a noble contempt of all his enemies, who would have induced him to retrace the cause of virtue and truth. He entered upon a high encomium of Huss; and declared he was ready to follow him in the glorious track of martyrdom. He then touched upon the most defensible doctrines of Wycliffe; and concluded with observing that it was far from his intentions to advance anything against the state of the Church of God; that it was only against the abuse of the clergy he complained; and that he could not help saying, it was certainly impious that the patrimony of the Church, which was originally intended for the purpose of charity and universal benevolence, should be prostituted to the pride of the eye, in feasts, foppish vestments, and other reproaches to the name and profession of Christianity.

"The trial being over, Jerome received the same sentence that had been passed upon his martyred countryman. In consequence of this, he was, in the usual style of popish affectation, delivered over to the civil power: but as he was a layman, he had not to undergo "the ceremony of degradation. They had prepared a cap of paper painted with red devils, which being put upon his head, he said, "Our Lord Jesus Christ, when He suffered death for me a most miserable sinner, did wear a crown of thorns upon His Head, and for His sake will I wear this cap.

"Two days were allowed him in hopes that he would recant; in which time the cardinal of Florence used his utmost endeavors to bring him over. But they all proved ineffectual. Jerome was resolved to seal the doctrine with his blood; and he suffered death with the most distinguished magnanimity.

"In going to the place of execution he sang several hymns, and when he came to the spot which was the same where Huss had been burnt, he knelt down, and prayed fervently. He embraced the stake with great cheerfulness, and when they went behind him to set fire to the fagots, he said, "Come here, and kindle it before my eyes; for if I had been afraid of it, I had not come to this place.' The fire being kindled, he sang a hymn, but was soon interrupted by the flames; and the last words he was heard to say these, 'This soul in flames I offer Christ to Thee.'"

The elegant Pogge, a learned gentleman of Florence, secretary to two popes, and a zealous but liberal Catholic, in a letter to Leonard Arotin, bore ample testimony of the extraordinary powers and virtues of Jerome whom he emphatically styles, A prodigious man! FOXS BOOK OF MARTYRS, John Foxe, Edited By: Wm. Byron Forbush, p 144-146.

"Basle was a great centre of spiritual activity. The printers were not afraid to issue books branded as heretical, and from their presses such works as those of Marsiglio of Padua and of John Wycliff went out into the world. Brethren of striking gift and ability were among those who met with Hubmeyer for consideration of Scripture. Of one, Wilhelm Reublin, it is recorded that he expounded the Holy Scriptures in so Christian and excellent way that nothing like it had ever been heard before so that he gained great numbers. He had been a priest in Basle and during that time, at the celebration of the feast of Corpus Christi, had carried a Bible in procession instead of the monstrance.

"He was baptized, and later when living near Zurich, was expelled from the country so continued his preaching in Germany and Moravia. There were often brethren present from abroad through whose visits connections with churches in other lands were maintained. Among these was Richard Crocus from England, a learned man who exercised great influence among students, that came also from France and from Holland.

"In 1527 another conference of brethren was called, in Moravia, at which Hubmeyer was present. It was held under the protection of Count Leonhard and Hans Von Lichtenstein; the former was baptized on this occasion by Hubmeyer, who himself had been baptized two years earlier by Reublin. At that time 110 others had been baptized, and another 300 were baptized afterwards by Hubmeyer, among them his own wife, the daughter of a citizen of Waldshut. The same year Hubmeer and his wife escaped with the loss of everything, from an advancing Austrian army and reached Zurich, but there he was soon discovered by Zwingli's party and thrown into prison.

"The cities of Canton and of Zurich were at this time completely under the influence of Ulrich Zwingli, who had begun the work of Reformation in Switzerland even earlier than Luther in Germany. The doctrine of the

Swiss Reformers, differing in some respects from those taught by Luther; and, had spread over many of the Cantons and far into the German States.

"The Zurich Council arranged a disputation between Hubmeyer and Zwingli in which the former, broken by imprisonment, was overwhelmed by his robust opponent. Afraid of being delivered into the hands of the Emperor, he went so far as to retract some of his teaching, but immediately repented bitterly of this fear of man and besought God to forgive and restore him. From there he went to Constance, then to Augsburg, where he baptized Hans Denck.

It was In Nikolsburg, in Moravia, Hubmeyer was very active as a writer, printing some sixteen books. During his short stay in the district about 6,000 persons were baptized and a number in the churches rose to 15,000 members. The brethren were by no means of one mind on all points, and when the enthusiastic preacher Hans Hut came to Nikolsburg and taught that it was not Scriptural for a believer to bear arms in the service of his country or for the self-defense, or to pay taxes for carrying on war, Hubmeyer opposed him.

In 1525, a controversy arose relative to baptism and legitimately led to the rejection of infant baptism. Those which had been baptized as infants saw the fallacy of this practice. Philip Schaff says, "The demand of rebaptism virtually unjbaptized and unchristianized the entire Christian world, and completed the rupture with the historic Church. It cut the last cord of union of the present with the past."

In regard to Hubmeyer In 1527 King Ferdinand forced the authorities to give Hubmeyer up to him, and brought him to Vienna, where he insisted on his being tortured and executed. Hubmeyer's wife encouraged him to remain firm, and a few months after his arrival in Vienna he was brought to the scaffold set up in the Market Place. He prayed with a loud voice: "Oh, my gracious God, give me patience in my martyrdom! Oh, my Father, I thank Thee that Thou wilt take me today out of this vale of sorrow, Oh Lamb, Lamb, who takest away the sin of the world! Oh my God, into Thy hands I commit my spirit: From the flames he was heard to cry out, "Jesus, Jesus!" Three days later his heroic wife was drowned in the Danube, thrown from the bridge with a stone around her neck.!

IT HARDLY SEEMS that a defense of The Doctrine of the believer's Baptism as set forth in Holy Scripture should be needed when The Reformers, themselves, understood baptism to be the immersion of the total person into Water, just as did the more ancient scholars. The problem arises from wrong concepts relative to The Nation of Israel and the idea God has no future plans for that nation!

Pedo-Baptism, as the 'replacement' of The Sign of Circumcision that God had ordained for Israel as His People, was believed by some to be a *needed* 'sign' for The Church in order that infants of believers would (and should have) participation in The New Covenant for His Church. Martin Luther was challenged on the matter of whether an infant has Faith as needed for baptism, but, his answer was, "PROVE that THEY HAVE NO FAITH!" AND, with this teaching, Salvation is tied to baptism as an INTEGRAL PART OF SALVATION, *rather than* a Testimony to Conversion and to the entering into New Spiritual Life in Christ.

HOWEVER, the CLEAR STATEMENT by our Lord that of such (children) IS The Kingdom of God, all should CLEARLY UNDERSTAND that the little children BELONG TO HIM, by THE RIGHT OF PURCHASE, as is true of EVERY person He has REDEEMED! NEITHER ADULTS *or* infants have a SAVING benefit from baptism or any other works of man, as has been clearly declared by Scriptures such as Ephesians 2:8-9, Titus 3:5, etc.

"In France the Cathari were strong enough in 1167 to hold a council at St. Felix de Carman near Toulouse. It was attended by Nicetas of Constantinople, to whom the title of pope was given. He was accompanied by a Catharan bishop, Marcus of Lombardy. Contemporary reports represent the number of heretics as very large. Contemporary reports represent the number of heretics as very large. They were compared by William of Newburgh to the sand of the sea, and were said by Walter Map to be infinite in number in Aquitaine and Burgundy. By the end of the twelfth century they were reported to have followers in nearly 1000 cities. The Dominican Raineruys gave 4,000,000 as a safe estimate of their number and declared this was according to a census made by the Cathari themselves." HISTORY OF THE CHRISTIAN CHURCH, VOL.V, P. 473.

THE WORD "BAPTIZE", *Gr. Baptidzo "a word peculiar to N.T. and ecclesiastical writing, immersion, submersion"(y 1)= To dip repeatedly, to immerge, submerge." (2)= to cleanse by dipping or submerging, to wash, to make clean with water."* **Thayer Greek Lexicon**

Liddell and Scott, Greek Lexixon: "Baptidzo, to dip, to immerse, to sink...." "There is no evidence that Luke and Paul and the other writers of The New Testament put upon this verb meanings not recognized by the Greeks."

Scapula: *baptizo* "to dip, to immerse, as we do anything for the purpose of dying it."

Schleusner: *baptizo* "Properly, it signifies to *dip,* to immerse in water."

Schrevelius: *baptizso* "To baptize, to *merg,* to bathe."

Parkhurst: *baptizo* "To *dip,* immerse, or plunge in water."

Greenfield: *baptizo* "To *immerse,* immerge, submerge, sink."

Green: *baptizo* "To dip, *immerse,* to cleanse or purify by washing."

Schottgen: *baptizo* "To merge, *immerse,* to wash, to bathe."

Passow: *baptizo* "To *immerse* often and repeatedly, to submerge."

Stockfus: *baptizo* "Properly, it means *to dip,* or immerse in water."

Sophocles: *baptizo* "*baptizo,* to dip, to *immerse,* to sink."

Martin Luther: "The term *baptism* is a Greek Word. It may be rendered *a dipping,* when we dip something in water, that it may be entirely covered with water." – *cited by Du Veile on Acts 8:38.*

Martin Luther "Baptism is that dipping into water whence it takes its name. For, in Greek, to baptize signifies to dip, and baptism is a dipping.... Baptism signifies two things, --death and resurrection; that is, full and complete justification. When the minister dips the child into the water, this signifies death; when he draws him out again, this signifies life;..... not that I think it necessary to do so, but that it would be well that so complete and perfect a thing as baptism should also be completely and perfectly expressed in the sign." – (Romans 6:4). *History of the Christian Church, Vol. 7, p.218, 219.*

Whitsius: "It cannot be denied that the native signification of the word *baptzein,* and *baptizein,* is to plunge or dip." – Econ. Covenants, p. 1213.

Melancthon: "Baptism is *immersion* into water, which is made with this admirable benediction." – *Melancthon Catecism P. 15*

John Calvin: "The word baptize signifies to *immerse;* and the rite of immersion was observed by the ancient church." – *Institutes, B.IV., ch. 15, Sec. 19.*

"From these words of John (Ch. 3:23) it may be inferred that baptism was administered, by John and Christ, by *plunging the whole body under the water." Commentary on John 3:23.*

"Here we perceive how baptism was administered among the ancients; for they *immersed* the whole body in water." - *On baptism, Chapter 3, p. 56.*

John Wesley: "Buried with Him—alluding to the ancient manner of baptizing by *immersion." Note on Romans 6:4*

Bishop Fell: "The primitive fashion of *immersion* under water, representing our death, and elevation again out of it, our resurrection or regeneration." – *Note on Romans 6:4,5.*

Archbishop Tillotson: "Anciently those who were baptized were *immersed,* and *buried* in water, to represent their death to sin; and then did rise up out of the water to signify their entrance upon a new life. And to these customs the Apostle alludes." (*Re: Rom. 6:4; Col. 2:12*) – *Works, Vol. I., p. 179*

Bishop Bossuet: "To baptize signifies to *plunge*, as is granted by all the world." – *Stennett against Russen, p. 174.*

Dr. Doddridge: "It seems the part of candor to confess, that here (Rom. 6:4) is an allusion to the manner of baptizing by *immersion*, as most usual in those early times." – *Family Expos. On Rom. 6:4*

Neander: "The usual form of *submersion* at baptism, practiced by the Jews, was passed over to the Gentile Christians. Indeed, this form was the most suitable to signify that which Christ intended to render an object of contemplation by such a symbol: the *immersion* of the whole man in the spirit of a new life." – *Planting and Training, p. 161.*

Dr. Dollinger: "The Baptists are, however, from the Protestant point of view, unassailable, since, for their demand of baptism by submersion, they have the clear text of the Bible; and the authority of the Church and of her testimony is not regarded by either party." – *Kirche and Kirchen, 337.*

Note: Whitby, Stackhouse, Bishop Bossuet, Brenner, Von Colin, Hagenbach, Winer, Augustine, Bingham, Van Oosterzee and Coleman have left writings confessing that for *the first thirteen centuries,* immersion was the prevailing form of baptism. These Pedobaptist scholars concede that for *thirteen hundred years* immersion was the prevailing form of baptism, departed from only in special and extraordinary cases. And that even when abandoned by the Latin, or Roman Church, it was retained by the Greek, and other Oriental churches, which do to this day preserve the original form of that sacred rite." – *E.T. Hiscox*

We conclude this series of personal statements with the testimony taken from: **THE CATHOLIC ENCYCLOPEDIA:** "II. ETYMOLOGY. – The word *baptism* is derived from the Greek word, *bapto*, or *Baptidzo*, to wash or to immerse." – *Vol II, p. 259.*

"The most ancient form usually employed was unquestionably immersion. This is not only evident from the writings of the Fathers and the early rituals of both the Latin and Oriental Churches, but it can also be gathered from the Epistles of St. Paul." who speaks of baptism as a bath (Ephesians v 26; Rom., vi, 4; Tit., iii,5). In the Latin Church, immersion seems to have prevailed until the twelfth century. After that time it is found in some places even as late as the sixteenth century." - *Vol. II, pps. 261, 262.*

Is it not both striking and strange that 1200 years of the practice of immersion are not adequate to hold the Church steady??

Chapter XV
THE PRESENCE OF GOD
IN BAPTISM

T
HE INFINITE PRESENCE of God was hardly cultivated with the tenacity of James, but the "deadly drifting" of Hebrews 2:1 was constant! The great spirit of prayer, cultivating the awesome power of God and the deep consciousness of Him was neglected, both the diligent, fervent training; and, above all else, the baptismal service was ignored! The strong awareness of being pleasing to God in true soul-searching was needful and the true Presence of Father, Son and Holy Spirit must be passionately held precious.

In the time of my child hood, false teaching, or no teaching was given! This is truly a holy hour in the life of the Child of God; and when uncertainty prevailed, the death and resurrection of Christ was very vivid to me. I recall the awe of that experience in my own life; and, the snowfall coming down from heaven blanketing all in perfect white, in the very moment of my baptism, it all seemed beautiful and very precious to me. It is clearly a sacred hour as an infinite number of teachings are occurring and the human mind is being transformed (II Corinthians 3:18). This Child of God is experiencing a holy coronation.

The Will and Work of God are ordered, and, should be heeded, that the first steps of the believer may be bold and forthright. Seldom is there the heart devotion or the comprehension for the individual to become properly aligned to travel with David in Psalm 16:8 "I have set the Lord always before me; because he is at my right hand, I shall not be moved."

IT IS WELL that the Child of God be alerted to the transformation that is occurring in experience and of the enormous challenge that is being set before him, far greater than the perfection that is being aspired to!

"Being born again, not of corrujptible seed, but of incorruoptible, by the Word of God, which liveth and abideth forever." I Peter 1:23. The Living God is there, living and working in you. Phil. 1:6!

We may readily wonder WHY ISRAEL'S leaders would hesitate to put into firm practice the teachings their Holy Scriptures carefully taught them; that the prophets spoke so clearly that every woman in Israel hoped to be the mother of the Messiah; that Simeon and Anna bore witness to Him (Lk. 2:21-35), and, that Herod believed the record, seeking to kill the Lord Jesus. The Lord Jesus instructed them for three days, at the age of twelve! It is stunning that they would listen to Him for three days at the age of twelve and then do the outrageous things they did. (Lk 2:42); *Besides* His daily teaching them after "He came to be about thirty years of age" (Lk.3:23) and, that these are records that cannot be destroyed. Israel submitted to the baptism of John; "Then went out to him Jerusalem, and all Judea, and all the regions round about the Jordan, and were baptized of him in the Jordan, confessing their sins." After Redemption was complete in the Risen Christ, they refused to be obedient to Him and suffered the awful price of their defiance! To obey him meant like treatment of Christ; and, they were terror stricken of that prospect!!

Would you not agree that the allowing and authoring of doctrines without a true and firm basis or Command of Holy Scripture opens the way for floods of false teaching and division that can only be supported by 'assumptions' and 'human reason'? Out of these poor procedures has proceeded horrible apostasies, from the days of the Savior until today. The ridiculous abandoning of solid ground on which to build our faith leaves the Church without a defense against modern agnosticism. This is a stance that totally abandons many of The Scriptures Own Claims to be The Infallible, Infinite, Eternal Word of The Eternal God Who cannot lie, and changes not!

***THE HORRIBLE APOSTASIES** of the current time are to be laid at the door of the degenerate liars of corruption. A converted Methodist 'minister' confessed openly that he went to the street corner to have his laughs with 'buddies', telling smutty stories! That isn't half of the* *problem! More than 60% of practicing 'ministers' have swallowed 'some of' the evolutionary garbage and doubt the inspiration of Scripture, yet The Word of God says, Pasa Graphe Theopneustos "Every Scripture is God-Breathed" "All Scripture is given by inspiration of God, and is profitable for doctrine, for reproof, for correction, for instruction in righteousness, that the man of God may be perfect, thoroughly furnished unto all good works." II Timothy 3:16,17. "For the prophecy came not at any time by the will of man, but, Holy Men of God spake as they were borne along by the Holy Spirit." I Peter 1:21. One statement is all that is really necessary but the Whole Fabric of Scripture is built upon this fact!*

GREAT NUMBERS of the Jews were expecting the Messiah to come from Heaven. The Land was devastated! Order would no longer be established than the Egyptian and Syrian armies would be back at their games in the ideal place where it would not bother either of them. Their carnage and devastation could be left behind for Israel to deal with! They returned to their lands with no destruction at all to be seen in their lands, following their return from the Captivity.

"Then they that feared the Lord spoke often one to another; and the Lord hearkened and heard it, and a book of remembrance was written before Him for them that feared the Lord, and that thought upon His Name.

AND THEY SHALL BE MINE, saith the Lord of Hosts, in that day when I make up my Jewels; and I will spare them, as a man spareth his own son that serveth him.

Then shall ye return, and discern between the righteous and the wicked, between him that serveth God and him that serveth Him not. Malachi 3:16-18.

The tragedy of blindness relative to infant baptism, when those who tied Salvation to baptism, chose to believe that one must be baptized to be saved, steps were taken which should never have been taken to enforce their beliefs and foist their convictions upon those who accepted Regeneration as a Totally Supernatural Experience. I believe this to be a tragic work of Satan which has contaminated the Holy Process of Truth!

For a period of time there was acceptance in the Reformation camp of immersion; but those who came to John for baptism were preparing for this event which they so graphically misunderstood. With their rejection of their king, came the postponement to a future day. The Kingdom of Heaven is a rule of the Heavens over the earth. It is a Spiritual Kingdom, offered in a bonafide manner during our Lord's ministry, Israel defiantly declared, "Let Him be crucified!" "His blood be on us and on our children!" The Kingdom was postponed. (Matthew 27:22, 23. 25). The horrible mistreatments that have filled two thousand years cause us to shudder!

"The Jews of the Diaspora developed great zeal in making the true God known among the heathen, and large numbers were prepared for conversion to God because of their testimony. In the third century B.C., the translation of the Hebrew Scriptures into Greek was accomplished in the Septuagint version, and as Greek was, both at that time and long afterwards, the chief medium of intercommunication among the peoples of various languages, an invaluable means was supplied by which the Gentile nations could be made acquainted with the Old Testament Scriptures.

The "Jews for the most part had not accepted the gospel, whereas Gentiles had embraced it in large numbers. Some might argue that the Jews' refusal to accept it frustrated the divine purpose. But Paul rejects this conclusion. It has, he points out, been a recurring feature of Israel's history that some members of the nation had responded to the call of God, while others (usually the majority) had been disobedient.

The gospel had been plainly set forth before the Jewish people of Paul's day, as the messages of the prophets had been set before their ancestors, so none could say that they had not heard it. Even so, there remained a chosen remnant of Jewish believers in Christ, and as in earlier days so now it was in the faithful remnant that the hope of the people's future was embodied." PAUL, APOSTLE OF THE HEART SET FREE, F.F' Bruce, p.333

Israel, as a Nation, remains as a sign of the ages. The Jew is still in the Hand of God, and he that touches Israel touches the "apple of God's Eye." I find it fascinating that "The Eye" of God has fascinated scientists as "it is fixed on US" according to a current science article, as the heavens are constantly scanned! A massive eye formation has been discerned that is focused on the earth!

The number of Jews in the United States rose sharply, but no large scale attempt was made to convert them. The Jews in the country increased from about three thousand in 1818 to nearly three million in 1914. However, only slight attention was paid, by either Roman Catholics or Protestants, to missons to the Jews. Here and there a Jew became a Roman Catholic, through attendance at a Roman Catholic school through acquaintance with Roman Catholics, or through being a patient in a Roman Catholic hospital. CHRISTIANITY IN A REVOLUTIONARY AGE, Kenneth Scott Latourette, p.80.

(The number of Jews given in America's 2010 census is 5 million 275 thousand,) Israel is central to The Mind of God! "Who hath heard such a thing? Who hath seen such things? Shall the earth be made to bring forth in one day? Or shall a nation be born at once? For as soon as Zion travailed, she brought forth her children." Isaiah 66:8

"After these things came Jesus and his disciples into the land of Judaea; and there he tarried with them, and baptized.

"And John also was baptizing in Aenon near to Salim, because there was much water there: and they came, and were baptized." John 3:23-24.

"Jesus Christ, the God-Man, the Prophet, Priest and King of mankind, is, in fact, the centre and turning point not only of Chronology, but of all history, and Key to all its Mysteries. Around Him, as the sun of the moral universe, revolves at their several distances, all nations and all important events, in the religious life of the world are brought into absolute focus; and all must, directly or indirectly, consciously or unconsciously, contribute to glorify His Name and advance His cause." HISTORY OF THE CHRISTIAN CHURCH, VOL. 1, P. 56-57.

It is most striking that what has happened to Israel, Isaiah 59:10 "We grope for the wall like the blind, and we grope as if we had no eyes; we stumble at noonday as in the night; we are in desolate places like dead men." The call to prayer for clear leading of the Holy Spirit is overshadowed by the blindness of humanity because all have sinned! Hitler in his wretched attempt to heap upon the Jews every indignity, after taking away their property and finances, forced them to be baptized as Christians! But, they survived every hideous indignity and move forward to a glory unspeakable!

It seems that Jeremiah 3:14-17, casts doubt on the vain efforts to preserve the ark and it is doubtful if the 'red heifer' has a great deal to do with the return of Christ. But, it is very obvious from the 'times and seasons' 'which God hath put in His Own Power," that the time is drawing very near!

THE TRAGIC conclusion men have reached regarding Israel is very unfortunate to say the least. The God of Israel gave to us a Holy and Infinite Word. It is impossible in the Absolute for The God of Israel to lie! He will proceed on schedule and in the manner He has stated.

"NOW the Lord had said unto Abram, get thee out of thy country, and from thy kindred, and from thy father's house, unto a land that I will shew thee:

"AND I will make of thee a great nation, and I will bless thee, and make thy name great; and thou shalt be a blessing:

"AND I will bless them that bless thee, and curse him that curseth thee: and in thee shall all families of the earth be blessed." Genesis 12:1-3.

THIS PROMISE shall be kept with Father Abraham. He had a son when he was 100 years old, because God will keep His Word! The following scenario is impossible!!

That Israel as a Nation was utterly and forever rejected!

In Genesis 17:1-8, The Almighty God made a Covenant with Abraham: v.7-8 "And I will establish my covenant between Me and thee and thy seed after thee in their generations for an EVERLASTING covenant, to be a God unto thee, and to thy seed after thee. And I will give unto thee, and to thy seed after thee, the land wherein thou art a stranger, all the land of Canaan, for an EVERLASTING possession; and I WILL BE THEIR GOD."

Judges 2:1 "AND an angel of the Lord came up from Gilgal to Bochim, and said, I made you to go up out of Egypt, and have brought you unto the land which I sware unto your fathers; and I said, I will never break my covenant with you."

Jeremiah 33:13-17 "in the cities of the mountains, in the cities of the vale, and in the cities of the south, in the land of Benjamin and in the places about Jerusalem, and in the cities of Judah, shall the flocks pass again under the hands of him that telleth them, saith the Lord.

"Behold the days come, saith the Lord, that I will perform that good thing which I have promised unto the house of Israel and to the house of Judah.

"In those days, and at that time, will I cause the Branch of Righteousness to grow up unto David; and he shall execute judgment and righteousness in the land.

"In those days shall Judah be saved, and Jerusalem shall dwell safely: and this is the name wherewith she shall be called, The Lord our Righteousness.

"For thus saith the Lord; David shall never want a man to sit upon the throne of the house of Israel;"

Jeremiah 31:33 "..this shall be the covenant that I will make with The House of Israel: After those days, saith the Lord, I will put my law in their inward parts, and write it in their hearts; and will be their God, and they shall be My people."

Jeremiah 33:25,26 "THUS SAITH THE LORD, If My Covenant be not with day and night, and if I have not appointed the ordinances of heaven and earth; THEN will I cast away the seed of Jacob, and David My servant, so that I will not take any of his seed to be rulers over the seed of Abraham, Isaac, and Jacob: for I WILL cause their captivity to return, and have mercy on them."

Ezekiel 37:21-28 "..THUS SAITH THE LORD GOD; Behold, I will take the children of Israel from among the heathen, whither they be gone, and will gather them on every side, and bring them INTO THEIR OWN LAND: and I will make them one nation IN THE LAND UPON THE "MOUNTAINS OF ISRAEL; AND one king shall be king to them all; and they shall be no more two nations, neither shall they be divided into two kingdoms any more at all: neither shall they defile themselves any more with their idols, nor with their detestable things, nor with any of their transgressions: but I will save them out of all their dwelling places, wherein they have sinned, and will cleanse them: so shall they be my people, and I will be their God.

> "And David my servant shall be king over them; and they shall also walk in my judgments, and observe my statutes, and do them. And they shall dwell in the land that I have given unto Jacob my servant, wherein your fathers have dwelt; and they shall dwell therein, even they and their children, and their children's children for ever: and my servant David shall be their prince for ever. Moreover I will make a covenant of peace with them; it shall be an everlasting covenant with them: and I will place them, and multiply them, and will set my sanctuary in the midst of them for evermore.

> "My tabernacle also shall be with them: yea, I will be their God, and they shall be my people. And the heathen shall know that I the Lord do sanctify ISRAEL, when My sanctuary shall be in the midst of them for evermore."

THESE PROMISES OF GOD to THE TWELVE SONS OF JACOB AND THEIR DESCENDENTS cannot be taken from them BY ANYONE!! These are a MERE SAMPLING of God's

Promises to The Nation of Israel; and, it is total dishonesty to deny them.

This swamp of dishonesty has bred many doubts of the believer's own personal security, founding it in a lineal descent from another believer, rather than in the Finished Work of Salvation by Messiah Christ. His promises to the Nation of Israel stands as absolutely as does the Saving Work of Christ for ALL BELIEVERS and FOR HIS CHURCH, HIS BRIDE!

A. That Israel's Covenants were transferred to His Church!

NEITHER assumption is correct! The ABRAHAMIC and The DAVIDIC Covenants are as eternal as every Promise God has put on RECORD for His Church. Covenant Theology ASSUMED, (without GOD SAYING SO!), that baptism was the replacement of circumcision; and, that Israel's future is spiritualized into God's New Testament Church! This made believer security questionable.

Which it most certainly is not! The glory of God's People, Israel; and the Glory of The Church are both distinct and eternal!!

FURTHERMORE, the baptism of the Cathari is solid rock! All groups of the Cathari are agreed; and, their striking intellectual interpretation of Holy Scripture exceeds that of the 'established church' that was accepted by the Reformers.

Since Schmidt wrote his *History of the Cathari*, it has been common to represent Catharism as a philosophical system... 'Theirs was a daily faith and practice.' Their view alone makes it possible to understand how the movement gained rapid and widespread acceptance in the well-ordered and prosperous territory of Southern France, a territory in which Cluny had exercised influence and was established.

In the 12th Century, the Cathari agreed that they stood distinct from the Roman Church, believing they themselves constituted the Church of the righteous: believing that they were the true Church, and had the sole right of preaching the Gospel, having received the imposition of hands and had done penance according to the teachings of Christ and the Apostles. Therefore, they taught that "Its fruits proved that the established Church was not the true Church. The true Church endures persecution, does not prescribe it. The Roman Church sits in the place of rule and is clothed in purple and fine linen. The true Church teaches first. The Roman Church baptizes first. The true Church has no dignitaries, prelates, cardinals, archdeacons, or monks The Roman Church is the woman of the Apocalypse, a harlot, and the pope is anti-Christ. *See The History of The Christian Church, Vol V, P.474-5.*

The depositions at the Cathari's trials indicate that the Cathari made large use of Scripture. The treatises of Bonacurus, Ermengandus, and other writers in refutation of Catharan teachings abound in quotations of Scripture, a fact indicating the regard the heretics had for them. They put spiritual interpretations upon the miracles and freely allegorized parables.

False teachings were rampant, the ideologies present c.1250 could not be safeguarded against evil and it was extremely difficult to know the truth of many current teachings. It was a much later time before it became possible to "compare Scripture with Scripture."

Chapter XVI

PERFECT REST IN BAPTISM

NEANDER'S VIEW may be found in Kitto, Cyclopedia, 1:287 – "infant baptism was established neither by Christ nor by his apostles. Even in later times Tertullian opposed it, the North African church holding to the old practice." The newly discovered Teaching of the Apostles, which Bryeunios puts at 140-160 A.D., AND LIGHTFOOT AT 80-110 A.D. SEEMS TO KNOW NOTHING OF INFANT BAPTISM.

THE AGONY AND SUFFERING of the beautiful Redeemer that followed The (First) Last Supper were a clarion call and challenge that was readily, even eagerly entered into for centuries following the crucifixion! Our Lord said: "But I have a baptism to be baptized with; and how am I constrained till it be accomplished! Suppose ye that I am come to give peace on earth? I tell you, Nay; but rather division;

"For from henceforth there shall be five in one house, divided; three against two, and two against three." Luke 12:50-51.

THE CHRISTIAN FAITH is the faith of the broken heart. Our Lord was the Man of Sorrows. Much of His adult life was spent in the Mount of Olives, where He communed with God, Alone! Many have pondered why Joseph vanished from the household. But I have a further question: WHY did Joseph of Arimathaea furnish the tomb? Luke 23:50-53.

"And in the day time he was teaching in the temple; and at night he went out, and abode in the mount that is called the Mount of Olives." Luke 21:37.

Martin Luther preached a strong message on the conversion of the soul. He stated "Learn from St. Paul that the Gospel teaches Christ that He came, not to give a new law by which we should walk, but that He might give Himself an offering for the sins of the whole world." 'Luther also felt very strongly that immersion was the proper method of baptism, but saw that there was no way in which he could advocate it without giving up his control in a unified form of government that was absolute in its cohesive nature. He revealed Christ to the multitudes and that the Saviour to whom each one was invited to come, without intervention of priest or saint or church or sacrament, not on account of any goodness in himself, but as a sinner in all his needs, to find in Christ, through faith in Him to be the perfect salvation, founded in the perfect work of the Son of God.

Regarding the Abrahamic Covenant: "Under that covenant circumcision was administered to children as a sign of their participation in the relation in which their parents stood to God. The children of Christian believers have therefore a similar right to the ordinance which has replaced circumcision."
– *The Westminister Dictionary of the Bible, p. 59.*

Circumcision and Baptism are two totally different things! There is NO Scripture that even suggests these to be one and the same thing! Covenant Theology has invented many things. Christ's Atoning Death covers infant salvation and security in the most ABSOLUTE terms!! The tying of the salvation of infants to their baptism corrupts the teaching of CLEAR Scripture Statements of ALL PROMISES OF ETERNAL SALVATION TO "WHOSOEVER"!! Baptism, as we have already seen, is one of the two ORDINANCES for His Church; and NOT a PART of the FINISHED Work of SALVATION for ALL OF HIS OWN, WITHOUT REGARD TO AGE, AND NOT OF WORKS WHICH CORRUPTS THE PERFECTION OF IT!!

The sweetness of infants and little children is deeply treasured by the Savior. They are to be tenderly loved and treasured. *It must be firmly stated that our Lord purchased all creation and all babies, irrespective of baptism, are redeemed by the Blood of The Lamb. The statement that baptism has replaced circumcision is not correct or Holy Scripture would have so stated. It has not. Baptism is the first act of obedience for the believer. Baptism is not required for Salvation. When Jesus said, "Suffer little children, and forbid them not, to come unto me: for of such is the kingdom of Heaven,." He meant what he said.*

Matthew 19:14 He was stating a fact! ALL LITTLE CHILDREN HAVE CARTE BLANCHE ENTRY INTO HEAVEN. They were redeemed by the Blood of The Lamb, and baptism has nothing to do with it!

"'God', says Calvin (IV.xvi.5), 'did not favor infants with circumcision without making them partakers of all those things which were then signified by circumcision.' Similarly, under the new dispensation, the baptism of the body of the infant is the sign and seal of the baptism of the soul by the Holy Ghost." – *Dogmatic Theology, Wm. G.T. Shedd, Vol. II, p. 576.*

That is a very radical statement not to have an ounce of Scripture upon which to establish a doctrine!!

THE ABRAHAMIC COVENANT *commands* ISRAEL in specific wording relative to responsibilities and with specific promises. No such Scriptures are to be found relative to denial of His Promises to Israel; or, to the REAPPLICATION of His Promises, consigning them to The Church, or to its infants!! To FABRICATE SUCH ASSUMPTIONS that are PRESUMED to be THE WILL OF GOD is not just dangerous. It is DISASTEROUS.Circumcision is ASSUMED to be a type of baptism. Circumcision was a SIGN *GIVEN* to *ISRAEL'S* covenant head, Abraham, and the circumstances are stated in Romans 4:11 – "And he received the SIGN of circumcision, a SEAL of the RIGHTEOUSNESS OF THE FAITH WHICH HE HAD YET BEING UNCIRCUMCISED..." In Abraham's case, his faith PRECEDED his circumcision. Therefore additional twists are necessary for applying it to babies who have not exercised faith. But, the principle was, that ALL infants have the same coverage, hence, has nothing to do with the experience of the child. Circumcision was a purely covenant relationship restricted to Israel! But, the security of infants is to be a security (Col. 1:16) insured as part of God's creation in which God breathed the breath of 'lives', which He owns as His Perfect creation. Heb. 2:9. They are perfectly Redeemed!

AFTER TIMOTHY'S BAPTISM, Paul yet circumcised him (Acts 16:3) "Him would Paul have to go forth with him; and took him and circumcised him because of the JEWS which were in those quarters: FOR they knew all that his father was a Greek." – If baptism had REPLACED circumcision, would Paul have virtually denied it by such an action?

FURTHERMORE, in Galatians 2:3-5, where efforts were made to fasten Israel's sign onto the CHURCH, Paul and his companions refused to permit Titus to be forced into this rite.

THE VERY FACT that circumcision remains *ISRAEL'S* SIGN is sufficient proof that it has NOT been *REPLACED* by baptism.

In Galatians 2:7-9, we read: "but contrariwise, when they saw that the Gospel of THE UNCIRCUMCISION was committed unto me, as the Gospel of THE CIRCUMCISION was unto Peter;

"(For He that wrought effectually in Peter to the apostleship *OF THE CIRCUMCISION*, the same was mighty in me toward the GENTILES:)

"And when James, Cephas, and John, who seemed to be pillars, perceived the grace that was given unto me, they gave to me and Barnabas the right hands of fellowship; that we should go unto the HEATHEN, and they unto the CIRCUMCISION."

(INASMUCH as ISRAEL'S PROPHETS declare that..NOT THE CHURCH.....but ISRAEL will be given ALL THEIR PROMISED LAND in the future......... **EVERY OTHER PROMISE** God ever gave to His Beloved Nation of Israel..... (AND THE SCRIPTURE CANNOT BE BROKEN), would be *ABSOLUTELY BROKEN* were ISRAEL to be REPLACED by THE CHURCH. *IF GOD BROKE HIS PROMISES TO ISRAEL, ON WHAT GROUND CAN THE CHURCH FEEL SECURE IN HER PROMISES??* WHY would THE CHURCH that is promised a "FAR MORE EXCEEDING AND ETERNAL WEIGHT OF GLORY" want to take away ISRAEL'S gifts and promises? Canaan in all its glory doesn't COMPARE with The HEAVEN promised to believers.

Not only Israel's SIGN but also her *clear **unconditional promises*** are by this philosophy shamelessly taken by The Church because of the COVENANT idea that The Church has totally displaced The Nation of Israel in The Economy of God FOREVER! This has been the SEED PLOT for most of the fertile theological doubt and double talk of modern times, the questioning of Divine Inspiration.

God promised ISRAEL The Land of Palestine FOREVER (Gen. 13:14-15), but this is denied by Pedo-Baptists, as this is appropriated to *mean* *HEAVEN.* CANAAN is NOT *HEAVEN!*

THE RESULT of Covenant teaching was that even during The Reformation, ANTI-Semitic feelings ran so deep that the pages of history have been stained with tragic records. In looking at the tragedy of false teaching, just survey carefully the awful power of Satan to deceive, to twist, to corrupt, to defile and to put the Church in crisis mode. When God says "SUBMIT YOURSELVES, THEREFORE TO GOD. RESISST THE DEVIL, AND HE WILL FLEE FROM YOU. Draw nigh to God and He will draw nigh to you", James 5:7,8a! *Unless we do just that*, we will become confused, distraught and become useless as servants of God! (This is SO IMPORTANT!!!).

Some idea of this is seen in Martin Luther's attitude which is recorded as follows: (Even Luther, Peter, etc. were subject!)

RELATIVE TO the Jews dispersed throughout the world: "He went so far as to advise their expulsion from Christian lands, the prohibition of their books, and the burning of their synagogues and even their houses in which they blaspheme our Saviour and the Holy Virgin. In the last of his sermons, preached shortly before his death at Eisleben, where many Jews were allowed to trade, he concluded with a severe warning against the Jews as dangerous public enemies who ought not to be tolerated, but left the alternative of conversion or expulsion." – *History of The Christian Church, Vol. VII, p. 62.*

The very foundation of core beliefs held by advocates of Covenant Theology rests on the false premise that God has transferred His Abrahamic and Davidic Covenants to The Church, linking infant baptism with the belief that:

    (1)   Baptism has saving merit. (2) – It is the RIGHT of all children OF CHRISTIANS. (3) – It is a covenant sign which will INSURE

the infant's salvation. (4) – It marks out the infants of Christians as possessing assurance of salvation; and, that other infants do not have that promise.

PLEASE NOTE WHERE THIS LEADS: "A first consequence of this sacramental justification of baptism is that the eternal rite becomes absolutely necessary to salvation. Since a work has to be done in the individual, it is obvious that there can be no salvation WITHOUT this cleansing and renewal. But since the means appointed for the accomplishment of this work is baptism, there can be no salvation, without the proper means of grace." – *Sacramental Teaching and Practice in the Reformation Churches, G.W. Bromiley, (A Pathway Book). Dr. Bromiley is "Rector of St. Thomas' English Episcopal Church, Edinburgh, Scotland."*

IT IS CLEAR that infant baptism developed from the belief that baptism is a *sacrament,* i.e., NECESSARY to salvation. Webster says, "*SACRAMENTALISM,* The doctrine that the sacraments are necessary to salvation." – *Webster's New World Dictionary of the American Language.*

Such unBiblical beliefs not only dishonor God, they have wrought disaster in His Church. Not ONE shred of evidence can be adduced from the Scriptures to sustain either the philosophy or its practice. Dr. Charles M. Mead, of Andover, *Resigned, 1882* makes the following statement:

"Though a Congregationalist, I cannot find any Scriptural authorization of pedobaptism, and, I admit also that immersion seems to have been the prevalent, if not the universal, form of baptism at the first." - Dr. C.M. Mead, in a private letter, dated May 27, 1895. – *Systematic Theology, p. 952.*

THE PRACTICE of religion NOT FOUNDED ON **SCRIPTURE** is dangerous... "...Charles M. Mead and Joseph H. Thayer, who had studied in Germany and were beginning to use the historical-critical approach to the Bible, resigned, giving as their reason that they had conscientious scruples against repeating their endorsement of the creed every five years." – *Christianity in a Revolutionary Age, Vol. III, Kenneth S. Latourette, p. 159. (Without Biblical Text to support their teaching, Mead and Thayer moved into the troubling apostate camp of higher criticism.*

Chapter XVII

THE PRINCIPLES IGNORED IN INFANT BAPTISM

" Professsor A. H. Newman in Bap. Rev., Jan 1884.- "Infant baptism has always gone hand in hand with State churches. It is difficult to conceive how an ecclesiastical establishment could be maintained without infant baptism or its equivalent. We should think, if the facts did not show us so plainly the contrary, that the doctrine of justification by faith alone would displace baptism. But no! The *establishment* must be maintained. The rejection of infant baptism implies insistence upon a baptism of believers. Only the baptized are properly members of the church. Even adults would not all receive baptism on professed faith, unless they were actually compelled to do so. Infant baptism must therefore be retained as the necessary concomitant of a State church."

"But what becomes of the justification by faith? Baptism, if it symbolizes anything, symbolizes regeneration. It would be ridiculous to make the symbol to forerun the fact by a series of years. Luther saw the difficulty; but he was sufficient for the emergency. 'Yes' said he, 'justification is by faith alone. No outward rite, apart from faith, has any efficacy.' Why, it was against *ioera operata* yet baptism is the symbol of regeneration, and baptism must be administered to infants, or the state church falls. With an audacity truly sublime, the great reformer declares that infants are regenerated in connection with baptism, and that they are *simultaneously justified by personal faith.* An infant eight days old believe? 'Prove the contrary if you can!' triumphantly ejaculates Luther, and his point is gained. If this kind of personal faith is said to justify infants, it is wonderful that those of mature years learned to take a somewhat superficial view of the faith that justifies?

237

"Yet Luther had written: "Whatever is without the word is by that very fact against God"; see his Briefe ed. De Wette, II:202; J. G. Walch, De Fide, in Utero, There was great discordance between Luther as reformer, and Luther as conservative churchman. His Catholicism, only half overcome, he broke into all his views of faith. In his early years, he stood for reason and Scripture; in his later years he fought reason and Scripture in the supposed interest of the church." SYSTEMATIC THEOLOGY, P. 953, 954.

Pfeiderer, Philos, Religion, 2:342-45, quotes from Lang as follows: "By mistaking and casting down the Protestant spirit which put forth its demands on the time in Carlstadt, Zwingle, and others, Luther made Protestantism lose its salt; he inflicted wounds upon it from which it has not yet recovered today; and the ecclesiastical struggle of the present is just a struggle of spiritual freedom against Lutheranism," E. G. Robinson: "Infant baptism is a rage of Romanism. Since regeneration is always through the truth, baptismal regeneration is an absurdity." See Christian Review, Jan. 1851: Neander, Church History 1:311,313; Coleman Christian Antiquitties, 258-260; Arnold, in Bap. Quarterly, 1869:32; Hovey, in Baptist Quarterly, 1871:75.

The Covenant System of Theology has presumed to modify or abrogate the direct Command of Christ; and, by that assumption has brought upon itself the very chilling Judgment of Almighty God, in maintaining that baptism takes the place of circumcision under the Abrahamic covenant,(But, Scripture does not say so) then proceeding to use an altered form of baptism, which cannot be substantiated by Scripture, seeing it is not baptism, but sprinkling.

THE PRINCIPLES OF THEOLOGY called An Introduction to the Thirty-nine Articles, produced by W.H. Griffith Thomas, is a volume of more than 500 pages, setting out, article by article, the doctrines of the Reformed Faith. It is a structured theology from the Covenant Theology point of view, which has chosen to claim an unbroken structure from Adam to the Second Coming of Christ.

ARTICLE TWENTY SEVEN of the thirty nine articles has been carefully read, as it is clearly the best statement to be had on the matter, that I have found; please be my guest, although, I reserve the right to inject a rebuttal, as we approach their classic presentation in THE PRINCIPLES OF THEOLOGY, by, W.H. Griffiith Thomas, pps. 371-386.

"BAPTISM (And, I inject *baptizo*) is not only a sign of profession, and mark of difference; whereby Christian men are discerned from other that be not Christened, but it is also a sign of Regeneration or new Birth, whereby, as by an instrument of New Birth, whereby, as by an instrument they that receive baptism rightly are grafted into the Church; the promises of forgiveness of sin, and of our adoption to be the sons of God by the Holy Ghost, are visibly signed and sealed; faith is confirmed, and Grace increased by virtue of prayer unto God.

"The Baptism of young children is in any wise to be retained in the Church, as most agreeable with the institution of Christ.

"This represents the Article of 1553, with only slight verbal alterations. The last paragraph at that time was thus worded,... 'Mos ecclesiae baptizandi parvulos et laundardedus est, et omnino in Ecclesia rettinendus' – "The custom of the Church to christen young children is to be commended, and in any wise to be retained in the Church," 'In 1563 the Article 'sign and seal of our new birth. which was changed in 1571 to the present phase, "sign of regeneration or new birth."

"It is essential to consider this, first of all. What is the primary and original idea of Baptism as distinct from any results arising out of it? As Scripture does not state or define this meaning we must derive it from usage. Three Baptisms are mentioned in the New Testament: Jewish (Heb. 9:10); John the Baptists; Christian. There must, therefore, be some common characteristic of all three with specific differences. Two Greek words are found in this connection: *Baptisma, and Baptismos*. The former is used for John's Baptism and Christian Baptism; the latter for the Jewish "washings" or 'Baptisms (Mark 7:4; Luke 9:37,39; Heb. 9:10). This word is never employed to describe the ordinance of Baptism in the Christian Church. Then, too, the English words "Baptism" and "Baptize" are literal renderings of the Greek, and require proper interpretation. Another difficulty is that the one 'Greek preposition is associated with Baptism and yet has four renderings in the English: *into* (Rom 64:3); *unto* (Matt.3:3) *for* (Acts 2:38) *in* (Matt. 28:19)."

It seems that the violent hatred that grew through the ages made it impossible to reconcile and concede the correctness of Scripture in the matter of baptism. But the wickedness of burning those who held to immersion, refusing to bend on the matter is a matter for God to handle and I think He has done that in the inability of the Protestant movement to retain a spirit of oneness; and, I find the multiplicity of denominations, comparable to a reference toward the plurality of offspring of The Great Harlot in Revelation 17:5.

The return of the Protestant churches to the Catholic system, I have every reason to believe will be brought about by an amiable pope, a congenial atmosphere, and a Bible which is already used by both Catholics and Protestants, The New International Version. "The custom of the Church to Christen young children is to be commended, and in any wise to be retained in the Church." This general, cautious, and yet definite statement is particularly valuable in view of modern teachings and tendencies in the direction of indiscriminate Baptism, and in its position is in thorough harmony with the teachings of the Church through the ages."

You will notice that he does not use 'sprinkling' but baptism in all except where he makes one quote. The simple reason he does not use Sprinkle is because the Bible uses baptism and baptism means immersion. He is very careful NOT to say "its position is in thorough harmony with the teachings of the Word of ALMIGHTY GOD!" Why not? Scripture has nothing whatsoever to say about infant baptism sprinkling! It is absurd!

"Is there any rule of the Universal Church compelling Infant Baptism? When we consider that St. Augustine, son of a Christian mother, was not baptized until he was of full years, may we not accept the principle of freedom as regards Infant Baptism, especially in Missionary districts. There are many who are doubtful even of the advisability of indiscriminate Infant Baptism in some districts of England. Although we do not agree with them, it must be recognized that there is no Catholic rule compelling Infant Baptism" AN ARTICLE BY DR. HEADLAM, *Church Quarterly Review,* VOL. LXXVII, p. 418 (January,1914); see also *English Church Manual!* On "baptism," by Principal Grey.

AGAIN, no appeal whatsoever to the Holy Scriptures!! Let it be what will!! The apostasy that has spread like a prairie fire is most certainly an earnest call to prayer for the apostate church, that "the eyes of their understanding may be enlightened" there is no preaching the simple Gospel Message, in fact, I pray they understand! The tenderness and caring of the martyrs is amazing!

IF THE GREEK WORD means immersion, and, it most surely does, properly defined, I am totally in the dark as to how under heaven Reformed Theologians can insist on sprinkling instead of immersion.

MANY DISTINCT and dramatic principles that surround the sacred institution of baptism are totally ignored by the institution of infant baptism. There is no command for infants to be baptized but they most surely have a protective security in Christ's finished work. Election belongs to the saints and it is only for the saints. Until a person is born again, he is lost. The Gospel is for everybody "For whosoever shall call on the Name of The Lord shall be saved." If they accept it, they are elected; and, if they don't accept it, they are clearly not elected. But that has everything to do with believing on the Lord Jesus Christ. Does God know from eternity who will receive the Gospel? Of course He does! But we don't; and, we must passionately work and pray and give the Word lovingly to every person.

I find it very strange that people believe that some people are elected to Salvation; and, that some are not so elected. Some are NOT elected and some condemned to Hell! I have no doubt that some harden their heart until God adds his hardening with it! Pharaoh did that! But anyone who wants to come to God may do so. "God is not willing that any should perish, but that all should come to repentance." II Peter 3:9.

DR. LEWIS SPERRY CHAFER, a master Presbyterian scholar, one of the leading and best organized theological minds of all time, says, "Any consideration of the general theme of ritual baptism is not complete unless some attention is given to pedo or infant baptism. Here again there is difference of opinion and practice, but the same demarcation which divides over mode of baptism is not found at this point. Though the great majority of affusionists practice pedo-baptism, some practice it and have infants baptized by dipping in water. The pedo baptism problem is not so much one of mode, then, as of baptizing infants at all.

Those who reject infant baptism do so with emphasis upon the idea that ritual baptism must be restricted to believers, therefore it could not apply to children. The same company declares that they find no warrant in the New Testament for the practice. On the other hand, the very large proportion of the professing church do baptize infants and for various reasons. (1) By some who practice pedo-baptism it is assumed that there is saving merit in ritual baptism. (2) It is believed by a large percentage that there is some connection between the rite of circumcision as required for the Jewish child according to the Old Testament and the baptism of children according to the New Testament. In the attempt to establish and magnify its one-covenant idea, Covenant Theology has contended for this supposed relationship between the two dispensations. Israelites, however, were not partakers of their covenants on the ground of circumcision; they were born into covenant relationship to God. Therefore, it is not demonstrated that children by baptism become "children of the covenant."

To be consistent those who baptize infants because of an assumed covenant relationship should baptize only male children and only on the eighth day." – *L.S. CHAFER. Systematic Theology, Vol. VII, p. 41-42*

LET IT BE CLEAR to our hearts that God's Holy Spirit is no respecter of persons, times, seasons, rituals or contrivings; but we, in taking His Yoke upon us, are to serve in love and in discernment as we are taught of Him, "for the Love of Christ constrains" us.

May we love ALL of God's beautiful people; and, learn much truth through every God-provided channel, as His Scriptures give us understanding. Childhood training becomes the core of our being;

and we must do our teaching according to the infinite Word of our Eternal, Loving, Righteous, Gracious God, just as *It has been given; and, do it FAITHFULLY.*

ONE OF THE INFINITE principles of Scripture learning is that God used the two most precise and expressive languages of man to give us His Truth; and, it is to be treasured above all earthly ties, as we devote ourselves to truthful and accurate teaching of His Holy Word. NONE of it is adaptable to our prejudices. THANK GOD this does not make us treasure our childhood teachers less, but, rather, even MORE!..BECAUSE of the BOND OF LOVE.

HOWEVER "Assumptions" and "attempt to establish and magnify "the idea", "various practices", etc...if something is not commanded then, the "practice" of it is NOT **obedience! We ought to obey God, rather than man!**

BUT, let us, as believers, at all times build relations in The Body of Christ, with the 9-fold fruit of The Spirit: Love, joy, peace, longsuffering, gentleness, goodness, faith, meekness, temperance." This is God's provision and basic to obedience! It is deeply profound and knits our hearts together in love.

BECAUSE INFANT BAPTISM *is not taught, in The New Testament, Baptists do not practice it.*" – *The World Book Encyclopedia, Article on* "Baptists", *Vol. B, p.71.*

IT IS VERY INTERESTING TO NOTE that "Rantidzo", The New Testament Greek Word for 'sprinkle', is found only in the following Texts: Hebrews 9:13,19,21; 10:22; 11:28; 12:24; and in I Peter 1:2. NONE of these pertain to baptism. IF SPRINKLING were BAPTISM, this word "rantidzo" would doubtless have been used in those passages where "baptism" is the subject set forth. (IN EVERY TEXT, *baptizo* is total immersion). But in ALL passages, WITHOUT EXCEPTION, where BAPTISM is the subject, "baptizo" is the Word used.

MOREOVER, The Greek Septuagint Version, used side by side with the Hebrew Text, in translation, gives the Greek rendering of *"tabal"*, in II Kings 5:14, KJV, "dipped." The Greek Septuagint as "*baptidzo,*" as Naaman, in obedience to Elisha, dipped himself in Jordan. The Church of England scholars, who translated under the auspices of King James, did not hesitate in this translation. In The New Testament Text of Revelation 19:13, The King James Version says: "And He was clothed with a vesture *dipped* in Blood and His Name is called The Word of God." There, the translation of the word "*baptidzo*" *as 'dipped'*, is without hesitation translated "dipped", because, again, there would be no implications, relative to use of sprinkling as a form of baptism, in this Text. Decision in both cases was to deliberately translate the Greek Text, *baptidzo,* to The English Text in the understood FORM of the word, as DIPPED.

LIGHTFOOT, one of the most distinguished and influential men of the Westminster Assembly, a teacher; and, master scholar, says: "That the baptism of John was the *immersion* of the body, in which manner both the ablutions of unclean persons; and, the baptism of proselytes was performed, seems evident from those things which are related of it; namely, that he baptized in the Jordan, and in Enon, because there was much water; and, that Christ, being baptized, went up out of the water." – *On Matthew 3:6.*

The Church of England, in its break with Rome, continued the use of sprinkling as a mode of Baptism. When the translators of The King James Version were preparing the copy of Holy Scripture for King James, for his approval, there was fear of the king's violent rejection of their work, were it to appear in conflict with the king's own baptism; nor, would The Church of England have endorsed it. therefore, lest it be rejected, the letters in The Greek New Testament word *baptizo* of the Greek Text were transliterated into the English Text, to form the word, 'baptism'. Thus, with the king's endorsement, this became The King James Version of Holy Scripture for England and English speaking peoples everywhere.

SURELY THE DEFINITION of the Word and the consistency of usage given to the word, give us the plain meaning it has conveyed throughout Greek common culture. THE FACT that the colorful Greek Language is so exact in its meaning, rules out any broader meaning than that it was meant to convey. THEREFORE, interpretation has always been so uncomplicated, that, even though the Greek Church baptizes infants, they do so by immersion only.

These authorities, by no means, stand alone in their clear concepts as will be noted later, but, let us first consider The Scriptural Basis upon which this matter rests. I believe you will find this, likewise, to be self evident. Scholars in BOTH camps of Scripture interpretation have to understand that The Word of God shall NOT be twisted to fit interpretations. Scriptures that are treated as mere interpretations to be played with and twisted is obviously in the hands of fools! God plainly says what He means and means what He says!

WERE GOD TO *NOT LITERALLY FULFILL HIS PROMISE TO ABRAHAM AND DAVID, WHEN HE SAID "IN ISAAC SHALL THY SEED BE CALLED" and "DAVID SHALL SIT UPON HIS THRONE", WE WOULD FORFEIT OUR OWN SECURITY THAT RESTS UPON THE ETERNAL WORD OF THE ALMIGHTY GOD OF HEAVEN AND EARTH THAT CHANGES NOT! (TRAGIC RESULTS remain YET in the false teaching of the apostate church of today!) EVERY PROMISE GIVEN TO ISRAEL WILL BE FULFILLED TO ISRAEL!*

EVERY PROMISE GOD HAS GIVEN IN THE WORD OF GOD WILL BE FULFILLED...not to someone else, but to the designee!!

Years ago, a ship and its crew were lost at sea because of one error made by a crew member who broke the tiny tip off his knife in the frame of the ship's compass, while cleaning it, pulling the compass hand slightly to one side. But distance increased their problem as the angle widened until they were miserably off course. Doctrinal error has, through the centuries, created similar confusion in God's Spiritual Kingdom; Both The Verbal Teachings of our Lord; and, the Written Text of New Testament Scriptures declare a departure from the Truth (The Apostasy of the Last Days) to be an event man is to expect, NOT the conversion of the world; and, that Christ's Millennial Reign will FOLLOW His Second Coming in Glory.

Some Church Bodies took the position there would never be such a period on earth; and, declared themselves to be A' millennial, (No millennium). Most believed The Church would convert the world; and produce the 1,000 year Peace. This belief is Post Millenial. Premillenial people believe Christ will come before the millennium. Some have anticipated Papal rule of the world, This it seems, continued to be the position of The Catholic Church; and, of the larger segment of the Reformation Churches under Martin Luther and John Calvin as well.

Ulrich Zwingli, Swiss patriot and protestant reformer took issue with these teachings. In regard to The Divine Presence in the elements of Communion, Zwingli held the position it is memorial and anticipatory in character, being a continual 'reminder' of His Death; to be observed 'until He comes.' Elsewhere, freedom of personal faith was not tolerated by "State Church" Polity; and, persecution of nonconforming Christians as heretics fostered the climate that encouraged the migration of Christians to America from lands that persecuted church dissidents.

Now, for purposes of clarity, may God guide our hearts well, as we look at the truth, that the eternal wellbeing of children who die in infancy are secure beyond question. The Holy Spirit's personal revelation of Truth to the individual's heart, is already an absolute certainty since Christ tasted death for every human. The ground of Christ's Blood Atonement and tender grace is in the Absolute; and, *is not* secured by that child's baptism, since water baptism secures salvation for no one. The Holy Scriptures are our single basis for practicing baptism; and They do not ONCE command the baptism of infants! The eternity of God's work is all that is needful.

IT IS OUR PRAYER that Biblical Truth we have considered might have been helpful to you, thus far, for preparing your heart to deal well with problems each of us face, in our walk through life. Satan is attacking and deceiving humanity with intensifying force.

FOR INSTANCE: One deeply devout mother, of whom we learned, lost her baby at birth. Being unable to get him 'baptized', her own life was finished in the absolute agony of believing her baby was lost forever just because she had been unable to have him baptized.

The use of 'baptism' and 'communion' as ties to the church to instill mortal fear becomes a false 'religion.' But, the person who uses 'freedom' to resist God's call also has his own false religion. Both are tragic. But, right teaching avoids both. Multiplied millions drift in uncertainty, believing that observance of baptism and communion IS or SECURES their salvation, yet are unsure they will go to Heaven!!

IN Matthew 5:18, OUR LORD said, "For verily I say unto you, Till heaven and earth pass, one jot or one tittle shall in no wise pass from the Law, till all be fulfilled." (OUR LORD is saying that the smallest Hebrew letter, the youth, or the rough breathing marking used in His Holy Text of Scripture will neither be dropped or made to have different meaning, or become obsolete. Interpreters need to know there is ABSOLUTE accountability of teachers of Scripture.

II Timothy 3:16, 17 "ALL SCRIPTURE is given by inspiration of God, and is profitable for doctrine, for reproof, for correction, for instruction in righteousness: "That the man of God may be perfect, thoroughly furnished unto all good works."

MARTIN LUTHER'S extant writings and recorded statements are very clear in regard to his own personal belief that baptism was by immersion. However, his decision to follow the course he did was made in view of his own baptism; and, the destructive rebellions that would have halted the Reformation movement. Even the wisest, most faithful church leaders have human limitations and failings. Thank God for the man that had the moral and spiritual courage to nail his 95 Theses to the cathedral door; and, declare, "Here I stand!" Very many of the knowledgeable church leaders did not have his kind of courage; and, remained in their places of leadership, ignoring false teachings that had gripped the mother church.

PHILIP SCHAFFS HISTORY OF THE CHRISTIAN CHURCH, *Vol. VIII p. 546 regarding The Reformation in French Switzerland* states of Calvin and Luther "..the former went back to the ultimate root in a pre-mundane unchangeable decree of God; the latter looked at the practical effect of saving grace upon their favorite dogma,

in opposition to Romanism, which weakened the power of divine grace, magnified human merit, and denied the personal certainty of salvation.

Augustine (354-430 A.D.), Bishop of Hippo: "..regards the elect as an inner circle of the baptized; and holds that, in addition to the *baptismal grace of regeneration*, the elect receive from God the gift of perseverance to the end, which puts into execution the eternal and unchangeable decree of election." *Creeds of Christendom, Vol. 1 p. 640.* Augustine is adopted by Christianity.

Life, Truth, Doctrine, Ability, Thoughts, Works, Trust and Influence upon others, are great Gifts from God; and every person faces both life and eternity as accountable stewards of The Eternal God of Heaven and Earth! Matthew 12:34-36; Luke 16:1-2. Thank God He offers forgiveness in His Son. It is, however, incumbent upon us that we understand and maintain responsibility!! It is essential that we learn of Him! Matthew 11:28-30!

In John 3, a Jewish teacher, Nicodemus, came to his Messiah Christ. When Jesus told him, "Ye must be born again" and, "that which is born of the flesh is flesh; and, that which is born of The Spirit, is spirit", his thinking could not make the hurdle! Christ's Word, by the Holy Spirit, our Teacher, converted him!

THERE ARE *TWO BAPTISMS*! SPIRIT Baptism and WATER baptism. As to Spirit Baptism, this is a spiritual occurrence of Birth, not only into the Spirit World, but Into The Family of God as His children: I Corinthians 12:13, "For by One Spirit are we ALL Baptized INTO One Body..!" When this occurs, we are conscious a new dimension has been added to our understanding.

The simultaneous nature of the experience relates to entry BOTH into the Body of Christ and into, Thereby, The Family of God, as Members of The Body of The God Man, Christ Jesus, God Incarnate, of His Flesh and of His Bones!! This is rarely, *if ever*, simultaneous with the administering of WATER baptism. They are decisively distinct baptisms!

The records of Covenant Theologians acknowledge this fact, admitting existing cases of wicked living among those who receive water baptism, such as Simon the sorcer; and Julian the apostate, etc. as well as those who, through the Church Age have lived wicked lives:

Re: Baptismal Regeneration and Fall from Grace *p638-39*: in #81 *The Interpretation of The Articles, V,1* The Creeds of Christendom: "The Articles teach also the possibility of falling away from grace (XVI.) AND THE DOCTRINE OF GENERAL BAPTISMAL REGENERATION (XXVII.). This seems to exclude an absolute decree of election 'to everlasting life,' which involves final perseverance as a necessary means to a certain end. Hence the attempts to explain away either the one or the other to save the logical consistency of the formulary." *CREEDS OF CHRISTENDOM, VOL.1, p. 638.*

"Baptismal regeneration is taught indefinitely in Article XXVII., more plainly in the Catechism, and in the baptismal service of the Liturgy, which pronounces every child after baptism to be regenerated." –CREEDS OF CHRISTENDOM, VOL.1, p.639

"Wonderful indeed, very wonderful, that to some of his own sons, whom he has regenerated, and to whom he has given faithfulness and charity, God does not give perseverance." CREEDS OF CHRISTENDOM, VOL.1, p. 640.

THE TRAGEDY of failing to discern and distinguish between the two baptisms has gendered the teaching of 'falling from grace'. This GROSS UNCERTAINTY about personal relationship with God has resulted in an even larger agnosticism. The doubts and multiple numbers of false alternatives to Gods giving a New Birth has created horrible confusion without any cause whatsoever!

I trust you have taken note that in all of this conglomerate confusion, NO EFFORT has been made to appeal to Scripture for Its OWN Answers to such folly, that has generated foggy doctrines and erroneous activities, instead of bringing Glory to God. This has fostered and fathered innumerable false ideas and gendered a human philosophy of total uncertainty. It is a climate, extending even to the point of questioning whether our very existence has any reality of any kind! Many philosophers of today take refuge in this 'last resort' effort to deal with life's reality! Man is blind, by nature, and on his way to an eternal Hell, without God and without hope, until he receives The Lord Jesus Christ, The Messiah of Israel, The Eternal Son of God, man's Savior, as Redeemer and Lord!

In Isaiah 55:8-9, God declared an existing barrier between the human mind and God's Mind, between man's thoughts and His thoughts and between man's ways and His ways. Luke 2:41-50; 4:22; John 7:14, 15.

When we become believers in The Lord Jesus Christ, Son of God, Head of His Church and Messiah of Israel, we begin a New Life of relationships in two realms of authority. We have an even larger responsibility to our fellow man, but we have been called to walk with God (as Enoch did).

The Church will, one day, experience the 'catching away' such as that man did, to meet The Lord in the air. I Thessalonians 4:13-17. As to the spiritual realm, it was The Holy Spirit Who regenerated us into that realm by His Baptism, upon our trusting in Jesus Christ our Lord; and He is our Keeper!

Our water baptism serves three purposes: (1) It declares our state to be that of sinners, responsible for Christ's Death, who, by faith died with Him; and, have accepted His invitation to share all the benefits of Christ's Resurrection Life forever. (2) It is our open identity with His Church on earth as a part of a local body of believers that have been commissioned of God to bear witness to a lost world as we become a faithful, participating part of His locally identified Family. (3) It is the visible witness of a past, truly experienced New Birth into God's Family. At the time water baptism is administered by a fellow believer, the experience of regeneration is already a fact of history; and, is just being openly and publicly confirmed and recognized. Responsibility embraced extends into BOTH realms of experience. Evidences of the two realms: Matthew 11:28-30; Romans 8:5-13; II Corinthians 3:12-18.

Chapter XVIII
THE PUZZLES OF BAPTISM

JOHN 14:15 "If ye love me, keep my commandments."

THE CATHOLIC ENCYCLOPEDIA is its own witness to the fact that immersion was the first method of baptizing. Some of the Reformed theologians have indicated the same. Obviously and without warrant, the Catholic Church has proceeded to Sprinkle! The Reformation churches have followed suit, ignoring the plain teachings of Scripture. The reason for both groups to continue to sprinkle is a mystery to me. Anytime baptism is spoken of, the word, *baptizo,* in its needed tenses are always used, never, *rantizo.*

THE COMMAND of our Lord, in Matthew 28;18-20, to His disciples, to preach The Gospel to every creature, baptizing them in The Name of The Father; and, of The Son; and, of The Holy Spirit is a command to be diligently obeyed. The baptism cannot be conducted as directed without the preaching of the Gospel and the absorbing of Spiritual truth.

WHY SHOULD WE BE AMAZED at the conflict and confusion generated by the Doctrine of Baptism? God set a husband and wife in The Garden of Eden, beginning a home. Satan divided it. They began their family: Satan divided it. The older son killed his brother. God began the Nation of Israel. Satan divided it. Our Lord, in Matthew 16:18, declared "Upon this Rock, I will build My Church." Satan has used men and The Ordinances, themselves, to divide it.

The silence of Scripture as to the practice of sprinkling is strong evidence it is not to be done.

DR. L.S. CHAFER, again, in his Summary of Ritual Baptism, says "In approaching the theme of ritual baptism it is recognized that over this subject the most bitter divisions have been allowed to arise in the church------divisions and exclusions for which it is difficult to account in the light of two facts: (1) the great majority of those who are given to separations confess that there is no saving value in the ordinance and (2) all who look into it with freedom from prejudice recognize that fruitful, spiritual Christians are to be found on each side of the controversy. In a work on Systematic Theology, which purports to be faithful in declaring all aspects of Biblical doctrine, the consideration of ritual baptism cannot be eliminated, though to do so would be easier and to avoid countering good men would in itself not be desirable." – *Systematic Theology, Vol VII, p.34 (I* believe the facts must be printed.)

IF WE ARE TO OBEY our Lord's Command, then it must be obeyed the way He gave it. JOHN'S BAPTISM has already been demonstrated to have been by immersion. The great old Catholic cathedrals built prior to the 13th Century have been cited..... not as having fonts, but large baptisteries! Following The Great Schism, The Greek Church continued to immerse as the Greek *baptizo* directed.

St. Augustine (354-430), bishop of Hippo, N. Africa "first clearly introduced.. wholesale exclusion of all un-baptized infants from heaven.." "The Roman Catholic Church.. teaches..the salvation of all baptized, and the *condemnation* of all *un-baptized* children.." THE CREEDS OF CHRISTENDOM, VOL.1, p.37

AS TO INFANTS, when our Wonderful Lord PURCHASED WITH HIS OWN BLOOD, His ENTIRE CREATION, man was CERTAINLY not excluded! Hebrews 2:9. Nor does the use of water (in whatever quantity) give them Salvation! Nor will our Righteous God condemn his unoffending creature, made in His Image! The sanctifying of ALL innocent little children was MOST CERTAINLY *an integral part of our Holy Redeemer's eternal purchase!!*

AS TO THE POWER OF THE CHURCH TO MODIFY OR ABROGATE the Written Word of God, and the Spoken Word of

The Lord Jesus Christ, the Reformation Church is in the proper company of the mother church! It is hardly necessary, Neither Church carries that right! Or, that baptism takes the place of circumcision, baptism doesn't take the place of anything of anything!

There are 59 references in the New Testament that God was beginning a NEW THING! The Old Economy was done! It was finished. Not only did the Lord Jesus Christ state that it was finished, so did The Word of God! Think about it! The drama of ritual was over!

FOR 400 YEARS Israel had witnessed that exclamation point with its totally brazen sky! There was no Word from Heaven!

In Mark 1:27, "And they were all amazed, insomuch that they questioned among themselves, saying, What thing is this? What new doctrine is this?"

Matthew 9:16,17 "No man putteth a piece of new cloth unto an old garment, for that which is put in to fill it up taketh from the garment, and the rent is made worse.".

"Neither do men put new wine into old bottles: else the bottles break and the wine runneth out and the bottles perish: but they put new wine into new bottles, and both are preserved."

Why did the Lord Jesus say, in Matthew 26:28, Mark 14:24, "This is My Blood of THE NEW TESTAMENT? The significance of the 'obedience'(like baptism) becomes a spiritual act of obedience. No elements are changed!

Not only must The Church accept its new role, it must do so with a willingness to die; it must accept total transformation and witness to it by being 'crucified unto the world, (and be baptized to demonstrate it); and, (let the) the world be crucified' to us!

You will not find the word 'crucified' in the Old Testament but you will find it at least 38 times in the New Testament. Furthermore, it must be with mature minds and with forthright will that people step into the waters of baptism! The standard for acceptance into the church must be at least as good as it is in Deuteronomy 6:1-25!

AGE OF ACCOUNTABILITY is usually, correctly or incorrectly, believed by most to be twelve years of age, because The Savior, The Eternal Lamb of God, was twelve years of age at the second mention in Holy Scripture of his being taken to the temple in Jerusalem BY HIS PARENTS and the reason his parents went three days before checking his whereabouts was that he had just taken the full responsibility of Manhood as he rebuked his parents with the words, "Wist ye not that I must be about my Father's Business!". That, significantly, is the Last Word that Scripture records of the parent-Child submission, as He went with them to Nazareth "and was subject unto them." Luke 2:49-52. This obedience was always subject to His Father's Call.

THE TEACHING OF CHILDREN BY PARENTS IS AN AWESOME RESPONSIBILITY.. and, it CANNOT be sluffed off with a few drops of water in infancy!! The MOST SERIOUS of parental RESPONSIBILITIES is the teaching of their OWN children, making VERY sure those children KNOW and LOVE THE SAVIOR!! A child's OWN faith is God's channel of Salvation; and, great numbers of children experience The New Birth, as they believe The Word of God, during those years.

LET IT BE emphatically understood that no one but The Holy Spirit of God is capable of doing what must be done in setting forth the Truths that are so clearly taught in Scripture; and those who proclaim it had better know they are speaking by the Holy Spirit. We should, therefore, understand that our responsibility is to Him rather than to man or even to the church with which we are affiliated. THE NEW BIRTH is The Holy Spirit's OWN Regenerating Process!

God's Holy Spirit can only teach us as we are ready to be taught. Our real learning processes begin by our asking God to show us the Truth and by declaring our willingness to obey Him. God will teach no man who resists His teaching, therefore He keeps the treasures of His Truth for those who commit themselves to obey Him. This moment is a wonderful time to make this commitment. Let us pause and commit ourselves to God with a resolute readiness to obey God after every fact has been carefully considered. "Then Peter and the other apostles answered and said, We ought to obey God rather than men." Acts 5:29.

OUR LOVING GOD *OWNS and MAKES SECURE ALL* infants and children too young to discern good and evil. Jonah 4:11; Matt. 19:14. One of the most revolting and God-dishonoring ideas today in existence is that our God, Who is no respecter of persons, would condemn undiscerning children to eternal Hell. God's Criteria for judging the lost is that it shall be 'according to their works.'

THE DEATH AND RESURRECTION of our Lord Jesus Christ insures the release of the material universe from the curse of sin under which it has groaned and travailed "in pain together until now", Romans 8:19-23!! THEREFORE, by what concept can anyone suggest of Him the horrible injustice of consigning conscious little ones, into whom He has breathed the breath of 'lives', Genesis 2:7, (Hebrew plural), arbitrarily, *without personal cause,* to a place in the flames of an eternal Hell, or to Limbo?

ON WHAT GROUND can GOD'S DECLARATION in Hebrews 2:9 be canceled out? There, He EMPHATICALLY declares: "But we see Jesus, who was made a little lower than the angels for the suffering of death, crowned with glory and honor; that He by THE GRACE OF GOD should TASTE DEATH FOR EVERY MAN!" I can think of no action that would be more cruel than that of consigning infants to Hell who were born into unchristian homes through NO CHOICE OF THEIR OWN.

CHRISTIAN BAPTISM must find its methodology of obedience as to its valid observance in the CLEAR TEACHINGS of the Bible, God's Holy, Eternal Word, as The Living Breath of God. In John 6:63, The Lord Jesus declared, "It is the Spirit that quickeneth: the flesh profiteth nothing. THE WORDS that I speak unto you, THEY are SPIRIT, and they ARE Life!!"..to be obeyed!

THE PROBLEMS of infant baptism clearly stem from the fact that it has no support of Command in the Scriptures. The Truth of God must be taken with intelligent and responsible candor.

FIRST, --THERE IS NO EXPRESS COMMAND that infants should be baptized. NO ONE is saved by water baptism!!

SECONDLY, --THERE IS NO CLEAR EXAMPLE of the baptism of infants.

THIRDLY, -- ASSUMPTIONS are NOT valid as COMMANDS !!

FOURTHLY, -- PRACTICE of Anti-Biblical ideas is HERESY!!

Biblical Truth Concerning Infants

II SAMUEL 12:19-23 "And when David saw that his servants whispered,. David perceived that the child was dead: therefore David said unto his servants, Is the child dead? And they said, He is dead. ---

"And he said, while the child was yet alive, I fasted and wept: for I said, Who can tell whether God will be gracious to me, that the child may live?

"But now he is dead, wherefore should I fast? Can I bring him back again? I SHALL GO TO HIM, but he shall not return to me."

It is clear that David had absolute confidence that he would spend eternity with his child which he had begotten in an adulterous relationship, in spite of the circumstances and apart from ANY ritual. There is nothing to indicate that ANYTHING was done directly to this child, to secure its eternal safety. If some rite were needed for its security, The Holy Spirit would have made it known.

MATTHEW 18:1-6 – "At the same time came the disciples unto Jesus, saying, Who is the greatest in the Kingdom of Heaven? And Jesus called a little child unto him, and set him in the midst of them,

"And said, Verily I say unto you, Except ye be converted, and become as little children, ye shall not enter into the Kingdom of Heaven. Whosoever therefore shall humble HIMSELF as this little child, the same is GREATEST in the Kingdom of Heaven.

"And whoso shall receive one such little child IN MY NAME receives ME. But whoso shall offend one of these little ones which believe in Me, it were better for him that a millstone were hanged about his neck, and that he were drowned in the depth of the sea. MATTHEW 18:10 – "Take heed that ye despise not one of these little ones; for I say unto you, that *in Heaven* THEIR ANGELS do ALWAYS behold the Face of My Father which is in Heaven."

IN MATTHEW 19:13,14, NONE would have 'forbidden', if Jesus and His disciples had been in the habit of baptizing infants: "Then were brought unto Him little children, that He should PUT HIS HANDS ON THEM and PRAY: and the disciples rebuked them.

But Jesus said, Suffer little children, and forbid them not, to come unto me: for of such is The Kingdom of Heaven."

MARK 10:15 – "Verily I say unto you, whosoever shall not RECEIVE the Kingdom of God AS a little child, he shall not enter therein."

Would you say the little child should receive it "unconsciously", or "trustingly"? The trusting little child would have been conscious of the tender, loving hands of the Lord Jesus.

THE "ALL AUTHORITY" OF Matthew 28:18-20, the Authority for judgment in John 5:19-27, and the Unlimited Authority displayed in Philippians 2:5-11, under which EVERY KNEE shall bow, has a unique magnificence which will require ALL to rightly confess Him to be that ONE Who is FULL of GRACE and TRUTH. The same blood of Jesus Christ which covers the **INANIMATE CREATION** that was "made subject to vanity, NOT WILLINGLY, is surely sufficient to cover helpless infants who are without the capability of making their own personal decision.

From Acts 16:15,33,40, NEANDER says that "we cannot infer infant baptism, For I Corinthians 16:15 shows that the whole family of Stephanas, baptized by Paul, were adults (I Cor. 1:16 It is impossible to suppose a whole heathen household baptized upon the faith of its members included infants.

I CORINTHIANS 16:15 – "I beseech you brethren, (ye know the HOUSE OF STEPHANAS, that IT is the firstfruits of Achaia, and that THEY have ADDICTED THEMSELVES to THE MINISTRY of the saints.)"

IT IS SURELY IN KEEPING with The Nature of our loving and gracious God to show mercy toward a being created in HIS OWN Image who has had no opportunity to exercise their own will positively for or against God. Furthermore, all judgment which God exercises toward EVERY individual is based upon that person's works; and, not upon the works of ANYONE ELSE at that last great judgment of the unsaved dead. Revelation 20:13

CONVERSELY, if the sprinkled infant who has been born of Christian parents were justified on that premise, then he would be justified on the basis of his parents' works and faith which THEY exercised for the procurement of his salvation...not upon those personally authored by the child. No Scripture can be produced to support such a theory for the principle is contrary to revealed truth.

OUR ONLY MOTIVE must consistently be to search out the Truth of God, **OBEY IT, and spread it.** There is no object to be gained by ignoring truth or perpetuating falsehood. Surely there are not many ways to Heaven, since Jesus said, "STRAIT is THE GATE..narrow is THE way, which leadeth unto life.." SHOULD WE NOT SEEK TO WALK IN IT TOGETHER?

Biblical Truth Relative to The Life Principle, is that life shall last forever and shall give account to God.

ECCLESIASTES 3:14 "I know that whatsoever God doeth, it shall be for ever: nothing can be put to it, nor any thing taken from it: and God doeth it, that man should fear before Him."

INASMUCH as God doesn't even annihilate natural born humans, once life has begun, termination of ETERNAL life is unthinkable.

"Baptismal Regeneration and Fall From Grace: The Articles teach also the possibility of falling away from grace (XVI.) and the doctrine of baptismal regeneration (XXVII.). This seems to exclude an absolute decree of election 'to everlasting life,' which involves final perseverance as a necessary means to a certain end." – *CREEDS OF CHRISTENDOM, p. 638.*

When a new member of the human race arrives, his new baby cry is witness he *has* ARRIVED alive into the family circle! Spiritual Birth, likewise, is ARRIVAL into God's Family Circle ALIVE. Until that has OCCURRED, there is nothing to witness to. Water baptism is a witness or testimony to an observing world of an experience THAT HAS ALREADY OCCURRED!! And for the added reason that we are not reborn of corruptible things. Water, as everyone knows, is corruptible.

Spiritual Birth, likewise, is arrival ALIVE into God's Family; and water baptism is God's witness His child has already become part of God's Family Circle. I Corinthians 12:13 is HIS SPIRIT Baptizing, or placing His New Born Child into The Body of Christ eternally!! It is IMPOSSIBLE that this should EVER be reversed!

"TRULY, TRULY, I say unto you, He that heareth My Word, and believeth on Him that sent Me, HAS everlasting life, and SHALL NOT come into condemnation (judgment); but IS passed FROM death UNTO LIFE!!!" St. John 5:24

"My sheep hear My Voice, and I know them, and they follow Me:

"And I give unto them Eternal Life; and they shall NEVER perish, neither shall any *man* pluck them out of My Hand. (Please notice that the word 'man' is italicized to remind us it doesn't exist in the Holy Scriptures in the Greek Text. So, in each text of Scripture.)

"My Father, which gave *them* Me is greater than all; and no *man* is able to pluck *them* out of My Father's Hand.

SATAN was THERE when man was placed in The Garden. He is ACTIVE in every newborn human; and that activity does not cease until that human draws its last breath on earth. He continues his presence after the NEW birth STILL until that last breath on earth.

SATANIC PROBLEMS began for man when he was placed in the garden. They begin for the believer, hence for The Church, the very moment the New Birth occurred in man. Satan's weapon is deceit; and, even born again humans remain amazingly gullible. For this reason, apostasy (drifting from the truth) began the day The Church began. Hebrews 4:1, "...fear..lest..any of you should seem to come short of it.".…More properly: "lest any of you should…drift from (the truth)!" The Conflict of the Ages continues in the professed church until The True Church is caught up to meet The Lord in the air (I Thessalonians 4:13-17); and the apostate religious system is spewed into the Tribulation Period. (Revelation 3:13-17; 17:3-18; Jude 3,4). There will be a merger of ALL apostates under Antichrist into one false religious system, stemming from the beast and false prophet.

Few professed believers in the early years of The Church held a copy of Holy Scripture in their hands, as it had to be prepared with minutest care by hand copying. In much of the professed church this continued far past 1450 when the printing press was invented. Therefore, false teachings and false beliefs became rampant!

During the 20th century, an American preacher of The Gospel visited Africa and witnessed a pastor, whose ONLY BIBLE was eight (8) pages of The New Testament. He preached to his church every week from these eight pages!! His congregation had not a shred of Holy Scripture! NO WONDER the church is ignorant of God today!!

Most Americans HAVE some type of 'copy' of the Bible. Just a few years ago, The Gideons visited our universities to give Bibles to all who would take them. These representatives had scarcely left one campus before the trash cans were glutted with the unread Bibles. Are America's problems the judgment of God?

Drifting humanity, without God and without hope, dares to meddle with the life principle, involving the human embryo. Can you visualize what the results would be if this knowledge fell into the hands of demonic minded men?! Warning needs to be given in every realm; but, Spiritual Truth of Baptism is our topic here; and, already, we must note the divisions within the Pedo-Baptist Camp, making it VERY CLEAR that deviations only branch into more deviation. The Pedo-Baptist camp has introduced the erroneous teachings of: (1) baptismal regeneration. (2) falling from Grace. Both of which are very serious misunderstandings and tragic false teachings.

THE GREEK LANGUAGE uses eight (8) tenses in order to avoid just these types of problems. The Greek 'present' is the durative tense in that there is no termination point. (God lives in the eternal present, Infinite in Presence) and, The Life He gives does not end. 'Falling from Grace' is a wicked teaching, completely destroying Faith and Trust, creating multiple uncertainties. Then there is the aorist tense that makes it clear that what God does, has eternal implications. But, as Ecclesiastes told us, "Whatsoever God doeth, it shall be forever!" God gives us HIS OWN KIND of life. John 5:24; 10:28-30; Romans 8:35-40; I John 5:11-1

The Regeneration of man is The Work of God that involves All Three Persons of the Eternal Godhead; and God conforms NOTHING to man's thinking: Isaiah 55:7-11. If we are saved, we BELIEVE GOD!!! We either believe Him, or we don't. We are either saved or lost. Limbo and purgatory are Satan's deceptive falsehoods. Since Messiah Christ's Finished Work of Redemption, His redeemed people, at death, are "present with the Lord." Philippians 1:23. Lives like that of 'just Lot', II Peter 2:7, saved 'as by fire' are with Him. I Corinthians 3:15. His Work is Done!!

CHAPTER XIX
PRESSING FOR THE PRIZE IN BAPTISM

" I PRESS TOWARD the mark for the prize of the high calling of God in Christ Jesus." Philippians 3:14. The master builder Isaiah 26:3 "Thou wilt keep him in perfect peace, whose mind is stayed on thee." Where is your focus?

I believe it to be extremely dangerous to deliver obedience to a system rather than to the Holy Word of God!!

"And when the tempter came to him, he said, If thou be the Son of God, command that these stones be made bread.

"But He answered and said, 'It is written, Man shall not live by by bread alone, but by every word that proceedeth out of the mouth of God." Matthew 4:3,4.

"But I say unto you that every idle word that men shall speak, they shall give account of it in the day of Judgment." Matthew 12:36.

"But he said, Yea, rather, blessed are they that hear the Word of God, and keep it." Luke ll:28.

There is no justification for believing that eternal life is drawn from another human being. God has no step children.

LET US CONSIDER CAREFULLY The **PROPOSALS** that are evident in the assumed premise for infant baptism Dr. Shedd sets forth in his SYSTEMATIC THEOLOGY, *Vol. II, p.574-578.Par,2, Pg.576:* "The infant of the believer receives the Holy Spirit as a regenerating Spirit, by virtue of the covenant between God and his people.... The infant of the believer, consequently, obtains the regenerating grace by virtue of his birth and descent from a believer in covenant with God..."

P574, "The sacrament of Baptism is the sign and seal of regeneration. "The baptism of the infant of a believer supposes the actual or prospective operation of the regenerating Spirit, in order to the efficacy of the rite. The Westminster Confession (XXXVIII. iv.) teaches that 'the efficacy of baptism is not tied to that moment of time wherein it is administered; in other words, the regenerating grace of the Spirit, signified and sealed by the rite, may be imparted when the infant is baptized, or previously, or at a future time. The baptism is administered in this reference, and with this expectation. Baptism is to be administered, to be a sign and seal of regeneration and ingrafting into Christ, and that even to infants." Larger Catechism, 177.

"The infant of the believer receives the Holy Spirit as a regenerating Spirit, by virtue of the covenant between God and his people..... The infant of the believer, consequently, obtains the regenerating grace by virtue of his birth and descent from a believer in covenant with God; and not by virtue of his baptism. God has promised the blessing of the Holy Spirit to those who are born of his people. The infant of a believer, by this promise, is born into the church, as the infant of a citizen is born into the state..... They are church members by reason of their birth from believing parents; and it has been truly "said, that the question that confronts them at the period of discretion is not, will you join the visible church? But, will you go out of it?.......Church membership by birth from believers is an appointment of God under both the old and the new economies; in the Jewish and the Christian church....Baptism is the *infallible* sign of regeneration, when the infant dies in infancy. All baptized infants dying before the age of self-consciousness, are regenerated without exception. Baptism is the *probable* sign of regeneration, when the infant lives to years of discretion. It is possible that the baptized child of believing parents may prove, in the day of judgment, not to have been regenerated, but not probable.....

"A baptized infant, on reaching years of discretion, may to human view appear not to have been regenerated, as a baptized convert may. The fact of unregeneracy, however, must be proved, before it can be acted upon. A citizen of the state must be presumed to be such, until the contrary appears by his renunciation of citizenship, and self-expatriation. So a baptized child, in adult years, may renounce his baptism and church membership, become an infidel, and join the synagogue of Satan, but until he does this, he must be regarded as a member of the church of Christ....

"The *mode* of baptism which is by far the most common in the history of the Christian church is sprinkling or pouring. From the time of Christ to the present, a vastly greater number have been sprinkled than have been immersed. At the present day, sprinkling is the rule throughout Christendom, and immersion the exception. The former mode is catholic; the latter is denominational." DOGMATIC THEOLOGY, W.G.T. Shedd, Vol. 2, p.578.

"Are infants, dying in infancy, included in the decree of reprobation? This is another critical crucial point in the Augustinian system and the rock on which it sits.

"St Augustine expressly assigns all unbaptized children dying in fancy to eternal damnation, because of original sin inherited from Adams transgression. It is true he mitigates their punishment and reduces it to a negative state of privation of bliss, as distinct from positive sufferings. This does credit to his heart, but does not relieve the matter for '*damnatio*' though '*levissima*' and '*mitissima*' is still '*damnatio*'

"The scholastic divine made a distinction between *poena damni* which involves no active suffering, and *poena sensus,* and assigned to infants dying unbaptized to the former but not the latter. They invented the fiction of a special department for infants in the future world, namely, the *limbus Infantum* on the border region of hell at some distance from fire and brimstone. Dante describes their condition as one of "sorrow without torment." Roman divines usually describe their condition as a deprivation of the vision of God. The Roman Church maintains the necessity of baptism for salvation, but admits the baptism of blood (martyrdom) and the baptism of intention, as equivalent to actual baptism. These exceptions however, are not applicable to infants, unless the various desire of Christian parents be accepted as sufficient vicarious desire of Christian parents be accepted as sufficient.

"Calvin offers an escape from the horrible dogma of infant damnation by denying the necessity of water baptism for salvation, and by making salvation dependent on sovereign election alone, which may work regeneration without baptism, as in the Old Testament saints and the thief on the cross. We are children of God by faith and not by baptism, which only recognizes the fact. Calvin makes sure the salvation of all *elect* children, whether baptized or not. This is a great gain. In order to extend election beyond the limits of the visible means of grace, he departed from the patristic and scholastic interpretation of John 3:5, that "water means the sacrament of baptism, as a necessary condition of entrance into the kingdom of God. He thinks that a reference to Christian baptism before it was instituted would have been untimely and unintelligible to Nicodemus. He, therefore, connects water and Spirit into one idea of purification and regeneration by the spirit." HISTORY OF THE CHRISTIAN CHURCH, Philip Schaff, Vol VIII, p.556, 557.

* * *

THERE IS NOT ONE New Testament word of support for these astonishing claims. NO BIBLICAL COMMAND to baptize infants exists in the entire Bible, either forthcoming from our Lord, or from the Inspired writers of Scripture. It is not the wide PRACTICE but the BIBLICAL BASIS which justifies a Christian BELIEF and PRACTICE. BELIEF is REQUIRED. Acts 8:37.

"The blood of the martyrs was the seed of the Church." At The Conversion of Constantine, heathen temples were made into "churches"; Christianity was made 'the religion of the Roman Empire,' adding internal issues. Polycarp, disciple of The Apostle John is the last recorded person we have who knew the Apostles. Irenaeus was his disciple. Polycarp died at the stake in Smyrna's public square for his faith, under the emperor, Marcus Aurelius Antonius, at the age of eighty six.

IN CHURCH HISTORY: "The first clear reference to the baptism of infants is in a writing of Tertullian in 197, in which he condemns the practice beginning to be introduced of baptizing the dead and of baptizing infants. The way for this CHANGE, however, had been prepared by teaching concerning baptism, which was DIVERGENT from that in the New Testament; from early in the second century baptismal regeneration was already being taught." E. H. Broadbent, *THE PILGRIM CHURCH, p.8,9.*

"Constantine sat among the fathers at the great Council of Nicaea, (held at Nicea, Bithynia, on the south coast of the Black Sea in 325 A.D.) giving legal effect to its decrees, Gregory of Nazianzum, St. Chrysostom, and St. Augustin, who had mothers of exemplary piety...were not baptized before early manhood." Philip Schaff – HISTORY OF THE CHRISTIAN CHURCH, Vol.II, p.258 (*Postponement of baptism was due to the teaching that for a baptized believer to commit ONE of the SEVEN deadly sins was eternally fatal*)

Righteous Noah, second father of the race, precedes Abraham in providing all infants, following the Flood, equal righteous ancestor coverage along with Abraham, thus insuring there have been none who was not, in like manner, securely sheltered by the umbrella of a faith exercised by a righteous ancestor, had that been required!

ROMANS 5:17-18 – "FOR IF BY ONE MAN'S OFFENCE death reigned by one; MUCH MORE they which receive abundance of grace and of the GIFT of righteousness shall reign in life by ONE, JESUS CHRIST.

"Therefore as by THE OFFENCE OF ONE judgment came upon all men to condemnation; even so BY THE OBEDIENCE OF ONE, the free gift CAME UPON ALL MEN unto justification of life."

ROMANS 5:12-21 sets out the broad portrayal of The Fall of man in Adam; and, the ABSOLUTE cover of that sin by The Second Person of

The Eternal Godhead! ON WHAT GROUND shall ANY human state otherwise?

OUR LORD HIMSELF in Matthew 18:3-5; 19:14 states clearly His full acceptance of little children. NO conditional requirement is given; NOR, is there even the subject of baptism present anywhere in or even NEAR that Text of Scripture.

GOD'S SPIRIT in I Corinthians 14:6-11 makes it TRANSPARENTLY CLEAR that the True Doctrinal Teachings of Holy Scripture are TOO CLEAR to be DEBATABLE. Things which are necessary for Salvation and for pleasing God are not vague or unclear!

YOUR ATTENTION IS INVITED to certain Bible Texts which have been used without warrant but which even in vague reference seem to serve effectively as dissolvers of doubt in restive hearts.

MATTHEW 19:14 – "But Jesus said, Suffer little children, and forbid them not, to come unto me: for of such is the kingdom of heaven." Were these little children to approach Him by baptism, He would have so directed. There is no connection with baptism in this entire passage of Scripture.

The Household Covenant

THE HOUSEHOLD COVENANT idea has deep natural appeal; and, parental responsibility to love and tenderly teach every child is paramount to the development of childhood faith. However, it is essential that children learn OBEDIENCE and grow accordingly. We, too, are to OBEY... not ASSUME!

Lydia's Household

ACTS 16:15 – "And when she was baptized, and her household, she besought us, saying, if ye have judged me faithful to the Lord, come into my house, and abide there. And she constrained them."

v.40 "And they went out of the prison, and entered into the house of Lydia: and when they had seen the BRETHREN, they COMFORTED them, and departed."

There is no basis in this text for the ASSUMPTION that infants were present. Lydia was a "seller of purple" from Thyatira, across the sea from Philippi where she was converted. As was the usual case in Bible times, her household doubtless included her hired servants as it did in the case of Abraham (Gen. 17:26-27). Nor is there any record that Lydia had a husband, either living OR dead!

The Philippian Jailor

ACTS 16:32-34 – "And they spake unto him the Word of the Lord, and TO ALL THAT WERE IN HIS HOUSE.

"And he took them the same hour of the night, and was baptized, he and all his, straightway.

"And when he had brought them into his house, he set meat before them, and rejoiced, BELIEVING in God WITH ALL HIS HOUSE."

EVERY MEMBER of that household first heard the Word of the Lord (Romans 10:17), and then EVERY ONE of them BELIEVED prior to baptism. We welcome such blessed individual response to the Word of God and covet this joy for all Christian parents through the clear presentation of the Scriptures and the voluntary, personal response of the individual child. The Bible knows of no other kind of "household salvation." In fact, even the Israelites who received the Covenant of Circumcision had no assurance of personal spiritual well-being apart from personal obedience to the Scriptures. Deut. 6:1-25; 11:1-32.

The Household of Stephanas

I Corinthians 1:16 – "And I baptized also the household of Stephanas:..." Yet BEFORE HE HAD COMPLETED THIS LETTER, we find Paul saying by Inspiration (I Corinthians 16:15-16): "I beseech you, brethren, (ye know the house of Stephanas, that IT is the firstfruits of Achaia, and that THEY have ADDICTED THEMSELVES TO THE MINISTRY OF THE SAINTS), "That ye SUBMIT yourselves unto SUCH, and to every ONE that HELPETH with us, and LABOURETH."

It is obvious that there were no infants here since all in the household have addicted themselves to the minstry, that they have authority, AND that they LABOR.

Matters of General Reference

I Corinthians 7:14 – "For the unbelieving husband is sanctified by the wife, and that the unbelieving wife is sanctified by the husband: else were your children unclean; but now are they holy."

If this Scripture authorizes the baptism of infants, then it also endorses the baptism of unbelieving husbands and wives.

Neither baptism nor eternal salvation is in view here, but rather the sacred marriage relationship, which this entire chapter is all about. This Scripture, therefore, must also be eliminated as a proof text for infant sprinkling because the subject of baptism does not enter the text of this chapter.

Galatians 3:1-29 – The entire point of this chapter is to set forth the fact that the covenant that God gave to Abraham could only be entered by FAITH; and, NOT by ritual.

v.22 – "But the Scripture hath concluded all under sin, that the promise by FAITH of Jesus Christ might be GIVEN TO those that BELIEVE.

CLEARLY, only by BELIEVING, can mature persons participate in that covenant. Infants and children are 'His' with added angel care, certainly during the innocent years. Matt. 18:1-6,10.

ROMANS 4:11 – "And he (Abraham) received the sign of circumcision, a seal of the righteousness of the FAITH which he had YET BEING UNCIRCUMCISED: that he might be the *father* of all them that BELIEVE, though they be not circumcised; that RIGHTEOUSNESS might be IMPUTED unto them ALSO:"

THE BIBLE knows of no way to become a spiritual child of Abraham without exercising the same kind of faith which he exemplified. As hard as it is to face facts as they are, we are not at liberty to stand for less than the whole truth of God.

THE BELIEVER'S WITNESS to his or her faith is always subject to, and rests upon THE CLEAR COMMANDS of HOLY SCRIPTURE. When NO SCRIPTURE can be found which COMMANDS that infants be baptized, HOW can their baptism properly be called "obedience"? Baptism cannot save. It only bears witness one has experienced Salvation. NOR was the thief on the cross denied entry into paradise through lack of it.

Chapter XX

PASSION OF OBEDIENCE IN BAPTISM

THE PASSION OF OBEDIENCE comes from the deep experience of the child of God in the conviction of sin and the infinite work of almighty God. Much like the life and death struggle of the beautiful butterfly escaping the chrysalis! This is essential to the formation of the life of beauty! But in the New Birth the meddlesome activity of others mars the working of the Holy Spirit and few become all that God intends. It often takes years to develop; and, most often never does except in measure!

"SAY IT WITH US," the soldiers screamed, kicking and punching the boys' faces and abdomens. "Allah is God, and Mohammed is his prophet. Say it!" The boys refused!

The four young Sudanese boys were firm. Their red blood began to flow across their skin, but they would not give up their faith in Christ!

They had seen their Southern Sudanese families murdered by sword-wielding Islamic fighters. Now they watched as their four young friends and relatives—the youngest only five years old—were beaten to death. There were fourteen boys and thirteen girls abducted in the raid that day. The girls have never been located and were likely sold as slaves or concubines in northern Sudan. All of the boys were tortured, but none relented. The next night the older boys escaped, still bearing the scars of the previous night. Not one renounced his faith. EXTREME DEVOTION, P.17

THERE IS AN UNBROKEN TRAIL of persecution back through the ages of time. In Britain and America it is largely 'behind the back,' lying and mocking. But the Jews have faced it wherever they have gone. In

Muslim countries, the news is silent. The holocaust is endured by the Jews as a house of horrors!

Matt. 10:22 "And ye shall be hated of all men for my name's sake: but he that endureth to the end shall be saved."

...IT IS INTERESTING if not significant that Exodus 2:10 tells us of Pharaoh's daughter regarding God's great Lawgiver: "And she called his name Moses: and she said, 'Because I drew him out of the water.'" (Moses, Heb. *Mosheh" means: "drawn"* or Coptic: *"drawn out."*) Jn. 12:32 "And I, if I be lifted up from the earth, will *draw* all men unto ME."

THE BIBLE with its WHOLE COUNSEL OF GOD is the SOLE BASIS of ALL CHRISTIAN FAITH; and, our obedience in this matter of BAPTISM is obedience to SCRIPTURE *COMMANDS*, not ASSUMPTIONS or PRESUMPTIONS, or, "I'll do it MY way!"

IN CONCECRATION of Mosaic priests, Lev. 8:5-6, "And Moses said unto the congregation, This is the thing which the Lord **COMMANDED** to be done.

"And Moses brought Aaron and his sons, and washed them with water." (At age 30, The Aaronic priesthood entered their work by a complete submersion, or bath, in their consecration.) The first 7 chapters of Leviticus presented FIRST, the blood offerings that were to be the total focus of these consecrated priests. THEN came the OBEDIENCE of the priesthood.

AS TO OUR LORD: Lk. 3:21-23 states: "Now when all the people were baptized, it came to pass, that Jesus also being baptized, and praying, the heaven was opened.

"And the Holy Spirit descended in a bodily shape like a dove upon Him, and a Voice came from Heaven, which said, Thou art My Beloved Son; in Thee I am well pleased."

"And Jesus Himself began to be about thirty years of age..." Mk. 1:12 "And immediately The Spirit 'driveth' him into the wilderness." (It is well to note The Presence of The Triune God, as well as God's note regarding "thirty years of age" as This Holy One, submitting in the absolute to The Holy Spirit, under Whose Power He had made His Commitment to do His Work and complete His Purpose on earth, Jesus, The Messiah, Christ was 'driven'. (or, moved by the Absolute Force of The Holy Spirit, to Whom His submission was, also, absolute! ALSO, to remember He is BOTH Offering AND HIGH PRIEST.)

THE NEW TESTAMENT CHURCH consists of the kind of Priesthood fully pre-figured by the Levitical Priesthood. But The Aaronic priesthood, is a figure of the Priesthood of Christ! Rev. 1:6, lit. *"And hath made us His Kingdom of priests unto God and His Father; to Him be Glory and Dominion FOREVER AND EVER. AMEN."*

IGNORANCE IN HIS CHURCH has made us to be, as His chosen ones (Jn. 15:16), unprepared to cope with life! God gave us new hearts and minds, but we must grow. Our hearts were changed that our renewing minds may learn and grow! May The Eternal God of Heaven and Earth wake His people to understand WHO HE HAS MADE US TO BE!!!! EVEN THE ETERNAL SON OF GOD, HIMSELF, WAS SUBMITTED IN THE ABSOLUE TO THE FATHER. We must grow into that perfection through diligent application, even though the final perfecting will be instantaneous, "in a moment, in the twinkling of an eye!"

Our Faith, prayer, and love must be made to grow; and, often the tempter tempts, misleads and cheats us out of growth!

II CORINTHIANS 4:1-4 – "THEREFORE seeing we have this ministry, as we have received mercy, we faint not;"BUT have renounced the hidden things of dishonesty, not walking in craftiness, nor handling the Word of God deceitfully; but by manifestation of the Truth commending ourselves to every man's conscience in the sight of God.

"BUT if our Gospel be hid, it is hid to them that are lost:

"IN WHOM the god of this world hath blinded the minds of them which believe not, lest the light of the glorious Gospel of Christ, Who is the

Image of God, should shine unto them." Ungodly men are DEAD. What excuse do WE have? Let's 'snuff out' excuses and set our house in order.

INASMUCH as we have looked IN VAIN for the CMMAND OF GOD to sprinkle infants, or to REQUIRE BAPTISM of infants, we rest in the eternal Grace of our Loving God as being the basis for the salvation of all little children. Baptism is not REQUIRED for the salvation of adults! THEREFORE it seems TOTALLY OUT OF ORDER to require such UNCOMMANDED action regarding unaccountable children! WERE SUCH COMMANDS TO APPEAR IN THE BIBLE, THEY WOULD BE OBLIGATORY ON *PARENTS*!! Commands *WERE* PRESENT IN *ISRAEL; but those commands were commands to TEACH; AND THOSE COMMANDS WERE TO PARENTS.* THEY were *the ones held accountable to God, not the children*! Deuteronomy 6:1-7. The responsibility was to teach and to train. It is the responsibility of Christian parents to do likewise; and doubly so!!

FURTHERMORE, the baptism of infants HAS STATEDLY been based on THE ASSUMPTION that God is finished with Israel;

and, has just automatically transferred their Covenants to His Church, WITHOUT HIS DECLARING SO; and retracting Israel's Covenants, WITHOUT DECLARING SO!! Has the Church been given THE LAND from the Nile to the Euphrates? NO SCRIPTURE DECLARES SO! Has God canceled his promise to Father Abraham? I have found no Scripture to this effect! In FACT, WE are told in Philippians 3:20-21 that all who are a part of God's Church have OUR CITIZENSHIP in HEAVEN!

There is no express COMMAND that infants should be baptized. There is no CLEAR EXAMPLE of the baptism of infants. The passages held to IMPLY infant baptism contain, when fairly interpreted, no reference that children or infants are present. In Matthew 19:14, none would have 'forbidden', if The Lord Jesus, The Christ of God, had ever baptized children, or, commanded it!

From Acts 16:15, 40; and Acts 16:33, 34, Neander says that we cannot infer infant baptism, for I Cor. 16:16 shows that the whole family of

Stephanas, baptized by Paul, were adults (I Cor. 1:16). As to I Cor. 7:14, Jacobi calls this text 'a sure testimony AGAINST infant baptism, since Paul would certainly have referred to the baptism of children as a proof of their holiness, if infant baptism had been practiced.

"MOREOVER, this passage would in that case equally teach the baptism of the unconverted husband of a believing wife. It plainly proves that the children of Christian parents were no more baptized and had no closer connection with the Christian church, than the unbelieving partners of Christians." – *Augustus Hopkins Strong, Systematic Theology, p. 951.*

IT IS THE WRITER'S BELIEF that the CLEAR STATEMENT of The Lord Jesus Christ, HIMSELF, in His COMMAND to 'forbid them not'; and, in His DECLARATION in Matthew 19:14 that of 'such' IS The Kingdom of Heaven,' PROVES ALL LITTLE CHILDREN TO BELONG TO HIM by HIS Choice, as we see in John 15:16!

THE ISSUE returns to whether God's Covenant is a FAITH covenant; or, a BAPTISM Covenant! The FOCUS begins with Genesis 15:6 in regard to Abraham: "And he BELIEVED IN THE LORD; and He counted IT to him FOR RIGHTEOUSNESS." His CIRCUMCISION was not commanded until Chapter 17!! BAPTISM *PROPERLY FOLLOWS* BELIEVING!

Genesis 17:11 – "And ye shall circumcise the flesh of your foreskin: and it shall be A TOKEN of the covenant betwixt me and you."

IF BAPTISM were the DOOR to Eternal Life; WHY would The Lord Jesus say in John 10:9, "I AM the Door. By ME if any man (any human) enter in, he shall be SAVED and go in and out and find pasture!"?? Innocents are His by His Choice. This is Clear!

I CORINTHIANS 15:22 – "For AS in ADAM *ALL* DIE, *EVEN SO* in CHRIST *shall ALL* be made ALIVE." PLEASE don't tell me that *CHRIST'S* Work is less effective than ADAMS, because I refuse to believe that! If the human nature brought sin and death to infants without ANY act on THEIR part; then, they are *ALL* LIKEWISE

AUTOMATICALLY covered by The Finished Work of The Lord Jesus Christ!.. NOT just PART of them! NOW, if any believe baptism has a PART in their Redemption, then, are they not denying GOD'S WORD in I Peter 1:18? "FORASMUCH as ye KNOW that ye were not redeemed with **CORRUPTIBLE** THINGS..!"

The New Birth, being Born of The Holy Spirit, lifts us into, and makes us participants in, The Uncorrupted Spiritual Realm of God's unfallen beings, never to leave it again. WATER is most certainly as corruptible as silver and gold! We either ARE, or we are NOT Redeemed (I Peter 1:19) by THE PRECIOUS BLOOD OF CHRIST!! Does not GOD declare we receive it BY FAITH? Innocents are trust incarnate!

ANYONE is at liberty to sprinkle their infant who wishes to...but, NO ONE can legitimately claim it is a COMMAND of God!! But, baptism *(baptidzo: immersion)* is a COMMAND for BELIEVERS!! It declares our death and Resurrection with Him!!

.HEBREWS 11 gives us the historical catalogue of FAITH; but, it says ABSOLUTELY NOTHING about BAPTISM. If baptism were PART OF the FAITH by which GOD declared them RIGHTEOUS, (rather than it being a WITNESS of it) I believe God would have DECLARED AND COMMANDED SO!

"BY FAITH Abel offered unto God a more excellent sacrifice than Cain, BY WHICH he obtained witness that he was RIGHTEOUS. God testifying of his gifts: and by IT he being dead yet speaketh, GOD testifying of his gifts:" Hebrews 11:4.

Hebrews 10:39 – "But we are NOT OF THEM who draw back unto perdition: but of them that BELIEVE to the SAVING OF THEIR SOUL."

The Church, Christ's Own Purchased Possession, sha 'be caught up together' in clouds to meet Him in the air! (I Thessalonians 4:13-17). Israel will be a Nation 'born at once' (Isaiah 66:8) when He reappears WITH His Church. The Eternal God of Truth leaves no room

WHATEVER for a discarded Israel or for a discarded Child of God! THE PARTNERSHIP IN BAPTISM. FOR WE ARE LABOURERS TOGETHER with GOD; YE are God's husbandry, ye are GOD'S building "According to the grace of God which is given unto me, as a wise masterbuilder, I have laid the foundation, and another buildeth on it. But LET EVERY MAN TAKE HEED HOW he buildeth upon it." I Corinthians 3:9-1 THE BAPTISMAL CEREMONY gives us license to comprehend the majestic occasion! Few comprehend the event! For they proceed from the baptismal service, walking away to live a life that is untaught!

THE BAPTISMAL ceremony began the order of instruction of the believer with the Lord. New breath! New Life! "I have been crucified with Christ: nevertheless I live; yet not I but Christ liveth in me; and the life which I now live in the flesh, I live by the faith of the Son of God, who loved me, and gave himself for me." Galatians 2:20.

"Let your conversation be without covetousness; and be content with such things as ye have; for he hath said, I will never leave thee, nor forsake thee." Hebrews 13:5.

It is teaching time! When the Apostle Paul was converted, he spent three years in the Arabian desert to get his life aligned with the Holiness of God and receive the Divine Instruction for his Mission to the Gentile Churches. Paul had been redeemed, justified, sanctified; and, now he was learning!

Paul had called himself 'a wise master builder'! If the proper procedure were followed, there would be an army of power filled men, women and children, exalting our Holy Redeemer to the death!! These folk could laugh in the face of death! Read the beautiful record of the hundreds of thousands of saints of God who walked boldly into the furnace!

IT WAS THE 20th CENTURY! The Pedo-baptists should have long ago brought world peace if their ideology were correct! Two special Christian friends had been tortured by the communists of Rumania, with all of the hideous, unspeakable tortures that could be applied to two Christian pastors: Archmandrite Ghiush and Richard Wurmbrand sat, surviving the cold and cruel treatment!! Would they go mad, as others had done? The two friends sat silently for a while.

Finally Richard broke the tense silence and asked, "are you sad?" To his amazement Archamandrite simply replied "Brother, I know only one sadness: that is not being given fully to Jesus!"

"It is often thought when the Reformation was established, Europe was divided into Protestantism: (whether Lutheran or Swiss) on the other hand, and Roman Catholics on the other. The large numbers of Christians are overlooked who did not belong to either party, but who, most of them, met as independent churches, not relying, as the others did on support of the civil power, but endeavored to carry out the principles of Scripture as in the New Testament times. They were so numerous that both the State Church parties feared they might come to threaten their own power and even existence.

In 1526 Zwingli chose to dialogue with Dr. Hubmaier of Bavaria of the Anaabaptist movement at Zurich. Dr. Hubmaier was expelled from Switzerland. Zwingli, who had first accepted immersion, then turned to advocate sprinkling. In 1527, the Anabaptists held a conference in Baden, where it was agreed (1) that only believers should be baptized. (2) that discipline should be exercised in the churches, (3) that the Lord's Supper should be kept in remembrance of His death. (4) that members of the church should not have fellowship with the world, (5) that it is the duty of the shepherds of the church to teach and exhort, etc. (6) that a Christian should not use the sword or go to law, (7) that a Christian should not take an oath. Mr. Sattler preached the word in many districts, and came in the Spring of 1527, he came to Wurttemberg. In Rottenburg he was arrested and condemned to death for his doctrines. In accordance with the sentence of the Court he was shamefully mutilated in the different parts of town, then brought to the gate, and what remained of him thrown on the fire! His devout wife and a number of other Christian women were drowned, and a number of brethren who were with him in prison were beheaded. This was just the first of a terrible series of such executions in Rottenburg.

"FOR WE ARE LABORERS TOGETHER WITH GOD, YE ARE GOD'S HUSBANDRY, YE ARE GOD'S BUILDING. I Cor. 3:9.

GOD THE HOLY SPIRIT has ALWAYS been present in the world as ADMINISTRATOR of God's affairs. Genesis 1:2. One of the most beautiful pictures of Divine Administration:

THE RING SYMBOLISM (PICTORIAL)

"AND PHARAOH SAID unto his servants, Can we find such a one as this is, a man in whom the Spirit of God is?

"And Pharaoh said unto Joseph, Forasmuch as God hath shewed thee all this, there is none so discreet and wise as thou art:

"Thou shalt be over my house, and according unto thy word shall all my people be ruled: only in the throne will I be greater than thou.

"And Pharaoh said unto Joseph, See, I have set thee over all the land of Egypt.

"And Pharaoh took off his ring from his hand, and arrayed him in vestures of fine linen, and put a chain of gold about his neck;

"And he made him to ride in the second chariot which he had; and they cried before him, Bow the knee: and he made him ruler over all the land of Egypt." Genesis 41:38-43

"SEE, I HAVE CALLED by name Bezaleel the son of Uri, the son of Hur, of the tribe of Judah;

"And I have filled him with the Spirit of God, in wisdom, and in understanding, and in knowledge, and in all manner of workmanship",.. Exodus 31:2,3.

"THEN was JESUS led up of THE SPIRIT into the wilderness to be tempted (Gr.-*Peirasthanai*, aor. 1, infin, pass. "to be tested.") of the devil." Matthew 4:1 (God cannot be tempted with evil.)

"IN THE LAST DAY, that great day of the feast, Jesus stood and cried, saying, If any man thirst, let him come unto me, and drink.

"He that believeth on me, as the Scripture hath said, out of his inner being shall flow rivers of living water.

"(But this spake He of The Spirit, which they that believe on Him should receive: for The Holy Spirit was not yet given; because that Jesus was not yet glorified.)" John 7:37-39.

"AND WHEN THE DAY OF PENTECOST was fully come, they were all with one accord in one place.

"And suddenly there came a sound from Heaven as of a rushing mighty wind, and He FILLED ALL THE HOUSE where they were sitting." Acts 2:1-2.

"BUT YE SHALL RECEIVE POWER, after that The Holy Spirit is come upon you; and ye shall be witnesses unto Me both in Jerusalem, and in all Judaea, and in Samaria, and unto the uttermost part of the earth." ACTS 1:8

"And His Name through Faith in His Name hath made this man strong, whom ye see and know: yea, the Faith which is by him hath given him this perfect soundness in the presence of you all. Acts 19:16.

(This is the point where we come to understand that Faith is the full operation of the Power of the Holy Spirit! Nothing happens but that He is the Doer of it! Sometimes it is 'assumed' and needs altogether to be accepted as Fact!)

THE WORD "UPON" used of the Holy Spirit's action is a word of intense, overpowering action by a Power Infinitely greater than one's own in a totally dominating action, as a massive, surging waterfall, carrying all in its path.

WHEN THE HOLY SPIRIT in Scripture took control of a person for God's service, human weaknesses and shortcomings were made subservient to Him! The Holy Spirit's INFINITE Power was given for Services that God,

Alone, could Perform! He Spoke! He Did GOD'S Work: He Empowered! He Wrought Conversions! The miracle son, SAMSON prefigures Messiah Christ; but, he also is a visual illustrating Supernatural Works performed through mortals in whom God is at Work! The word "upon" implies The Source is FROM HEAVEN! PRIDE has been a creature problem from the fall of Lucifer. THE CHURCH has been placed on alert!

IN JOHN 15:16 we are told *"YE* have not chosen *ME,* But, *I HAVE CHOSEN YOU, and ORDAINED YOU* that ye should *GO and BRING FORTH FRUIT,* and that your fruit should remain: that whatsoever ye shall ask of the Father in My Name, He may give it you."

JONAH was in the belly of the fish when the Light dawned; and he cried out in Jonah 2:9 *SALVATION IS OF THE LORD!* Are we getting the picture yet? God just doesn't need our help to save us!! He just commands us to BELIEVE IT, submitting to His Spirit.

MAN IS in a helpless, fallen state, capable of contributing NOTHING to the Salvation of God's creature, man.

"THEREFORE if any man (any human) be IN CHRIST, he is a NEW Creation! Old things ARE PASSED AWAY; behold, ALL things are become NEW!" II Corinthians 5:17.

When we speak of folk "passing away", they are DEAD to this world! When our Creator pronounces us NEW again, His first creation has now become better than "fixed"; and, He had no more help with getting it done, than He had when He made us THE The first time!! We are made NEW in Christ.! Ephesians 2:1

RESURRECTION of the old, however, makes the old form totally obsolete, because in His Working He has made us partakers of the Divine Nature, II Peter 1:4; with Christ Himself, as the Second Adam. He has been made to us Wisdom, Righteousness, Sanctification and Redemption, I Corinthians 1:30; and, having taken us with Him to the Cross, through the tomb, transforming us totally in His Own Glorious Resurrection so perfectly, Galatians 2:20, that He Himself has become OUR Perfection, because He lives eternally IN US, from the moment we received Him, for we are members of HIS Body! But not yet perfect I Corinthians 12:27. "In Him Dwells ALL THE FULLNESS OF THE GODHEAD BODILY and YOU ARE COMPLETE IN HIM WHO IS THE HEAD OF ALL PRINCIPALITY AND POWER. Colossians 2:9,10.

GOD'S COMMAND TO BAPTIZE, *BAPTIZO,* requires obedience to the WORD God chose to use, requiring BURIAL in water. The rising FROM those waters thus becomes pictorial of THE RESURRECTION to NEW LIFE! *RANTIZO* obviously does not qualify in giving an unbelieving world an adequate concept of the change called for in receiving and embracing His Holy Son, our Wonderful Christ! God used THAT Word in the Bible....just NEVER as a substitute for *BAPTISM!* We don't sprinkle a bit of dirt on dead people. They are given proper burial! Too many professed believers in Christ haven't been properly buried yet!! And, SADLY, Satan, once again, is being allowed to mar God's Message to a lost world in all parts of HIS Church! WE NEED HIS GREAT REGENERATING WORK WITHIN HIS CHURCH; AS WELL AS HIS OWN WORK OF *REAL AND TOTAL REDEDICATION AND REVIVAL WITHIN THE BODY!!* A LOST WORLD NEEDS HIS SALVATION! Colossians 3:1-4

DEATH is the experience of each of us when we are finished with this world; and, RESURRECTION is the only adequate answer to this part of fallen man's experience. WHILE RESURRECTION is in a thorough sense the true transformation of our being into a new creation, today, His Passionate, Divine Love in possessing us is the Real Power that transforms, burdens, energizes and utilizes us for His purpose to bring the whole world of lost humanity to Himself!

OUR SAVIOR'S MISSION WAS A CONVERTED, HOLY SPIRIT FILLED, INFINITELY CONTROLLED, EMPOWERED, VIGOROUS, PRODUCTIVE CHURCH TO GIVE HIM GLORY!

Chapter XXI

THE PEACE THAT COMES
IN BAPTISM

STEPHEN STOOD LIKE GRANITE, bold, passionate, faithful, The wolves had gathered for blood! He had prepared himself in every way: he had received Christ, had been baptized, and had become a master scholar! His infinitely inspired and masterful account of of God's classic work in history is plainly laid out!

"But he, being full of the Holy Spirit, looked up stedfastly into heaven, and saw the glory of God, and Jesus standing on the right hand of God,

"And said, Behold, I see the heavens opened, and the Son of man standing on the right hand of God.

"Then they cried out with a loud voice, and stopped their ears, and ran upon him with one accord,

"And cast him out o9f the city, and stoned him: and the witness laid down their clothes at a young man's feet, whose name was Saul,

"And they stoned Stephen calling upon God, and saying, Lord Jesus, receive my spirit.

"and he kneeled down, and cried with a loud voice, Lord, lay not this sin to their charge. And when he had said this, he fell asleep." Acts 7:55-60."Behold, I send you forth as sheep in the midst of wolves, be ye wise as serpents, and harmless as doves." Matthew 10:16 John the Baptist seemed to draw all Israel to him! And, the expectation was overwhelming! Evidently, the Apostles were shocked to find themselves at war with the establishment! They never got over it! The State Church, from it's founding rode the wave of acceptability and never awoke to the real calling of the church! Only a remnant became "called out"! The Ecclesia (The Church, "The called out assembly!"

FROM THE WORDS of the Great Commission it is obvious that a NEW THING is being done. "To wit, that God was in Christ reconciling the world unto Himself, not imputing their trespasses unto them, and hath committed unto us the Word of Reconcilliation." II Corinthians 5:19. He began an entirely new thing! The Bible is very explicit how infants are treated. There is no mystery about it. If there was to be some change in that, God certainly could, and would have done so. The change that He has made involves the will of the individual. He does nothing by proxy. From the earliest years infants are to be loved and tenderly taught. There is to be a gentleness and tenderness that causes children to respond with their very soul, thus making the child very tender, where it can be led into the sweetness of Christ.

GOD IS SPIRIT and they that worship Him, MUST worship Him in Spirit and in Truth. The son who grew to manhood, so tenderly is capable of leading and enfolding into the Way.

IT WAS THE 20th Century and Mr. Simpson had word that his son was dead! Muslim fanatics had slaughtered fifty people, his son was among them! Mr Simpson was very proud of the example of Christ that his son William had set! He had traveled 4,000 miles a year on horseback, preaching and teaching the Word and had established a small school on the Tibetian border!

NO! There is not the conversion of the world; but, that is the way we must work, prayerfully and tenderly and sacrificially! "Evil men and seducers shall wax worse and worse, with "wars and rumors of wars.. but the time is not yet!" II Tim 3:13; Matt. 24.

We were in Mammoth Cave and our guide turned off his light to illustrate for us absolute darkness. That is how dark it will become following the rapture; and, especially those following His Command, "Depart from me, ye cursed, into everlasting fire prepared for the devil and his angels!" Matthew 25:41; those wretched agonies of the horrible inferno of the awfulness of Hell, "..to whom is reserved the blackness of darkness forever!" Jude 13.

JESUS SAID, "I am come a light into the world." (John 8:12) "Ye are the light of the world." (Matt 5:14). When the Lord's own are taken out, the darkness will be near complete. Then Israel will begin to shine! When God said, "Let there be light:" "THERE WAS LIGHT". (Genesis 1:3). That was the true Light, which lighteth every man that cometh into the world. He was in the world, and the world was made by Him, and the world knew Him not." John 1:9, 10.

"BUT YE SHALL RECEIVE POWER, after that the Holy Ghost is come upon you: and ye shall be witnesses unto me both in Jerusalem and in Judaea, and in Samaria, and unto the uttermost parts of the earth." Acts 1:8. Thus the Word was spread!

"BROADUS, in his American Commentary on Matthew 3:6, claims that John's baptism was no modification of an existing rite. Proselyte baptism is not mentioned in the Mishna (A.D. 200). The first distinct account of it is in the Babylonian Talmud (Gemra) written in the 4th Century; it was not adopted from the Christians but was one of the Jewish purifications which came to be regarded, after the destruction of the Temple, as a peculiar initiatory rite. There is no mention of it, as a Jewish rite, in the O.T., N.T., apocyrypha, Philo, or Josephus." SYSTEMATIC THEOLOGY, A. H. Strong, p. 931.

The "confession of the Waldenses (those counted heretics by the Church of Rome) is completely fascinating to me. When the Church was persecuted horribly by Rome in the Ten Great Persecutions from the time of Nero, in 64 A.D. until the "Conversion of Constantine, in 313, Satan could not put out the Light! In fact, in spite of the blood and torture of those years one third to one half of the Roman Empire had been converted to Christ by observing the valor of the believers! While those who were confused and tired of suffering welcomed relief simply proceeded to accept the change. A great block of the True Church was firm in refusing to be counted a part of the State Church, withdrawing from the system in protest, and retaining some church records. which were sought by the religious system thrilled to be done with persecution and welcoming with open arms the freedom being accorded, but doubting and deeply troubled and confused by the wholesale sweep of evil into the church. Any who raised an opposing voice was branded "a heretic" and the persecution of those who were strong continued! Apostasy came fast and sweeping. Many proceeded to try to 'change things from the inside!'

BECAUSE I AM AMAZED at the astuteness of the Waldenses, I will proceed with "the confession of the Waldenses of A. D. 1615" with their introduction:

"(this confession belongs to the Calvinistic family, and is in part an abridgment of the Gallican Confession of 1559. It is still in force, or at least highly prized among the Waldenses in Italy. The occasion which called it forth entitles it to special consideration. It was prepared and Issued in 1655, together with an appeal to Protestant nations, in consequence of one of the most cruel persecutions which Romish bigotry could inspire. For no other crime but the simple, time-honored faith, the Waldenses in Piedmont were betrayed, outraged, mutilated, massacred, driven into exile, and utterly impoverished by the confiscation of their property and the burning of their villages. (See the frightful pictures of sufferings in the second vol. of Leger, an eye-witness.) The report of these barbarous atrocities roused the indignation of the Christian world. Oliver Cromwell, then Lord Protector of England ordered a day of humiliation and fasting, sent Sir Samuel Morland as a special commissioner to the Duke of Savoy (Charles Emanuel II.), opened a subscription with F2000 from his private purse and brought Protestant government to a sense of their duty, and Roman sovereigns (even the proud bigot Louis XIV,) to a sense of shame, the dispatches were written by his foreign secretary, the great Puritan post, in classical Latin and in the lofty spirit of his immortal sonnet, composed at that time,

'Avenge, O lord, thy slaughtered saints, whose bones Lie scattered on the Alpine mountains cold.'

Cromwell died too soon to finish this noble work of intervention in behalf of humanity and religious liberty. Of the more than f38,000 then raised by public subscriptions in England alone for the poor Waldenses, only f22,000 reached them: the remaining f16,333 Charles II unscrupulously wasted on his private pleasure under the pretext, worthy of a Stuart, that 'he was not bound by any of the engagements of an usurper and tyrant, nor responsible for his *depts.'* A fit illustration of the Spirit of the Reformation." THE CREEDS OF CHRISTENDOM, Philip Schaff, Vol.III, P. 757

When I began struggling with the topic of Baptism, and with why we had drifted into the troublesome blah indifference, I did not know that Christendom had been totally revamped and that Reformers agreed that a theology would be developed, knowingly, that would 'adapt' to all beliefs. They were naive, and were forced to confront reality, that Baptism was not an either, or situation without them being forced to conform. I am amazed at the insights of the Waldenses and the blood that would flow with the rage of the Reformation. I agree with every tenet of the Waldenses.

I firmly believe that Covenant Theology is absurd in the abstract and formed in the concrete. *I tremble and shudder to come to the conclusion that Protestant Churches will return to Catholicism! Revelation 17:5!*

"And there came one of the seven angels which had the seven unclean vials, and talked with me, saying unto me, come hither; I will shew unto thee the judgment of the great whore that sitteth upon many waters; with whom the kings of the earth have committed fornication, and, the inhabitants of the earth have been made drunk with the wine of her fornication." Revelation 17:1-6

These, I believe to be 'mystery Babylon's daughters! V.5, If she is a 'mother', she had daughters!

IT IS MOST EVIDENT in the CREEDS OF CHRISTENDOM, P.757-769, we have the complete Confession of the Waldenses, which sounds very Baptistic, and I believe the Biblical clarity with which it rings is the Biblically accurate truth for which we stand. I understand that our Lord said in John 6:53 "Verily, verily I say unto you, except ye eat the flesh of the Son of man, and drink his blood, ye have no life in you." Obviously, he puts a spiritual connotation upon that, over which the Jewish leadership stumbled; and, so did the harlot and her daughters!

It was most likely evident to Martin Luther, which brought a division between him, Zwingly and Calvin. But it was given verbatim in the Confession. They plead with The Church, that they 'may lead a quiet and peaceable life in all godliness and honesty' but the so called 'heretics' were the most devout of dedicated humans, treated like dirt, and worse for their passion, in The Inquisition!

"PUBLISHED WITH THEIR MANIFESTO ON THE OCCSION OF THE FRIGHTFUL MASSCRES OF THE YEAR 1655.

"Having understood that our adversaries, not contented to have most cruelly persecuted us, and robbed us of all our good and estates, have an intention to render us odious to the world by spreading abroad many false reports, and so not only to defame our persons, but likewise to asperse with most shameful calumnies that holy and wholesome doctrine which we profess, we feel obliged, for the better information of those whose minds may perhaps be preoccupied by sinister opinions, to make a short declaration of our faith, such as we have heretofore professed as conformable to the Word of God; and so every one may see the falsity of those their calumnies, and also how unjustly we are hated and persecuted for a doctrine so innocent. WE BELIEVE:

I.   "that there is one only God, who is a spiritual essence, eternal, infinite, all-wise, all merciful, and all-just, in one word all perfect; and that there are three persons in that one holy and simple essence: the Father, Son and Holy Spirit

II.   that this God has manifested himself to men by his works of Creation and Providence, as also by His Word revealed unto us, first by oracles in divers manners, and afterwards by those written books which are called the Holy Scripture.

III. That we ought to receive this holy Scripture (as we do) for divine and canonical, that is to say, for the constant rule of our faith and life: as also that the same is fully contained in the Old and New Testament; and that by the Old Testament we must understand only such books as God did entrust the Jewish Church with, and which the church has always approved and acknowledged to be from God: namely, the five books of Moses, Joshua, the Judges, Ruth, 1 and 2ⁿᵈ of Samuel, I and 2 of the Kings, 1 and 2 of the Chronicles, one of Ezra, Nehemiah, Esther, Job, The Psalms, The proverbs of Solomon, Ecclesiastes, Song of songs, the four great and the twelve minor Prophets: and the New Testament containing the four Gospels, the Acts of the Apostles, the Epistles of St. Paul—1 to the Romans 2 to the Corinthians, 1 to the Galatians, 1 to the Ephesians,

IV.   to the Philippians, 1 to the Colossians 2 to the Thessalonians, 2 to Timothy, 1 to Titus, 1 to Philemon, and the Epistle to the Hebrews; 1 of St. James, 2 of St. Peter, 3 of St. John1 of St Jude, and the Revelation.

V.   We acknowledge the divinity of the sacred books, not only from the testimony of the Church, but more especially because of the eternal and indubitable truth of the doctrine therein contained, and of the most divine excellency, sublimity, and majesty which appears therein; and because of the operation of the Holy Spirit, who causes us to receive with reverence the testimony of the Church in that point, who opens our eyes to discover the beams of that celestial light which shines in the depth of Scripture, and corrects our taste to Discern the divine Saviour of that spiritual food.

VI.   That God made all things of nothing by his own free will, and by the infinite power of his Word.

VII.   That he governs and rules by his providence, ordaining and appointing whatsoever happens in this world, without being the author or cause of any evil committed by the creatures, so that the guilt thereof neither can nor ought to be in any way imputed unto him.

VIII.   That the angels were all in the beginning created pure and holy, but that some of them have fallen into irreparable corruption and perdition; and that the rest have persevered in their first purity by an effect of divine goodness, which was upheld and confirmed them.

IX. That man, who was created pure and holy, after the image of God, deprived himself through his own fault of that happy condition by giving credit to the deceitful words of the devil.

X. That the man by his transgression lost that righteousness and holiness which he had received, and thus incurring the wrath of God became subject to death and bondage, under the dominion of him who has the power of death, that is, the devil; insomuch that our free will has become a servant and a slave to sin: and thus all men, both Jews and Gentiles, are by nature children of wrath, being all dead in their trespasses and sins, and consequently incapable of the least good motion to any thing which concerns their salvation: yea, incapable of one good thought without God's grace, all their imaginations being wholly evil, and that continually.

XI. That all the posterity of Adam is guilty in him of his disobedience, infected by his corruption, and fallen into the same calamity with him;, even the very infants from their mothers' womb, whence is derived the name of original sin.

XII. That God saves from this corruption and condemnation those whom he has chosen (from the foundation of the world, not for any foreseen disposition, faith, or holiness in them, but) of his mercy in Jesus Christ his Son; passing by all the rest, according to the irreprehensible reason of the freedom and justice.

XIII. That Jesus Christ having been ordained by the eternal decree of God to be the only Saviour and only head of his body which is the Church, he redeemed it with his own blood in the fullness of time, and communicates unto the same all his benefits by means of the gospel.

XIV. That there are two natures in Jesus Christ, divine and human, truly united in one and the same person, without confusion, division, separation, or alteration; each nature keeps its own distinct properties; and that Jesus Christ is both true God and true man.

XV.   That God so loved the world, that is to say, those whom he has chosen out of the world, that he gave his own So save us by his most perfect obedience (especially that obedience which he manifested in suffering the cursed death of the cross), and also by his victory over the devil, sin and death.

XVI.   That Jesus Christ having made a full expiation for our sins by his most perfect sacrifice once offered on the cross, it neither can nor ought to be represented upon any pretext whatsoever, as they pretend to do in the mass

XVII.   That the Lord Jesus having fully reconciled us unto God, through the blood of his cross, it is by virtue of his merits only, and not of our works, that we are absolved and justified in his sight' that we are united to Jesus Christ and made partakers of his benefits by faith, which rests upon those promises of life which are made to us in his gospel.

XVIII.   That this faith is the gracious and efficacious work of the Holy Spirit, who enlightens our souls and persuades them to learn and rest upon the mercy of God, and so to apply the merits of Jesus Christ.

XIX.   That Jesus Christ is our true and only Mediator, not only redeeming us, and that by virtue of his merits and intercession we have access unto the Father, to make our applications unto him, with a holy confidence that he will grant our requests, it being needless to have recourse to any other intercessor besides himself.

XX.   That as God has promised us regeneration in Jesus Christ, so those who are united to him by a living faith ought to apply themselves unto good works.

XXI.   That good works are so necessary to the faithful that they can not attain the kingdom of heaven without the same, seeing that God hath prepared them that we should walk therein; and therefore we ought to flee from vice, and apply ourselves to Christian virtues, making use of fasting, and all other means may conduce to so holy thing.

XXII.   That, although our good works can not merit any thing, yet the Lord will reward or recompense them with eternal llife, through the merciful continuation of his grace, and by virtue of the unchangeable constancy of his promises unto us.

XXIII.   That those who are already in the possession of eternal life in consequence of their faith and good works ought to be considered as saints and glorified persons, and to be praised for their virtue and imitated in all good actions of their life, but neither worshiped nor invoked, for God only is to be prayed unto, and that through Jesus Christ.

XXIV.   That God has chosen one church in the world for the salvation of men, and that this Church has one only head and foundation, which is Jesus Christ.

XXV.   That this church is the company of the faithful, who having been elected by God before the foundation of the world, and called with a holy calling, unite themselves to follow the Word of God, believing whatsoever he teaches them therein, and living in his fear.

XXVI.   That this Church can not fail, nor be annihilated, but must endure forever (and that all the elect are upheld and preserved by the power of god in such sort that they all persevere in the faith unto the end, and remain united in the holy Church as so many living members thereof).

XXVII.   That all men ought to join with that Church, and to continue in the communion thereof.

XXVIII.   That God does not only instruct us by his Word, but has also ordained certain sacraments to be joined with it, as means to unite us to Jesus Christ, and to make us partakers of his benefits; and that there are only two of them belonging in common to all the members of the Church under the New Testament—to wit, baptism and the Lord's Supper.

XXIX.   That Christ has instituted the sacrament of Baptism to be a testimony of our adoption, and that therein we are cleansed from our sins by the blood of Jesus Christ, and renewed in holiness of life.

XXX.   That he has instituted the Holy Supper, or Eucharist, for the nourishment of our souls, to the end that eating effectually the flesh of Christ, and drinking effectually his blood, by a true and living faith, and by the incomprehensible virtue of the Holy Spirit, and so uniting ourselves most closely and inseparably to Christ, we come to enjoy in him and by him the spiritual and eternal life.

Now to the end that every one may clearly see what our belief is to this point, we here insert the very expressions of that prayer which we make use of before the Communion, as they are written in our Liturgy or form of celebrating the Holy Supper, and likewise in our public Catechism, which are to be seen at the end of our Psalms; these are the words of the prayer:

'Seeing our Lord has not only once offered his body and blood once offered his body and blood for the remission of our sins but is willing to communicate the same unto us as the food of eternal life, we humbly beseech thee to grant us this grace that in true sincerity of heart and with an ardent zeal we may receive from him so great a benefit; that is, that we may be made partakers of his body and blood, or rather of his whole self, by a sure certain faith' the words of our catechism are the same, *Nella Dominica 53*.

XXXI.   That it is necessary the Church should have pastors

XXXII.   known by those who are employed for that purpose to be well instructed and of a good life, as well to preach the Word of God as to administer the sacraments, and wait upon the flock of Christ (according to the rules of a good and holy discipline), together with elders and deacons after the manner of the primitive Church.

XXXIII.   That God hath established kings and magistrates to govern the people and that the people ought to be jubject and obedient unto them, by virtue of that ordination, *not only for fear, but also for conscience' sake,* in all things that are conformable to the Word of God, who is the King of kings and the Lord of lords.

Finally, that we ought to receive the symbol of the apostles, the Lord's Prayer, and the Decalogue of fundamentals of our faith and our devotion."

CONCLUSION

" For a fuller and broader declaration of our faith, we do therefore reiterate the same protestation which was caused to be printed in 1503, that is to say that we do agree in sound doctrine with all the Reformed Churches of France, Great Britain, the Low Countries, Germany, Switzerland, Bohemia, Poland, Hungary, and others, as it is set forth by them in their Confessions: as also in the Confessions of Augsburg, as it was explained by the author, promising to persevere constantly therein with the help of God, both in life and death, and being ready to subscribe to that eternal truth of God with our own blood, even as our ancestors have done from the days of the Apostles, and especially in these later ages!

"Therefore we humbly entreat all the Evangelical and Protestant Churches, notwithstanding our poverty and lowliness, to look upon us as true members of the mystical body of Christ, suffering for his names sake, and to continue unto us the help of their prayers to God, and all effects of their charity, as we have heretofore abundantly experienced, for which we return them our most humble thanks, entreating the Lord with all our hearts to be their rewarder, and to pour upon them the most precious blessings of grace and glory in this life and in that which is to come. Amen." CREEDS OF CHRISTENDOM, 757-769, Philip Schaff.

The aim of true believers through the ages of time from the radical inclusion of the heathen into the membership of the church under Constantine, to and beyond The Reformation was the formation of a Biblical Church. I shiver at the blood, burnings and dismemberment of Bible believers by the countless hundreds of thousands who would not bow to misguided authorities. Nevertheless, millions of believers died the death of martyrs.

I find it absolutely stunning that the Reformation Church burned those who believed these things!! I think it is totally hideous!! May God have mercy that entire cities were wiped out to exterminate them! All they did was immerse believers, AS THE BIBLE TOLD THEM TO!! THE BIBLE IS THE INFINITE, INFALLIBLE, ETERNAL, VERBALLY AND PLENARILY INSPIRED WORD OF OUR SOVEREIGN GOD. ALL that remains to be said is that THE BIBLE TEXT is man's ONLY BASIS for Faith and Practice.

UNLESS you and I stand willing to embrace 'THE WHOLE COUNSEL OF GOD', our service to BOTH God and man becomes a fraud. GOD'S INVITATION to all who read these pages is a plea to make THE BIBLE (and, not the teachings of man) the basis of Faith. THERE IS NO OTHER BASIS FOR FAITH!

While we understand the anguish of division between ourselves and those we love, God calls us to take our correct stand IN LOVE, remembering that even our Lord declared:

MATTHEW 10:34-36 – "Think not that I am come to send peace on earth: I came not to send peace, but a sword.

"For I am come to set a man at variance against his father, and the daughter against her mother, and the daughter in law against her mother in law.

"And a man's foes shall be they of his own household."

IF MEN FAIL to accept the author's conclusions, this in NO WAY diminishes his love for ALL. The fact that some differ from him in their beliefs no more proves that he does not love them than the fact that God's refusal to condone man's evil acts does not disprove His declaration that He "loved the world." The proof God Loved the world is the Death of His Son for all mankind in their fallen state. OUR LOVE FOR OUR CHILDREN does not mean we give them their way about everything! In fact, if giving them their way proves anything, it proves that we do NOT love them. Our love for all mankind does not give us license to hold back Truth which can make the difference between Heaven and Hell for precious souls for whom our Lord Jesus Christ died.

FINALLY, the author has made no attempt to be a judge of the personal experience of people. God is the Judge of every man; and, to Him we must each give account.

IT IS HIS PRAYER that each reader shall FIRST, OBEY GOD in recognizing AUTHORITY over his or her life; and, that EACH shall come to his or her own personal conclusions and convictions, prayerfully allowing the Holy Spirit of God to form those conclusions and convictions as God's Own Spirit directs.

WHATEVER of these thoughts have been helpful to you shall make me eternally grateful for having had that privilege of spending time with the Word of God on the subject of BAPTISM.

WHATEVER your thoughts may be at this time, Friend, God has a deep and precious love for you as one for whom His Own Son gave His Life and His ALL. BELONGING TO HIM, BEING SURE OF HEAVEN and the BEAUTIFUL PRIVILEGE of having HIM as a PRESENT REALITY IN OUR HEARTS, to enable us for this life, through His Absolute, Sovereign Spirit, witnessing with our spirit, Romans 8:14-17, 26,27. This should cause us to be wise and caring enough to reach those we love for HIM, as we cherish and study with deepest diligence The Eternal Word of God, The Bible!

With this I leave the matter of Baptism and Martyrdom! Dark is the night of this hour with the Second Coming at the Door! What shall we then say to these things? If God be for us Who can be against us? Looking unto Jesus, the Author and Finisher of our Faith!...... "Because, when they knew God, they glorified Him not as God, neither were thankful, but became vain in their imaginations, and their foolish heart was darkenened. Professing themselves to be wise, they be came fools, and changed the glory of the incorruptible God into an image made like corruptible man, and birds, and four-footed beasts, and creeping things!" Goodbye, May

God be merciful!! God bless America!! "Our Father, Who art in Heaven, Hallowed be thy Name. Thy Kingdom come. Thy Will be done in earth, as it is in Heaven. Give us this day our daily bread. And forgive us our sins, as we forgive those who sin against us. And lead us not into temptation, but deliver us from evil. For Thine is the Kingdom, and the Power, and the Glory, Forever. Amen."

ABOUT THE AUTHOR

I was born to my parents, Laban and Florence Ford, in 1926. I attended U.G. High and have earned a Bible school diploma. My studies were done at Calvary College, Sue Bennett College, American College, and the Dallas Theological Seminary. I have spent more than fifty years in pastoral ministries, including in the student pastorate and interim pastorate at the Cornerstone Southern Baptist Church.